£14.95

D1390256

THE
POWER
OF
diversity

New Ways of Learning
and Teaching through
Learning Styles

Barbara Prashnig

Published by
Network Educational Press Ltd
PO Box 635
Stafford
ST16 1BF
www.networkpress.co.uk

© Barbara Prashnig, 1998

First published 1998
Reprinted 2000, 2001
UK edition published 2004

First published in 1998 by David Bateman Ltd, New Zealand

ISBN 1-85539-118-X†

Cover design by Shelley Watson
Printed by MPG Books Ltd, Bodmin, Cornwall

CONTENTS

If you find errors in this book,
please keep in mind that they are
there for a purpose.

I wrote something for everyone,
and some people are always
looking for mistakes.

Ever since I gained an awareness of learning styles and began developing our Working Style Analysis (WSA), I knew I had to write a book about this eye-opening concept and I knew it had to be a special book. A book which was hard to put down, containing the scientific concepts behind working, teaching and learning styles as well as giving a good overview of applications and practical advice on how to handle diversity in learning situations. But most importantly, it had to be enjoyable and easy to read. I imagined that if I had fun writing it, people might have fun reading it, talking about it and enjoying the knowledge they might gain from trying out what I invited them to do.

And that's when I finally took action. Knowing my own learning style, how I could work most effectively and which environment I needed to be creative, I had been dreaming about the perfect place for a long time. Armed with my laptop computer, a lot of suntan lotion, a suitcase full of reference books and half my collection of classical CDs, I retreated to Fiji for a few weeks over the Christmas break to write most of this book.

It was there that style differences became even more obvious to me. Watching the people of Fiji at the markets, in their villages and at their daily work, and the tourists at their hotels, on the beach and in the shops showed me how different and yet how similar human beings are. How difficult it often is to communicate, to interact and to understand one another. How much easier it would be if we all knew more about ourselves, our style differences and how we could get on with each other.

Six years have gone by since this book was first published in New Zealand and I observe with amazement the impact it still has on people around the world. In total it has been ten years of hard work of developing the Learning Style Analysis (LSA) for primary and high school students as well as for adult learners, and the Teaching Style Analysis (TSA) for educators; ten years of travelling the world and spreading the message. But it has also been ten years of enjoyment and immense pride about having created something people can accept, put to good use and pass on to others.

Since the first publication I have conducted training seminars and worked with educators in many different cultures – from the Arabic World to European countries, from the United States to Australia and China. Learning styles projects are underway in Canada, the USA, the UK, Norway, Finland and Australia, and it seems that educators everywhere are more willing than ever to accommodate learning diversity in their classrooms. I discovered that certain style features are universal, that the 'Diversity Concept' is understood and applicable anywhere because it deals with human beings.

This book has been translated into Swedish, Finnish and Norwegian and several other translations are pending. Our assessment instruments are available as software in Finnish, Swedish, German and Mandarin Chinese and has recently been translated into Norwegian, Danish and Spanish. I have realized it is a truly universal concept and I am grateful that modern technology as well as long-distance travel have made it possible to reach so many people. The biggest impact on 'spreading the word' was undoubtedly the expansion and greater reliability of the internet, which has made a huge difference in delivering LSA, WSA and TSA profiles via our website www.creativelearningcentre.com to anyone anywhere in the world who has access to email and a web browser.

There are now many schools, particularly in New Zealand, where learning style approaches are part of their new learning culture and have become the basis for improved teaching. I am particularly excited about a three-year project at Forbury Primary School in Dunedin which has completed its second year and is already showing remarkable results. For the first time in New Zealand's educational history, Learning styles and the 'diversity concept' have been accepted by the Ministry of Education as a promising intervention programme for achieving school success and turning a failing school around. My proposal to the Ministry for the pilot project was approved in November 2001 under the following conditions:

- NZ$400,000 over three years and continued funding depending on progress.
- Pilot programme monitored by Dunedin College of Education.
- New approaches to education based on individual learning styles.
- Teachers being trained in new instructional methods.
- Possible blueprint for other failing schools.

I feel honoured that you, the reader, have chosen to read, skim or browse through this book and I hope you can find plenty of interesting ideas which will excite you so much that you want to share them with others. I also hope that you are keen to continue learning about yourself, your family members, partners, friends, superiors, and about human diversity in general.

As you go through the book you will probably encounter some new ideas about human beings, why they do what they do and how you can handle diversity. Beyond that, and maybe more important for you as the reader, you will experience a new way of reading, a new way of information intake. In this book I am presenting to you a new style of text layout: the right-hand pages resembling newspaper columns and the left-hand pages filled with graphics, illustrations, quotes and exercises matching the text pages. I have chosen this style of text presentation to help you read the book faster if you wish, to remember better and have more fun doing it. The full scientific explanation for this so-called 'suggestopedic' style can be found in Chapter 6. You may find it confusing and challenging in the beginning (remember: your brain is not yet used to this style), but you will enjoy and benefit from it. So stretch your mental powers and have fun!

As with any book of this kind (semi-scientific, based on professional experience) it would have been impossible for me to put all the information together without the professional knowledge, advice, support, friendship and love of the many people I learned from and met along the way.

I want to express my gratitude to the many professionals, peers, colleagues and friends who influenced me most over the years and I would like to thank them sincerely for what they have done for me, even if they might not be aware of it.

On a professional level I would like to thank:

Jim Houghton of NEP for being my inspiring new publisher;
Dr Rita Dunn for opening my eyes to Learning Styles;
Dr Kenneth Dunn for accepting me as co-author for our new LSA and WSA models;
Dr Georgi Lozanov, Tony Stockwell and Charlotte Le Hecka for teaching me the art of Suggestopedia;

Dr Marion Diamond, Renate Nummela Caine and Robert Sylwester for exciting me about the 'learning brain', its functions, its chemistry and its unlimited potential;

Dr Jeannette Vos, Colin Rose, the late Charles Schmid, Douglas Webb, Stephanie Merritt, Don Campbell and Eric Jensen in the USA for helping me to understand and apply the concept of accelerated learning with all its magic;

Gordon Dryden with whom I share a passion about learning, for still supporting me after all these years in my search for the best methods in learning and teaching;

Anthony Robbins and Robert Kiyosaki for making me aware of my potential as an educator as well as a human being;

Alan Cooper for his courage to be the first principal in New Zealand to fully introduce learning styles into his school and trusting my professional advice;

Jeannette McCallum, Annette Joyce, Judy Dixon, Jill Courteaud, Michelle Morrison, Ann Marie Biggs, Mike Scaddan, Mary Grant and many other principals in New Zealand for accepting my training, for allowing the introduction of learning styles into their schools and for doing pioneering work;

Mike Allison for believing in my work and supporting my proposal to the Ministry of Education;

Janice Tofia, principal at Forbury Primary School in Dunedin, and staff members for being courageous enough to apply the learning styles concept under extremely difficult conditions and succeeding against all the odds;

Darrell Latham at COEC for supporting my work and promoting my seminars to New Zealand educators on a large scale;

EDNZ, Christine Milicich and the New Zealand Institute of Management for accepting creative learning techniques and the WSA and integrating them into their programmes;

Alan Marshall of Vibrant Learning Co in Melbourne for introducing learning styles to schools in Victoria, Australia;

Team Building Group in Copenhagen for introducing this concept to dyslexic students and to the business world in Denmark;

Bjørn Rosberg Anderson of BRA Empowerment in Bergen for translating the software into Norwegian, introducing the 'diversity concept' to a difficult market and for his involvement with the Norwegian version of my book;

Jim Roberts of TBS in Philadelphia for re-introducing learning styles to the USA;

Graduates of my teacher training programme 'Diploma in Holistic Education' and participants at my learning style seminars for their open-mindedness and their never-ending efforts in putting my suggestions into practice – often against all odds;

Managers and decision makers in corporations and organizations for allowing me to introduce creative learning techniques and the concept of diversity into their training programmes:
in New Zealand: ASB Bank, AMP, BMW, Air NZ, Apple Computers NZ, TVNZ, Star FM, Anchor Products, divisions of Fletcher Challenge, Westpac, Northland Health, Cooper Henderson Motors, Telecom New Zealand, Merck Sharpe and Dohme, Carter Holt Harvey, The National Bank of NZ, Wella NZ, the Salvation Army, Bay of Plenty Polytechnic, Manukau Institute of Technology, the Department for SMEs and the Graduate School of Business at Auckland University, MBA Programme;
in Australia: Aus-Meat, James Hardie Pipelines, Wella Australia, *Time* Magazine;
in Denmark: Lego and training staff at Hotel Legoland Conference Centre;
in Canada: NDSA for re-introducing learning styles to educators and for supervising a pilot project in high schools near Toronto;

in Finland: Jyväskylä University, Centre for Continuing Education for promoting my
  work, translating the software and supporting the 'diversity concept'; Atena Kostannus
  Oy for publishing my book in Finnish;
Norway: Kommuneforlaget in Oslo for publishing my book in Norwegian;
in Switzerland: Andrea Muller and Angela Hollington for spreading the word and
  organizing my seminars for teachers at International Schools in Europe;
in Sweden: Synapsen AB for having been a long-time business partner;
in the UK: the wonderful team at Network Educational Press for introducing the
  'diversity concept' and organizing seminars for educators;
Past and present staff at the Creative Learning Company for giving me all the back-up I
  need for my upfront work and for keeping the office going when I am away;
Alex Grayson for being not only the best GM and CEO a company could have but also
  for being a friend and most reliable support person during difficult times;
Mikhail Diatchenko for being a great programmer, webmaster and team member;
Belinda Clune for drawing the mind maps for my first and second books;
Lynton Blair for developing the original software programs;
Dr Yvonne Walus for developing the computer program for our new TSA;
Graham Biddle for his inspirational original artwork for our stationery and software;
Our team of national and international facilitators for sharing the same vision for students,
  teachers and schools, and for being such good team players;
Master Lin, Julia Biermann and Ken King for looking after my physical health with their
  wonderful healing methods.

And on a more personal level I'd like to thank:

My husband, Armin Prashnig, for believing in me, for always being there for me when I
  need him, and for accompanying me on the most exciting professional journey in my
  life;
My daughter Sigrun (Siggy) for giving me support and becoming a real friend as well as a
  most valued team member at CLC once again; without her help and tremendous
  computer skills I would not have been able to complete this book;
My late parents, Maria and Peter Stastny, for instilling in me the love for learning and
  giving me guidance to this very day;
My native Austria – my old home country – for giving me a solid education, excellent
  teacher training and a profound respect for human diversity;
My new home country – New Zealand – for giving me the freedom to do what I love and
  to live the life I have always wanted to.

Auckland, February 2004   Barbara M. Prashnig

*This book is dedicated to all educators
who are searching for better ways of teaching
to help their students find better ways of learning and
who by doing so begin to enjoy and rediscover
the delights of their profession.*

I love this book. It delivers a vital message of hope that is desperately needed by millions of students and parents around the world. Those are the millions who are stupidly and wrongly condemned to fail at school when they can just as easily succeed. This book shows how to achieve such results.

At its simplest, Barbara Prashnig's message is disarmingly clear:

- Everyone of us has a learning style, thinking style and working style as unique as our fingerprints.
- We each take in information, store knowledge and retrieve it in different ways.
- Parents and schools can now easily identify those individual styles, and so can businesses for their employees.
- It is imperative for schools, parents and organizations to cater to those individual differences.
- Unless that happens, millions more will be wrongly classed as school failures or learning disabled students and become dropouts because their learning style is not suited to their school's teaching style.

In some ways those dropouts are in illustrious company:

- Winston Churchill did poorly at schoolwork. He talked with a stutter and a lisp. Yet he became one of the greatest leaders and orators of the twentieth century.
- Albert Einstein was a daydreamer. He even failed mathematics early in high school. Yet he went on to become the greatest scientist of his age.
- Thomas Alva Edison was beaten at school because his teacher considered him 'addled' for asking so many questions.
- Beethoven's tutor said he was hopeless as a composer. He never learned to multiply or divide.
- Louisa May Alcott's teacher complained that she drew instead of doing addition.
- Emile Zola scored zero in his final literature examination.
- United States president Woodrow Wilson couldn't read until he was eleven.

And all had something in common. They had individual learning styles that were not suited to the style in which they were taught. Fortunately each seemed to have the temperament and drive to succeed by themselves – or with the help of loving parents and/or understanding mentors. For millions of others the same mismatch continues today. It is probably the biggest cause of school failure. And it need not be.

For most of the last three centuries, many school systems have been geared to teaching every child in one or two main ways – mathematically and linguistically. Even worse, today, so-called 'intelligence' tests have been devised to label those two main ways as the only forms of intelligence ... as if brilliant sporting achievers, musicians, painters, mathematicians, top sales people, orators, golf course designers, writers, accountants, lawyers, politicians, jewellers, architects, cooks, doctors and computer programmers all had the same talents.

For well over a century most schools have succeeded in graduating about 20 per cent of their students fully qualified for careers in management and the professions. Some schools have done a reasonably good job of schooling another 30-odd per cent to become craftsmen, tradesmen, clerks and typists. The other 50 per cent of so-called 'low achievers' have traditionally gone on to become manual or unskilled workers.

Today most of those unskilled jobs have gone. And we know that most of those school drop-outs are youngsters whose learning styles do not suit most school teaching styles. The amazing thing is how professionals in our education systems have perpetuated the myth that all learn in roughly the same way.

In my own case, I am very comfortable as a 'print-oriented visual' learner. I can happily skim-read book after book. At one stage, for seven years as a talk-show host, I averaged fifteen new books a week. I am also a morning person and I prefer to read stretched out on a bed or a sofa – before breakfast. I find great difficulty reading while sitting at a desk or table. Little wonder that I dropped out of school at the age of fourteen – and started learning.

I also store information in a different way: tactile/visually – by marking books with a highlighter and particularly by typing summaries. And I retrieve information by 'internal visualisation' – by recalling images in my mind's eye, or presenting it from visual slides.

As a youngster I flew through primary school. Fortunately a great headmaster identified my self-learning ability and introduced me to the wonders of the public library and its gifted librarians. Yet for me high school was a disaster. At 13 I was reading four mystery novels a *week*. But the teacher wanted me and every other third-former to read only one book a *year*: Shakespeare's *The Merchant of Venice*. Stagger through it over several months, regurgitate some of it in an exam – and you passed.

Every person reading this page would have collections of school students with different learning traits – not always with the same outcome. Over the last ten years at least 20 different methods have emerged to identify those learning styles.

Harvard professor Howard Gardner has argued extensively that we each have at least seven different 'intelligences'. More recently he has argued for an eighth: the naturalist intelligence. I would personally argue that visual and spatial abilities can be separate, and the love of nature is more a preferred learning style than a different form of intelligence. Amazingly, Professor Gardner leaves out one of the most important of all: the ability to create new ideas by recombining existing elements in new ways. But the overall logic of his argument is obvious from straight observation. Some children in the same family love playing the piano, others detest it. Some are almost magical in their ball-handling ability and can play table tennis, basketball and other sports almost instinctively. Yet others score highly in logic, while others are brilliant at painting.

Richard Bandler, John Grinder and Michael Grinder, in their pioneering work on Neuro-Linguistic Programming (NLP), present strong proof that generally we each have one dominant learning trait: visual, auditory or kinesthetic. They and others conclude, quite rightly, that it is the 'mainly kinesthetic', or physical learner, who misses out in most schooling systems – wrongly labelled 'hyperactive' or with a 'learning deficit disorder' when the real difference is in learning style. Despite strong research findings, it still amazes me that many NLP practitioners still make the ludicrous claim that 93 per cent of all learning is subconscious. Having proved that we all learn differently, they repeat, in a new way, that we are all the same! They also do not differentiate sufficiently between kinesthetic and tactile learning preferences, and Barbara Prashnig's field study findings are particularly valuable.

The husband and wife team of Ken Dunn, professor and chair at Queen's College, City University of New York, and Rita Dunn, professor at St John's University, New York, have isolated five different factors in their pioneering work on learning styles: environmental, emotional, sociological, physiological and psychological. These determine how human beings take in information, store and retrieve it. Together with Dr Ken Dunn, Barbara Prashnig has redeveloped the learning style model and also extended it into a working style model for people in the workplace.

But there are five major factors which, in my view, set Barbara Prashnig's work apart:

- While others rely largely on 'book research', Barbara has travelled the world to study with many of the leading researchers at first hand. She has studied learning styles, multiple intelligences, NLP, brain research and accelerated learning.
- She has then applied and tested their findings thoroughly in her new homeland of New Zealand: in primary/elementary schools, high schools, universities and in business settings.
- She has not taken one isolated aspect or method of learning and turned it into a new Holy Grail. Nor should she. If a child learns better through music, movement and touching, then Barbara's quest has been simple: find out how best to use music, movement and touch to enhance the learning process.
- Better still, she has used this multiplicity of experiences to fashion new ways to cater for the great diversity in students, teachers and workers alike.
- She also travels extensively to introduce her methods and test them in action in different cultures and to improve them continually.

Some of her findings were presented in an earlier book. I was honoured to be asked to contribute the preface. But this extended book is even more thorough, even more exciting, even more practical, even more essential.

I recommend it to teachers, trainers, parents and students alike. The world needs its message and the results it demonstrates and celebrates.

Gordon Dryden
Co-author of *The Learning Revolution*

This workbook is an introduction to diversity, different learning and working styles, new teaching methods and creative, accelerated learning techniques. It explains how to develop your learning potential in any environment. It can be read in a conventional manner or be used as a workbook for a self-study programme during which you will experience how these methods can be applied and find out how they work for you. If you are an educator or parent you can try out the recommendations or act upon your newly gained insights to help your students or children to have more fun and experience more success during the learning process.

If you decide to use this as a workbook, the following steps are recommended

1. You will have noticed that the **layout** of the book is rather unusual. On all the left-hand pages you will find **visuals**, **thoughts** and **graphs**, while the text on the right-hand pages has been written in **suggestopedic format** to speed up your reading and help you with your recall. If you want to find out more about suggestopedic methods go to page 159. You are also invited to **complete** the various **exercises and mind maps** throughout the book and use the empty spaces for your **own notes**.

2. To make the best possible use of your own **learning/teaching ability** please see **Appendix II** for obtaining your personal **Style Analysis**. If you want to find out about your students' or children's learning ability and discover their true **learning potential**, you can download LSA questionnaires and obtain their personal profiles via the internet from the NEP website in the UK and from the CLC website in other countries. The result – their **Learning Style Analysis** – will give you a detailed overview of their true learning needs, their **personal preferences**, their **dislikes** and their **flexibilities**. By knowing their strengths and weaknesses and by following the detailed **recommendations** given in the LSA report, they will considerably enhance their information intake skills, their study habits and their long-term memory. You will also be able to enhance your communication with them by understanding their style much better.

3. Decide where you want to work through this book – check your **physical environment** – is it arranged in a way that you feel **comfortable**?

4. Consider if you need absolute **quiet** or if you want to put on **background music** while you are going through this book. If so, refer to Chapter 6 (pages 161–169) to select the most appropriate **learning music** to keep your brain alert and your concentration high as long as you like. You can use the learning music recommended on pages 164 and 166 or choose your own music and switch it on **NOW!**

5. Prepare a **note pad**, a pen, several **sheets of blank paper** (A4 format or bigger) and at least five **coloured felt pens** or **highlighters** for your own note taking. As all the chapter overview mind maps are in black and white, you might like to colour them in after you have read the chapter to personalize them and to jog your memory.

6. Before you start working through the book, go to pages 156–157 and read about a very useful note-taking technique – **mind mapping**; create a **mind map** as a **summary** of these instructions and use this technique for summarizing each chapter you have read.

7. Browse through the whole book, look at the **mind maps** on the left-hand pages, particularly those with chapter overviews, or read the table of contents to gain an overview, the Big Picture, of the new learning content. This will especially help visual learners to remember.

8. To improve your **memory** and maximize your **retention**, make sure you read the book at a **time** when you are most alert and when you can concentrate easily. As **motivation** and **interest** are excellent learning enhancers, keep your **curiosity** high and reward yourself if you have discovered something new and exciting and when you can remember it!

9. However, if you are tired and still want to be **mentally alert** to read the book, do some **Brain Gym**® exercises as described on pages 154–155. They will help you to get energized, more alert and better focused. But if you feel you are too wound up, too uptight and stressed out to be able to concentrate, maybe some of the **Relaxation/Visualization** or **Centring Exercises**, as suggested on pages 148–151, might help you. Whatever it takes, help your body and brain to take in the information contained in this book with enjoyment and ease.

10. Now begin working through the book, learn a lot, remember it well, and most importantly – **ENJOY IT** and **HAVE FUN!**

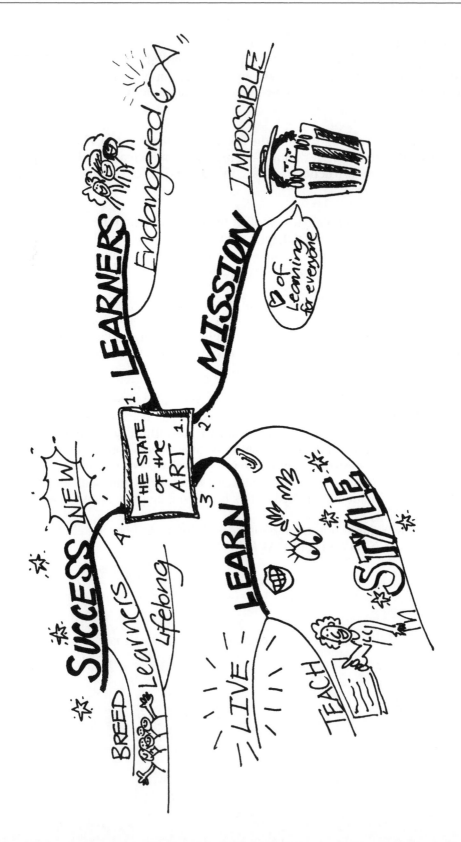

1. Learners – an endangered species

Over the past ten to twenty years many species, like whales, have been exposed to an <u>environment</u> which is no longer safe, which no longer supplies what their <u>basic needs</u> require for survival, and is threatening their livelihood. The results of such conditions are devastating not only for the species itself but also for the entire environment. Whenever a <u>species is decimated</u> or, worse, becomes extinct, there is always a <u>major upset in the balance</u> of any ecosystem.

environment

basic needs

species is decimated
upsets the balance

As we well know, this is presently happening on a huge scale worldwide. However, we tend to ignore it or prefer to believe that such events won't have the predicted negative impact.

If we compare the example from the animal kingdom with the situation learners find themselves in these days (especially in secondary and tertiary education), it is obvious that such learning environments are really <u>no longer conducive to successful and satisfactory learning</u>.

no longer conducive
to successful learning

Traditional education practices with a strong emphasis on mathematical and linguistic skills and formal delivery, using mainly <u>analytical, left-brain</u> teaching methods (as described on page 6), do not allow many students to develop life skills and learning abilities which would enable them to survive easily in our fast-changing world.

analytical, left-brain

Students cannot understand themselves as learners or what is happening to them, or why they cannot produce adequate results during their years of schooling. As a consequence, their <u>self-esteem</u> and <u>motivation</u> are <u>reduced dramatically</u> and finally their minds are lost for lifelong learning – they are literally <u>extinct</u> as a <u>learning species</u>.

self-esteem and motivation
dramatically reduced
extinct
as learning species

The results are dangerous for any human society and manifest themselves in climbing figures for crime rates, drug abuse, unemployment, alcoholism, divorce, child abuse, violence,

There Are Three Categories Of People:

The Ones That Make Things Happen,

The Ones That Watch Things Happen,

And The Ones That Wonder

What The Hell Is Happening.

economic recession, environmental problems, poverty, social unrest and, perhaps, even war.

It might not be obvious but the <u>social ills</u> every developed society is stricken with today seem to have their roots in <u>poor education</u>, dropoutism, underachievement and <u>low self-esteem</u> which can often be traced back to the parent generation.

social ills

poor education
low self-esteem

So, what can be done to <u>break the vicious cycle</u>, to prevent these developments continuing?

break the vicious cycle

2. Mission impossible – love of learning for everyone?

The claims that everyone can learn, that mass education is mental mass destruction and that this creates learning disabilities, are not new but sound like <u>provocations</u> because the generally held view, at least here in New Zealand, is that we have one of the best educational systems in the world – including our high school system.

provocations

Reality, however, seems to support the opposite: the number of underachievers in schools is on the rise; learning disabilities have become a fact of life; learning motivation goes down the longer students are in the educational system; nearly everyone is glad when school is finally over; and even many of those who successfully finish a degree find studying hard and frustrating.

As fond memories of school learning are rare, and in most people's minds knowledge acquisition seems to stop when they leave school, it is no surprise that <u>lifelong learning</u> is usually not part of our mindset. Yet most people appreciate the learning they experience in 'real' life; in fact over the years they usually get better at it and even enjoy it! However, as soon as they have to go back to <u>traditional training</u> situations or, even worse, to <u>formal learning</u> or <u>studying</u>, they immediately develop negative feelings – the same feelings they experienced through their school learning: anxiety, frustration, boredom, stress, decreased motivation.

lifelong learning

traditional training
formal learning/studying

And yet – considering the <u>human brain</u>,

human brain

HOW I FEEL ABOUT LEARNING
Pre-test

Please respond to these statements by ticking the appropriate box –
do it fast, without analysing.

	True	False
1. If I really want to learn something, I have to do a lot of studying and repetition.	☐	☐
2. Learning is something very interesting and pleasant for me.	☐	☐
3. I think I have a good memory.	☐	☐
4. Learning is hard work most of the time.	☐	☐
5. I think I've always been a good learner.	☐	☐
6. I wish I could concentrate better.	☐	☐
7. I don't think I'm very intelligent.	☐	☐
8. Often I think 'If only I didn't forget everything so quickly'.	☐	☐
9. If I can learn something new, I get the feeling of deep satisfaction and contentment.	☐	☐
10. If I think back to my time at school, I think 'Oh no! I'm glad that's over!'	☐	☐
11. I think learning is very hard for me.	☐	☐
12. I know I learn quickly.	☐	☐
13. Learning has hardly ever been fun for me.	☐	☐
14. Learning gives me satisfaction, happiness and contentment.	☐	☐
15. I can't imagine that I'll ever be able to master a difficult subject (for example, a foreign language, mathematics) easily.	☐	☐
16. Foreign languages have always been my favourite subject	☐	☐

Scoring, see page 324

it is quite clear that its <u>main function</u> is to learn, and that human beings can <u>increase</u> their <u>skills</u> and <u>knowledge</u>.

main function
increase skills/knowledge

Furthermore, given the amazing brain power every human being has, <u>learning</u> as well as studying and information intake <u>should actually be fun</u>, very <u>easy</u>, always <u>without stress</u> and should have <u>long-lasting effects</u>.

learning
should be
fun, easy, stress-free,
have long-lasting effects

If all that is really true, why do so many people have learning difficulties, a poor memory, concentration problems, and find information intake and skills acquisition often very stressful?

The answer is very simple and the reality behind it all is nearly too good to be true: the <u>key</u> to successful learning and working is knowing one's unique personal <u>learning</u> or <u>working style</u>, accepting one's strengths as well as one's weaknesses, and <u>matching personal preferences</u> as much as possible in any learning, study or work situation.

key
learning/working style

matching personal
preferences

The short pre-test on the opposite page can be used as a quick way of finding out your true <u>attitudes to learning</u>, which often go back to your early childhood.

learning attitudes

3. Learn, teach and live in style

People of all ages can learn virtually anything if allowed to do it through their own <u>unique styles</u>, through their own <u>personal strengths</u>. They are more capable of consistent performance if their working conditions suit their individual style preferences. Research over the past 25 years, mainly coming from St John's University in New York, has shown that human beings can learn any subject matter successfully when the <u>instructional methods</u> used are <u>matched</u> with their individual learning <u>preferences</u>. When <u>human diversity</u> is taken into account and <u>respected</u> in the learning process, in training situations or in skills acquisition, the <u>results are always positive</u>: the <u>learner</u> experiences

unique styles
personal strengths

instructional methods
matched with preferences
human diversity
respected

positive results for learner

Elements of Traditional Teaching

disciplined, ordered, logical, analytical
low emotional impact
meaning derived from content
strong emphasis on 3 Rs
sitting at desks – limited activities
stress on auditory mode
'chalk – talk – handouts'
lecture/didactic oriented
suppressing energy
little brain stimulation
belief that learning is difficult
mistakes recognized/corrected directly
strong association with failure
create tension and stress in student and teacher
low learning motivation
acceptance of students' mental state
content is fragmented/no Big Picture
finish when time is up
emphasis on quiet class
institutional rituals
school uniform
mass instruction/little room for individuality

Based on experience and handouts by Eric Jensen and Jeannette Vos

pleasure, gains a sense of accomplishment
without frustration and stress, experiences
increased motivation and is always <u>in control</u>
<u>of the learning process</u>.

in control of learning

Before you will be able to gain an insight
into the complexity of a person's style elements,
it is necessary to define what learning style is
and, as an extension of that, what working style is.

According to Drs Rita and Kenneth Dunn,
two of the leading researchers in this field,
'<u>learning style</u> is the way in which human beings
begin to <u>concentrate on</u>, <u>absorb</u>, <u>process</u> and
<u>retain new and difficult information</u>.' (1)

**learning style: how to
concentrate, absorb,
process, retain new and
difficult information**

Similarly, <u>working style</u> can be defined as
the way people in the workforce usually <u>absorb</u>
and <u>retain new and difficult information</u>, <u>think</u>
or <u>concentrate</u>, generally do their daily work
and effectively <u>solve problems</u>.

**working style: how to
absorb and retain new
and difficult information
think, concentrate,
solve problems**

4. A new success breed – lifelong learners in their own style

After having investigated why students do have
learning problems and why many people find it
so difficult to keep up their work performance,
it is obvious that the secret to success in learning
and teaching lies in knowing oneself, one's style,
one's potential and the resulting consequences.
The enormous benefit from all the aspects of
<u>self-knowledge</u> will be noticeable not only in
areas of learning, teaching and studying, but
also in one's personal and professional life.

self-knowledge

If people are allowed to learn and work through
their own styles and find suitable environments
for their activities, there is no limit to what
human beings can achieve, and they can actually
do it with much <u>less stress</u> and much <u>more joy</u>.

less stress and more joy

Teachers will be more understanding of their
students' <u>true learning needs</u> and more aware of
their own teaching style and the resulting style
matches or mismatches.

true learning needs

Ms Barbara M Prashnig
Director – Training and Research
Creative Learning Company Ltd
PO Box 5422, Wellesley Street
Auckland 1
NEW ZEALAND

Friday, 7th March 1997

Dear Barbara

I have just finished not simply reading, but also interacting (actually, it's the same thing for me), with your book 'Diversity is our Strength' and feel impassioned to write you a note of genuine, volcanically ardent appreciation. You have poured in your warmth, sincerity, and erudition onto the pages of the book, and anyone not interested in such material WILL be suitably 'metamorphosed'. (Your book was lent to me by a friend, can't find it in the shops here in Singapore.)

Your passionate spirituality, in the purest sense of the word, will prove to be an inspiration to humanity. I am certain that your presence in the learning ecosystem is as vital as oxygen is for our planet.

How wonderful that another terrific human being, Gordon Dryden, wrote the preface to your book. What a guy!

I believe your message needs to sweep across all continents. We seem to have largely lost touch with our essence. In truth, we see with our eyes, but observe with our brains. We hear with our ears, but listen with our minds. We touch with our hands, but feel with our hearts. We utter with our lips, but speak from our souls. We need to sense all by observing, listening, feeling, speaking, doing! For we sense with our spirit, and then, we embrace life! All this we were born with. What happened along the way? This is my question to us all, ergo your work has total relevance. Very well done, Barbara.

May I present you with a small token of my appreciation. It accompanies this letter and the title 'Superbrain' could just as easily apply to you!

Take care and God Bless

Dilip Mukerjea
Spiritual Entrepreneur (author of *Brainfinity* and *Superbrain*)

This will lead to better attitudes towards learning in a large group of students who cannot learn well with traditional teaching methods, who come to believe they are stupid and who are often lost for lifelong learning. If, however, they are encouraged to learn in their own way, <u>utilizing their unique style preferences</u>, they usually get very excited about learning tasks and can actually become lifelong learners.

utilizing unique style preferences

Everyone will also be more effective in their interpersonal relationships because <u>understanding human diversity</u> gives them new and better tools for interacting much more successfully.

understanding human diversity

When human beings <u>know their potential</u>, their unique style and how to go about effective information intake, they will naturally become what they are meant to be as a species: successful <u>lifelong learners</u> in their own style.

know potential

lifelong learners

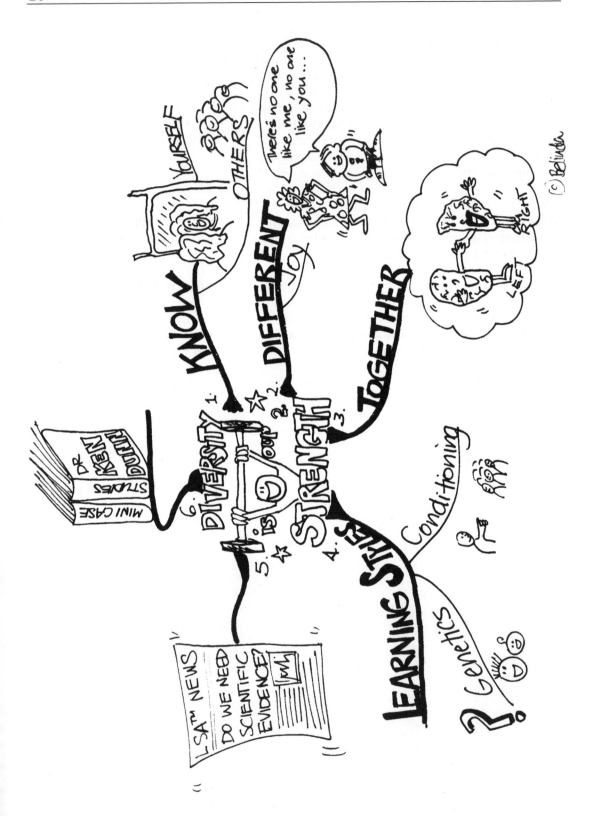

1. Getting to know yourself and others

Considering rapid developments in technology,
information overload, change in educational
and social systems in all modern societies, and the
breakdown of traditional business structures,
it is more important than ever that human beings
know what makes them tick, why they do things
they do or simply 'who they are' as a person.
This self-knowledge is not only vital for coping   **self-knowledge vital**
with our fast-changing world as we find it
at the start of the twenty-first century,
it is also immensely helpful as a tool which   **helpful as tool to**
facilitates understanding of people whom we have   **understand people**
to or choose to interact with in our private and
professional lives.

Only by knowing ourselves first will we ever be
capable of really understanding others and
less prone to misinterpret their communication   **less misinterpretation,**
or actions and misjudge their behaviour.   **misjudgement**

With better insights into our own and other people's   **insights into**
brain processes (and we are only at the beginning   **brain processes**
of a most exciting journey to this true last frontier)
it might be possible to utilize our brain power   **utilize brain power**
much better, have more fun doing so and ultimately
live in greater harmony, not only with ourselves   **live in harmony**
but, more importantly, with the people around us.

There are scientific tools available for finding out   **scientific tools**
style differences, and psychological tests have
been in use for a long time. They all give detailed
insight into various aspects of human behaviour,
thinking and personal preferences. Two of the
newest and most comprehensive instruments in
this area are the Working Style Analysis (WSA) for   **Working Style Analysis**
people in the workplace, and the Learning Style   **Learning Style Analysis**
Analysis (LSA) for students of all ages,
combining cognitive, biological, psychological
and social style aspects. The result is a very
detailed description of a student's preferences,

Listen teacher,
listen to me.
Don't look away.
See my eyes, they hold messages
that can make you understand me.
Hold my hand and your heart
will warm towards me.
Let me dance and sing you
my own songs which you don't know,
and you might smile as you have
never smiled before.
Hear me tell you a story
of my ancient past
and then, maybe, you can see
another person in me.

Emma Kruse Va'ai

flexibilities and non-preferences during the learning process, as fully described and explained in more detail in Chapter 4.

Alongside these researched tools there are also a great number of <u>non-scientific tools</u> available. Although they might not hold up to scientific scrutiny, they are usually a lot of fun and can be a light-hearted but nevertheless insightful <u>introduction</u> to the notion of <u>human diversity</u>.

non-scientific tools

**introduction to
human diversity**

One of the most astonishingly accurate and short tests about human diversity is from a very clever and entertaining book by Susan Dellinger, *Psycho-Geometrics* (1), which I like to use in my seminars because it is a lot of fun and people love to discover in a non-threatening way how different we all really are and that there is nothing wrong with being different. On the contrary, without diversity life would be very boring.

2. There is no one like me, no one like you – the joy of being different

As you begin to understand yourself and human diversity a bit more, the idea of *equal but different* might take on deeper meaning, and it is possible to appreciate some of the many <u>advantages</u> a new understanding of differences will bring:

advantages

- We can finally stop puzzling about ourselves and cherish our own individuality, <u>understanding more who we</u> are and the characteristics we have.

understanding ourselves

- We can help create <u>unity through diversity</u> in our private and professional lives by recognizing that different styles are needed in any group to make it work effectively.

unity through diversity

- We are able to <u>celebrate diversity</u> when we understand why children are often so different from their parents and why opposites attract (see Chapters 9 and 10).

celebrate diversity

Job Description of the Brain

Each brain hemisphere seems to be specialized in
different ways of processing information

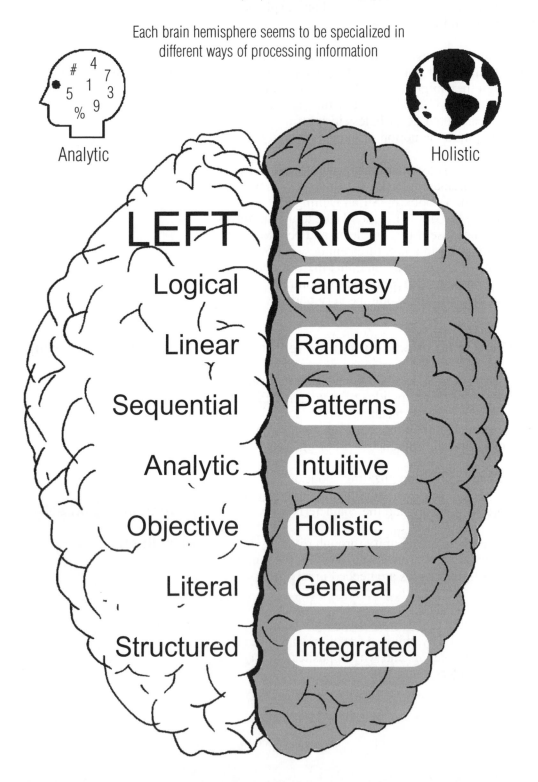

Analytic   Holistic

LEFT	RIGHT
Logical	Fantasy
Linear	Random
Sequential	Patterns
Analytic	Intuitive
Objective	Holistic
Literal	General
Structured	Integrated

3. Left brain–right brain – get your head together

Not all people process information the same way; therefore it is very important to know how different thinking styles translate into different learning and working styles. A good understanding of these basic style differences is vitally important for anyone who deals with people in all sorts of situations, not only in learning and training.

information processed differently

style differences

Over the past few years a considerable amount of information has become available about the differences between left-brain or analytical processing styles and right-brain or holistic styles. Although different authors have given these two different brain processing styles various names – as the list on the opposite page shows – they all fit the original terminology used by the Dunns. However, for our new instrument, the Learning Style Analysis™, we have chosen a different term for right-brain processing because we believe 'holistic' describes this brain processing style more accurately.

left-brain – analytical
right-brain – holistic

various names

right-brain processing holistic

Among the numerous examples of how these two distinctly different brain processing styles manifest themselves or how flexibility (when using both hemispheres equally) integrates both styles, the following descriptions are characteristic:

distinctly different
flexibility
integrates both styles

a) How do you find your way around a new city? Do you immediately purchase a street map and trace your route from point A to point B each time you leave your hotel, or do you 'feel' your way around, sensing where each place should be? Or do you alternate between map reading and following your nose, and intersperse visual clues with exact distances?

b) Consider these two people whom I know well. Both are successful; neither ever seems to change. One person does everything quickly in a set order all the time; his desk is neat; his briefcase has tidy compartments for office papers and to house documents; and his clothes match and are well organized. Another is forever losing his keys; his clothes, while expensive, are always somehow mismatched; and he finds all sorts of weird things in his pockets.

BASIC FUNCTIONS

LEFT HEMISPHERE	RIGHT HEMISPHERE
ANALYTIC Breaks down into details and component parts. No concern or interest for the whole.	**OVERVIEW** Sees the whole Big Picture. Correlates entire situation. Does not look at details. Synthesizes.
FOCUSES Focuses attention on fine detail. Zeros in on a small area of activity.	**DIFFUSE** Spreads out over a large area. Not concentrated in one place.
SERIAL Piece by piece, sequential. Auditory. Logic. Language. Mathematics.	**SIMULTANEOUS** Spatial relations. Visual. Rhythm and flow. Music. Managerial. Multi-operational.
TRY Conscious control and effort. Ego. Expressive. Struggle.	**REFLEX** Survival instinct. Impulse. Unconscious. Receptive.
BREAKING DOWN Figuring things out step by step and part by part.	**SYNTHETIC** Putting things together to form wholes.
TEMPORAL Keeping track of time, sequencing one thing after another.	**NON-TEMPORAL** Without a sense of time.
LOGICAL Drawing conclusions based on logic: one thing following another in logical order – for example, a mathematical theorem or well-stated article.	**INTUITIVE** Making leaps of insight, often based on incomplete patterns, hunches, feelings or visual images.

From: *The Children's Song Book*, by B. O'Hara

c) When I remember holiday preparations in our family, I always see my father planning every detail weeks in advance, every route and detour we might take, distances and places for sightseeing, with my mother making long lists of what to take and laying out everything at least one week before departure; the final packing was always done exactly two days before we set off! Although I realized that many preparations were necessary, it always bothered me that everything was done in such a precise way. My style of packing – until out of necessity I learned to get much more organized – was the following: leaving everything to the last minute, then grabbing what was available and throwing it into the suitcase which, of course, never closed properly. So either I had to sit it and force its locking or I would take pieces out, only to realize at my holiday destination that I needed exactly the things I had left behind. More than once I had to buy those missing items!

d) It's no accident that we learn the words of popular songs very easily – you don't have to make any effort to do that. You learn very quickly and remember for a long time because the left brain and the right brain are both involved. The left brain is processing the words and the right brain is processing the music.

Can you relate to these descriptions? Do they make sense to you? Then it's time to investigate how <u>left-</u> and <u>right-brain dominance influences</u> certain aspects of a person's <u>learning and working style</u>.

left/right-brain dominance influences learning and working style

Research on the Dunn and Dunn Learning Style Model has shown that <u>typical left-brain processors</u> prefer a learning or work environment that is:
quiet, brightly lit and formally designed.
They don't need snacking, and learn or work best alone or with an authority figure present.

left-brain processors

In contrast, most typical <u>right-brain processors</u> prefer so-called 'distractors':
noise or music, dim light, informal design,
snacking, mobility and peer interaction at work
or while learning or concentrating.

right-brain processors

It is quite obvious that <u>traditional classrooms</u> and workplaces were <u>designed with left-brain processors</u> in mind (by left-oriented designers, of course) and it is necessary, therefore, to <u>adjust workplaces</u> or <u>classroom environments</u> for people with right-brain preferences. And there are many more out there than we might like to think, particularly among younger students!

traditional classrooms designed for left-brain processors adjust workplaces, classroom environments

However, people who can <u>integrate</u> the use of <u>both hemispheres</u> are obviously better off because they can use their <u>flexibility</u> to adjust to any situation, whether it requires logical, <u>analytical and sequential</u> thinking skills, or <u>holistic, simultaneous and intuitive</u> approaches. Techniques for increasing flexibility are explained in more detail in Chapter 8. How these differences in brain processing styles can even <u>affect relationships</u> and communication <u>between males and females</u> we'll explore in Chapter 9. Knowing and accepting diversity is the first step, yet the true mastery in learning and teaching is <u>developing and applying methods</u> which <u>draw out</u> every learner's <u>full potential</u>.

**integrate
both hemispheres
flexibility
analytical – sequential
holistic – simultaneous,
intuitive**

**affect relationships
between males and females**

**developing, applying
methods draw out
full potential**

4. Learning styles – genetics or conditioning?

Why are we all so different and similar at the same time? What happens to our styles when we grow up? <u>Do our styles change</u> or do they remain the same throughout life?

style changes

The <u>search for explanations of human diversity</u> goes back centuries. Scientists have always been eager to find keys to unravel the mysteries of male and female differences, of character features or personality types. Although there is an ever-increasing amount of literature available in this field (see Bibliography and Further Reading) and research is continually going on in many institutions around the world, no one has so far come up with a <u>reliable conclusion</u>.

**search for explanations
of human diversity**

no reliable conclusion

To the best of my knowledge, the Dunn and Dunn Learning Style Model, from which both the LSA and the WSA are derived, is the only instrument containing scientifically researched <u>style elements</u> which are clearly <u>biological</u> and <u>remain fairly stable</u> over a lifetime. Research dating back to 1979 reveals 'that three-fifths of learning style is genetic; the remainder, apart from persistence, develops through experience'. (2)

**style elements
biological, remain stable**

Overview of Learning Style Models

Bandler-Grinder (NLP) (3)

The VAK Model is the basis for Neuro-Linguistic Programming (NLP – the study of 'words and nerves'), taking into account through which modalities (senses) people process and store information. Created in the 1970s, it is now widely used for counselling, learning and communication training.

McCarthy (4MAT System) (4)

The 4Mat System Model was developed in the early 1980s and is based on right- and left-brain dominance, giving insight into how human beings first perceive and then process information. It functions as a model for teaching and is used in schools for enhancing instructional techniques.

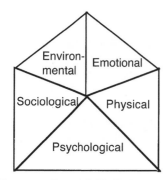

Dunn and Dunn (LSI, PEPS) (5)

The Dunn and Dunn Model was developed to help 'educationally disadvantaged' children. Research began in the late 1960s to identify individual preferences in students during the learning process. It is the most comprehensive and best researched learning style model and is available in two versions: LSI (Learning Styles Inventory) for school children and PEPS (Productivity Environmental Preference Survey) for adults.

When we developed the new, extended versions of
the WSA and LSA models (see pages 70 and 78),
we, of course, constructed the pyramids based on
these findings, and for many years the <u>division
between biological and learned elements</u> of the
new models seemed to hold well. Over the past
few years, however, more and more discussions
with educators and users of these assessment
instruments revealed that the divide might <u>not</u> be
<u>so clear-cut</u>, particularly in adults.

**division between
biological/learned
elements**

not so clear-cut

Several <u>new insights</u> are now emerging that even
some of the <u>learned/conditioned style elements</u> of
the model (see page 74) seem to have <u>biological</u>
(maybe even genetic?) <u>underpinnings</u>. Anecdotal
evidence seems to confirm that some learners are
much better off learning by themselves, can't be
with others when they need to concentrate, are
highly motivated from an early age and show
high persistence with learning tasks. Where does
this come from when children have not been
conditioned in this area? Is it possible that they
have been born with these features?

**new insights
learned/conditioned
style elements ≈
biological underpinnings**

Taking these considerations into account, we have
now added these two significant words to the <u>new
LSA-Adult pyramid model</u> as can be seen on
page 18.

**new LSA-Adult pyramid
model**

On the other hand, how much DOES <u>conditioning
alter our style features</u> in the <u>biological areas</u> (see
page 72) of the model? Can students change their
preferences for sound, light, study area and physical
needs during the learning process after years
of exposure to certain classroom environments
with certain rules, or do they just <u>become more
flexible</u>? Many students seem to <u>adjust</u> quite well,
get on with their studies and achieve good results,
but many others just can't, they don't fit in and
can't learn like some of their classmates, as every
teacher can confirm.

**can conditioning alter
biological style features?**

**become more flexible
adjust**

This has led to the realization that becoming
flexible in the biological areas is helpful but being
<u>conditioned into a style</u> which is not your own, is
<u>damaging</u> in many ways. It can lead to learning
problems, frustration and low self-esteem.

**conditioned into a style ≈
damaging**

Overview of Learning Style Models

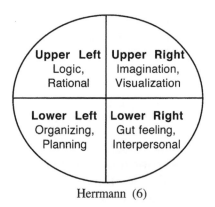

Herrmann (6)

The Brain Quadrants of the Herrmann Brain Dominance Model describe preferences for mental functioning and brain dominance. Based on brain-related research, it was created in the late 1970s and is being used in management training to enhance creativity and productivity of people.

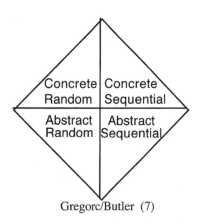

Gregorc/Butler (7)

The Gregorc Energic Model of Mindstyles, created in the mid-1970s, provides an organized way to consider how the mind works. It identifies four qualities found within four basic mediation channels. Butler refined it, and it is used for instructional strategies to enhance classroom teaching.

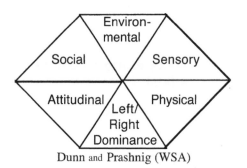

Dunn and Prashnig (WSA)

The Working Style Analysis is based on the original Dunn and Dunn Model but has been extended in two areas: sensory and left/right brain dominance. It was co-created in 1993, computerized in New Zealand in 1994, and is particularly applicable for people in the workforce and for career planning.

Nevertheless, the way human beings tend to take in information, process and store it, seems to depend more on <u>preferences</u> which are <u>inherent</u> rather than acquired and, despite conditioning in school or work environments, these preferences <u>don't seem to change</u>. We often don't know why we have them and when or where we acquired them; we only know they usually stay with us. They can often <u>disappear</u> for a while or might be <u>suppressed</u> because of particular circumstances but <u>tend to surface</u> time and again during the course of life.

inherent preferences

don't change

**disappear, suppressed
tend to surface**

When these <u>biological needs are matched</u> in learning or work situations, human beings can <u>concentrate much better</u> and for longer periods, are able to <u>improve their performance</u> and enjoy what they are doing.

biological needs matched

**concentrate better
improve performance**

5. Do we need scientific evidence?

One might think that most people would know their style elements but in my work with thousands of people I have experienced that comparatively <u>few are certain about</u> their real preferences, <u>their true style</u> and how they can function best.

**few know
their true style**

That's why we need <u>scientific evidence</u> – not only to <u>help individuals</u> come to terms with their own strengths and weaknesses, to convince them to <u>utilize their real abilities</u> much more confidently, but also to make it obvious to educators, trainers, teachers, parents and students themselves that there is no one 'best' way, <u>no one single style for</u> guaranteeing <u>successful learning</u> or studying, for information intake, problem solving and accomplishing tasks. Because when science 'proves' something, people are more inclined to believe it.

scientific evidence

helps utilize real abilities

**no one single style for
successful learning**

The old saying 'Do as I do' or 'Do as I say', often used by parents for their children, and between teachers and students, instructors and trainees, employers and employees, is definitely not the best approach in drawing out people's

Learning always consists
of two parts:

First – confrontation with new
information or experience;

Second – discovery of personal, individual
meaning.

A. W. Combs

abilities because it <u>does not take into account human diversity</u>. On the contrary, such a 'one fits all' attitude is very unjust to everyone and does <u>a lot of harm to the development of human potential</u>, resulting in low self-esteem, decreased motivation, high stress, anxiety and inconsistent performance. Disregarding diversity is <u>probably at the core of most social ills</u> today.

disregarding human diversity

harms development of human potential

at core of social ills

However, many people, particularly in education or in authority positions, are not yet ready to accept that <u>diversity has great advantages</u> and that there is always more than one way of accomplishing anything. They can only be convinced by <u>scientific evidence</u>, by hard statistical <u>facts and data</u> or by written reports as in personal profiles. They need time to reflect and reconsider, judge and evaluate. Then, armed with research results, the accumulated information and guidelines for implementation, they are ready to act upon these findings recognizing, finally, that the majority of people do need an <u>individualistic approach</u> rather than commonly practised mass instruction.

diversity has advantages

scientific evidence facts and data

individualistic approach

People never like being treated as numbers, neither in education nor in their daily work. Therefore it is crucial that we not only accept differences but begin to acknowledge and appreciate them.

6. Dr Ken Dunn – how to release your personal power

Thousands of students and adults have used our <u>important research</u> over a period of 30 years to release personal learning power. Research in more than 100 colleges and universities and responses from more than 3 million children and adults with nearly 20 national and international awards provide the base of validated <u>reliable results</u>. Success style is not only directly related to individual personal strengths important for the learning process, it is also a natural, <u>common-sense approach</u> to self-confidence, productivity and heightened motivation.

important research

reliable results

common-sense approach

Analysing 'what is' does not tell us 'what could be'.

BAD EDUCATION = SLAVERY

It enslaves people for life

Mini case study one

A young high school girl in California struggled to achieve a B average. Her parents and older brothers and sisters all received honours in high school and college. This obviously intelligent student was very unhappy with the manner in which her parents required her to study. When the parents asked me to help I interviewed the frustrated young lady to determine what was wrong with the rules of study established by her parents. With tears in her eyes she described her every evening torture. 'I have to go to my room, turn on the lights, sit up tall at my desk, shut the radio and TV off, and get rid of all the food and drinks until I finish. Then I get 78 or 82 on my tests and my parents say I should try harder.' Now the tears flowed uncontrollably. I asked her to tell me what her preferences were and to take a success style instrument. Then I reassured her that I would relate the results to her parents and that they would abide by her scores and follow my recommendations, at least for a trial period of one semester. She calmed down immediately and couldn't wait to answer the success style questions.

In checking the results and listening to her preferences it was easy to prescribe a new pattern of studying and learning at home. The young student preferred an informal setting – on the floor. She liked to nibble on fruit while working, and did not do well in bright light which caused her to squint and feel tired. During the interview she neatly packaged her success style preferences. 'I love my parents and I really want to BE with them when I'm studying. They watch television news and shows after dinner, and talk to my brothers or sisters when they visit. All I want to do is lie on the floor and study in the living room and have them all around while I work.'

It took some convincing but the parents had agreed to try the new study pattern based on the results of the questionnaire.

Six months later they called to thank me. 'The transformation is remarkable! Our daughter is scoring in the high nineties and smiles all the time now.' These well-intentioned parents had prescribed the right study patterns for the young student's siblings but they were absolutely wrong for her.

Mini case study two:

Jimmy was an 11-year-old who was labelled LD – Learning Disabled – because he couldn't seem to learn the multiplication tables. His mother had tried everything: a personal tutor, computer software designed to teach the tables, his friends, daily practice and so forth. The youngster was a B+ student in all subjects except maths, which he was failing. Jimmy's mother was a teacher who had just taken a workshop with me and agreed to test him for learning and success style preferences.

AUTOBIOGRAPHY IN FIVE SHORT CHAPTERS
by
Portia Nelson

Chapter One

I walk down the street.
There is a deep hole in the sidewalk.
I fall in.
I am lost ... I am helpless.
It isn't my fault.
It takes forever to find a way out.

Chapter Two

I walk down the same street.
There is a deep hole in the sidewalk.
I pretend I don't see it.
I fall in again.
I can't believe I'm in the same place.
But it isn't my fault.
It still takes a long time to get out.

Chapter Three

I walk down the same street.
There is a deep hole in the sidewalk.
I see it is still there.
I still fall in ... it's a habit.
My eyes are open.
I know where I am.
It is my fault.
I get out immediately.

Chapter Four

I walk down the same street.
There is a deep hole in the sidewalk.
I walk around it.

Chapter Five

I walk down another street.

He clearly was tactile and learned with his hands. He liked projects and building things. He liked puzzles and putting things together. Indeed, he could look at packaged devices and put them together correctly without spending much time on the manual of directions. 'I wonder if Jimmy could learn the multiplication tables with the flip chutes you taught us to make during the workshop?' asked his mom. 'I don't see why not!' I replied. Then I suggested that she place her decorated flip chute and a full set of multiplication tables flip chute cards on a food preparation table near the refrigerator because that's what an 11-year-old usually visits first when he gets home from school. Then I suggested that she just stand there and not say anything.

Jimmy came running in at 3.30pm, reached for the refrigerator after hugging his mom hello and stopped when he saw the half gallon decorated flip chute labelled the Green Learning Machine. 'Mom, what's that?' 'What's what, Jimmy?' 'This box. What does it do?' 'Oh, the flip chute! It has two slots and when you put a question in the top, the answer falls out the bottom,' said mom. He became very quiet and forgot about what was in the refrigerator. Finally he said 'I wonder if I could learn the multiplication tables with this flip chute thing?' 'I don't see why not,' she echoed my words and 'I just happen to have a whole set of multiplication cards that fit this green machine.'

Jimmy forgot about eating and ran upstairs to his room and placed the flip chute and cards on his bed – he was an informal 'horizontal learner'. At 6pm his dad came home and his mother called 'Jimmy, dinner's ready!' 'I'm not hungry, Mom. Is it OK if I keep playing with the flip chute? I like it!' His mother brought him a turkey sandwich and some milk on a tray but he kept putting the cards in with little time out for eating. Mom stayed up to see how long Jimmy would persist.

At 2am his lights finally went out. In the morning Jimmy came down with eyes a bit sleepy but flashing triumphantly. 'I know them! I know them! And I'm getting faster and faster. I'm using the stopwatch you gave me because our teacher wants us to do them in record time this year. I'm always last but not anymore. I'm going to be champ this Friday!' 'Now wait a minute, Jimmy. You didn't get 11x11 and 12x9 right away. You always had trouble with those ones.' '121 and 108.' 'How did you do it? That's wonderful! But why didn't you learn it with the tutor or with the computer?' 'Oh the tutor tried but she did the same things our teacher did and I couldn't remember them. And I hate the computer. Every time I got the wrong answer it made a buzz and everyone could hear I didn't get it right, <u>again</u>.'

'Well, why does the flip chute work?' 'It's great, I put the question in and then I see the answer right away. And when I was wrong I just put the card on the bottom and when it came up again I could see the answer in my head and I could get it right!' Jimmy was champ on Friday – two days after he started out using the tactile teaching machine. The flip chute held the key to his personal success style.

1. Old and new beliefs about learning and teaching

In the past, <u>traditional teaching methods</u> and
educational practices worked well for the
mainstream educational systems of Western
societies. These days, however, the same systems
have to cater for hugely <u>diverse student groups</u>
with vastly <u>different expectations</u> and attitudes
never encountered before. Despite these profound
changes, students and trainees around the world
are still being taught by educators and trainers
holding on to <u>outmoded beliefs</u> about learning
and even advocating these <u>archaic methods</u>.

traditional teaching methods

**diverse student groups
different expectations**

**outmoded beliefs
archaic methods**

It is therefore no surprise that <u>negative attitudes</u>
towards schooling in general, and traditional
learning in particular, are widespread, especially
among people who had <u>learning difficulties</u> or
found it hard to cope with <u>formal education</u>.
Their special ways of learning, their personal
learning styles and preferences were not
recognized and catered for, and that's why
they found learning so unrewarding.

negative attitudes

**learning difficulties
formal education**

Worldwide, teachers and trainers still succumb
to the following false beliefs:

1. *Students learn best when seated upright
   at a desk or table*.
   Research has shown that many human beings
   perform better in an <u>informal environment</u>.
   When someone sits on a hard chair, approximately
   75 per cent of the total body weight is supported
   by only ten square centimetres of bone. The
   resulting stress on the tissues of the buttocks often
   causes fatigue, discomfort and the need for
   frequent postural change.

seated upright

informal environment

2. *Students learn best in well-illuminated areas
   and damage their eyes when they read and work
   in low or dim light*.
   Research shows that many students perform
   significantly better in <u>low light</u> environments and
   that bright light makes them restless, fidgety and
   hyperactive. Dimmed light calms many learners
   down and helps them relax and think clearly.

well-illuminated

low light

Classroom 2000 Considerations

Some factors that should make us think about
the future of teaching:

- 80% of the children in their first year of primary school will enter careers that don't exist now, involving technology that hasn't yet been invented.

- Employees will change professions, not just jobs, four or five times during their working lifetime.

- 90% of the workforce will work for companies employing less than 200 people.

- The amount of information in the world is doubling every 2.5 years.

- When Year 2 students in the USA complete Year 12, the body of knowledge will have doubled four times since 1988.

- Today, engineers find that half their knowledge is obsolete in five years.

- Children in the year 2000 will live to 81 years old on average compared with 75 for children born in 1986.

- Graduates will have been exposed to more information in one year than their grandparents were in a lifetime.

- 90% of information and knowledge required in the year 2000 has yet to be invented.

Handout during a course on 'Classroom Strategies'

The younger children are, the less light they seem to need, but the need for light increases every five years throughout life.

3. *Students learn more and perform better in an absolutely quiet environment.* Research reveals that many adults think and remember best when <u>studying with music</u> in the background, and findings in New Zealand show that approximately 40 per cent of high school students prefer music or <u>noisy environments</u> for studying and are unable to concentrate when it is quiet. As there are always a few students in every group who need absolute silence, learning and training environments should cater for both needs.

absolutely quiet

studying with music

noisy environments

4. *Students learn difficult subjects best in the early morning when they are most alert.* Again, research has shown that this is definitely not true for all learners. When students were allowed to learn at their <u>best time of day</u>, their behaviour, their motivation and their maths scores improved. Not everyone can concentrate well in the morning and that's why <u>afternoon learners</u> as well as true '<u>night owls</u>' have a hard time in traditional education settings where difficult subjects are usually scheduled during the morning hours.

early morning

best time of day

afternoon learners
night owls

5. *Students who do not sit still are not ready to learn or are not learning properly.* Research findings have shown that students of all ages and generally more males than females <u>need mobility</u> while they learn. Most students who are <u>actively involved</u> in the learning process are likely to learn more, pay closer attention and achieve higher test marks than when they just have to sit and listen.

sitting still

need mobility
actively involved

6. *Eating should not be permitted in classrooms.* Many students concentrate better when they eat, <u>chew, drink or bite while learning</u>. One study revealed that students who <u>needed intake</u> and were allowed to eat while taking a test scored significantly higher than those who also needed intake but were denied it.

eating in class

chew, drink, bite
need intake

ABOUT SCHOOL

Anonymous

He always wanted to say things. But no one understood.
He always wanted to explain things. But no one cared. So he drew.
Sometimes he would just draw and it wasn't anything.
He wanted to carve it in stone or write it in the sky.
He would lie out on the grass and look up in the sky and it would be only him
and the sky and the things inside that needed saying.
And it was after that, that he drew the picture. It was a beautiful picture.
He kept it under the pillow and would let no one see it.
And he would look at it every night and think about it.
And when it was dark, and his eyes were closed, he could still see it.
And it was all of him. And he loved it.
When he started school he brought it with him.
Not to show to anyone, but just to have it with him like a friend.
It was funny about school. He sat in a square, brown desk
like all the other square, brown desks, and he thought it should be red.
And his room was a square, brown room.
Like all the other rooms. And it was tight and close. And stiff.
He hated to hold the pencil and the chalk, with his arm stiff and his feet
flat on the floor, stiff, with the teacher watching and watching.
And then he had to write numbers. And they weren't anything.
They were worse than the letters that could be something if you put them together.
And the numbers were tight and square and he hated the whole thing.
The teacher came and spoke to him. She told him to wear a tie like all the other boys.
He said he didn't like it and she said it didn't matter.
After that they drew. And he drew all yellow and it was the way he felt about morning.
And it was beautiful. The teacher came and smiled at him.
'What's this?' she said. 'Why don't you draw something like Ken's drawing?
Isn't that beautiful?' It was all questions.
After that his mother bought him a tie and he always drew airplanes and rocket ships
like everyone else.
And he threw the old picture away.
And when he lay out alone looking at the sky, it was big and blue and all of everything,
but he wasn't anymore.
He was square inside and brown, and his hands were stiff,
and he was like anyone else.
And the thing inside him that needed saying didn't need saying anymore.
It had stopped pushing. It was crushed. Stiff.
Like everything else.

It is believed that the teenage student who wrote this poem
committed suicide two weeks later.

7. *Generally, the older the students the easier*
   it is for them to adapt to a teacher's style.
   Although it is true that adult students require
   less teacher motivation and obviously also
   less structure, they continue to learn differently
   from one another, have varying needs and styles
   and require more options and clearly defined,
   appropriate objectives. Like younger students
   they find it equally hard to cope with teachers
   and trainers whose teaching styles do not match
   their own learning styles.

older students
adapt more easily

less teacher motivation
less structure
varying needs and styles
more options

These are just some fallacies about learning and
teaching that need to be put right.

What is the solution? As explained so far, it is
mainly that:

solution:

- everyone should have thorough knowledge of
  learning styles;

knowing learning styles

- educators must be ready to implement and
  maintain student-centred teaching methods,
  and cater for the needs of all learners as much
  as possible;

student-centred teaching

- parents must understand style differences
  in their children, support them in their true
  learning needs as much as possible and create
  a learner-friendly environment in the home.

understand
style differences
learning needs
home environment

2. Please, respect my individuality

Everyone who is a parent or works in education
these days has to be aware of human diversity
and has to do more than just acknowledge
differences among family members and students
in class. Teachers and educators alike must know
about learning style differences among human
beings, young or old. In our age of mass education
the old adages often heard by high school teachers
'We know what's good for our students' and
'Our methods have worked successfully for the past
one hundred and fifty years' have kept educators
from learning more about individual learning needs.
If teachers want to be successful in reaching all
their students, they will have to take into account
style differences, not only in their daily teaching
strategies but also in their preparations.

human diversity

individual learning needs

The incurable ACADEMIC,

watching a teacher successfully

using creative teaching methods:

'But would it work in

THEORY??'

When students in class can experience that their
individuality is accepted and they are allowed and
encouraged to learn 'their way', motivation goes up,
their schoolwork becomes more enjoyable, study
skills improve, and with these positive developments
their self-esteem increases.

individuality accepted

self-esteem increases

For parents it is similarly important to accept that
their children do have different learning styles and
that their learning needs might vary wildly from
their own. As we will see in Chapter 10, once
parents begin to understand and support their
children's individuality when it comes to learning,
school and homework, family life, communication
and interactions between parents and children can
profoundly change for the better, particularly during
teenage years. Beyond that, for everyone's peace
of mind, it is also necessary that children understand
their parents' styles and that their brains might
function very differently when it comes to learning
and information intake. This is particularly
important when family tensions are high and
understanding of each other is at a low point. I wish
I had understood the importance of style differences
and individuality years ago; it would have helped
me to avoid many family conflicts.

**parents understand
children's individuality**

parents' styles

During the past few years, since I have made
diversity the core idea behind any training session,
be it with teachers, trainers, parents, managers
or business executives, I have realized that it is
always the little things which make a big difference
to people.

diversity as core idea

little things/big difference

Around the world I have seen people in tears
after discovering their true style, when they finally
have the proof that they are not dumb and useless
at learning. I have experienced teachers in seminars
standing up and apologizing publicly to the audience
for the injustices they have done to their past
students. I have heard parents apologizing to their
children for not understanding their uniqueness
and trying to mould them into something they
will never be. And many people have shared their
experiences with me that when they began to work
or study through their strengths, they were much
more effective, and less stressed and frustrated.

The Paradigm Shift Question:

What is impossible

to do in your business (field, discipline,

department, division, technology etc.),

but if it could be done,

would fundamentally change it?

Joel Arthur Barker

Even their private lives benefited from truly
understanding diversity and acting upon it.
So the power of new insights can influence
behaviour, and even reshape people's values
and beliefs.

power of new insights

3. Paradigm shifts – signs of our times

Many new trends in education have made headlines
over the years but most of them were not here
to stay; they were merely preparing us for coming
changes or the high turbulence associated with
times of crises.

new trends in education

Most of the turbulence in education these days
is caused by two factors:

turbulence in education

1. The failure of old education paradigms, as well
   as unsuccessful attempts to prop up those
   outmoded systems. According to Joel Barker (1),
   paradigms are sets of rules and regulations that do
   two things:they establish or define boundaries,
   and tell us how to behave inside these boundaries
   so as to be successful.

education paradigms

sets of rules
define boundaries
how to behave

2. The creation and introduction of new paradigms.
   In times of crisis, people expect, often demand,
   great change. This willingness to accept
   great change produces two results crucial to any
   future development in education:
   a) more people, responding to the demand for
      great change, try to find new ways, in other
      words, new paradigms which will resolve the
      crisis and increase the likelihood of
      paradigm shifts;
   b) more people are willing to accept fundamentally
      new approaches to resolve the crisis and, by
      doing that, increase the opportunity to change
      paradigms. This mechanism sets the stage for
      radical change.

new paradigms

great change

new ways

new approaches
change paradigms

Joel Barker's general cycle of paradigm shifts (2)
can easily be related to the cycle of shifting
educational paradigms which has already begun
and is continuing to work in New Zealand
(some educational institutions and communities
are already going through Step 9!):

general cycle
shifting
educational paradigms
New Zealand

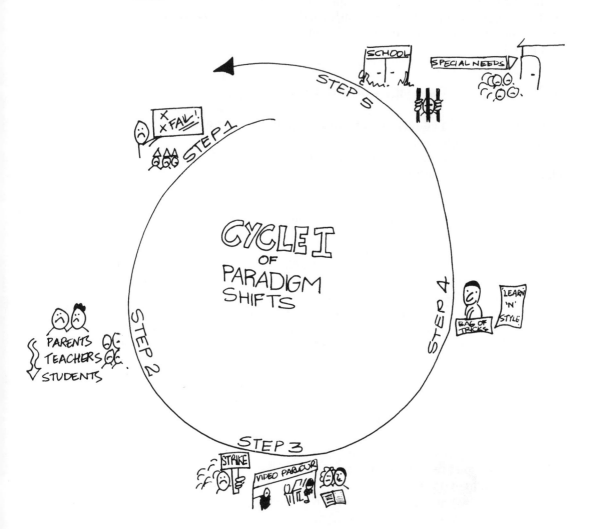

Step 1 *The established paradigm begins to be less effective*: traditional education methods fail and their general application to all students in New Zealand is no longer effective.

established paradigm less effective

Step 2 *The affected community senses the situation, begins to lose trust in the old rules*: parents are dissatisfied, teachers stressed out, students frustrated; there is more and more academic failure.

affected community begins to lose trust

Step 3 *Turbulence grows as trust is reduced – the sense of crisis increases*: teacher strikes become more frequent, underachievement and truancy increase, parents begin to look for new alternatives to traditional schooling.

turbulence grows crisis increases

Step 4 *Creators or identifiers of a new paradigm step forward to offer their solutions*: many of these solutions (like Suggestopedia, Brain Gym®, creative accelerated learning, matched instructions based on learning styles, and so on) have been around for a long time, yet generally disregarded by mainstream education.

paradigm creators offer solutions

Step 5 *Turbulence increases even more as paradigm conflict becomes apparent*: there are higher dropout rates, more and more so-called 'special needs' and 'learning disabled' or ADD (Attention Deficit Disorder) students, increased unemployment, domestic violence, drug abuse, gang activities and crime.

turbulence increases paradigm conflict

Step 6 *Affected communities are extremely upset and demand clear solutions*: economic downturn leads to reduction of government spending, ruling parties lose elections, alternative political groupings occur; there is breakdown of social and educational structures, social tension and unrest.

community upset demands clear solutions

Step 7 *One of the suggested new paradigms demonstrates the ability to solve a small set of significant problems that the old paradigm could not*: accepting new approaches to teaching and learning like '**everyone** can learn when taught with matched instructions based on their individual learning styles'.

new paradigm demonstrates ability to solve problems

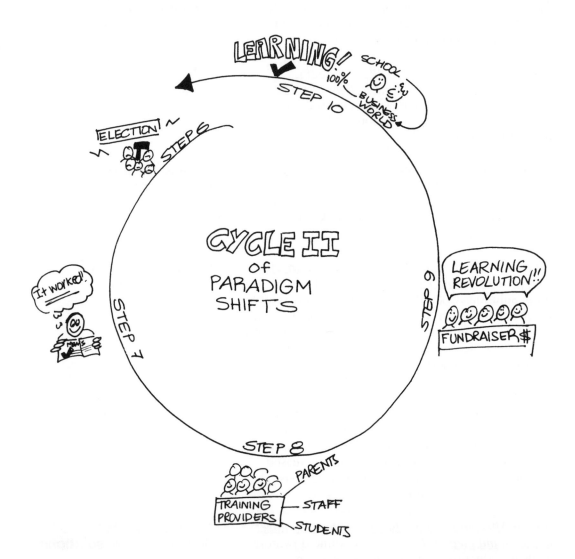

Step 8 *Some of the affected community accepts the new paradigm as an act of faith mainly out of desperation*: private training providers offer their services to groups of interested teachers who then successfully implement new holistic methods; individual, progressive schools join new and progressive change programmes, train their staff, assess their students' learning styles and begin to teach for diversity; at the same time they re-educate parents about these new methods. Very rapidly, sometimes after a few months, these schools experience dramatic changes for the positive in their students, teachers and their community.

**community accepts
new paradigm
out of desperation**

Step 9 *With stronger support and more funding, the new paradigm gains momentum*: more schools want to be part of the 'Learning Revolution'; they apply for funding from government and/or find new ways of co-operating with the business community to raise funds. The successful change process is monitored and documented, results are publicized widely. Finally, legislation makes it possible for every student in the country to have their learning styles assessed and be taught according to their individual preferences.

**stronger support
new paradigm
gains momentum**

Step 10 *Turbulence begins to wane as the new paradigm starts solving problems*: educators realize that these methods are not a fad or gimmick but help learners to develop their true strengths, their untapped potential; the affected community has a new way to deal with educational problems; the new learning methods seem successful and are transferred over into the business community which is pleased about the qualities and attitudes of students having gone through a successful education process.

**turbulence wanes
paradigm solves problems**

At this point, a combination of holistic education, learning styles and creative, accelerated learning methods has become the new standard in schools across the country and serves as a model for successful teaching strategies in other countries. With the affected community increasingly comfortable with the new prevailing paradigm, the level of tolerance for more new ideas drops dramatically and the cycle is complete. Now

**comfortable with
new paradigm
cycle is complete**

If you can come

through the snow and the rain

and the sleet,

you know you can

make it easily

when the sun is out

and everything is all right.

Malcolm X

society must wait for the next round of
significant problems in education (that this
newly accepted paradigm cannot solve)
to trigger a <u>new cycle</u>.

new cycle

If you think the described process does not apply
to your educational system, your society or your
country, and the proposed <u>solutions</u> seem
far <u>too simplistic</u>, <u>unworkable</u> and idealistic
because you believe the whole problem is much
more complex, just sit back and reflect on
these <u>possibilities of change</u>. Where does any
change begin? Who can and will instigate it?
What does it take to bring changes about? What
might be your own role in this change process?
Are you actively involved or are you trying to
avoid or even resist changes?

solutions
too simplistic, unworkable

possibilities of change

If, after answering these questions honestly,
all that business of change still seems too utopian,
too 'way out' for you, maybe you yourself are
locked into so-called '<u>paradigm paralysis</u>' –
<u>a mindset that is very limiting</u> because it tells you
only logically what's possible and what's not.
Be aware that that terminal disease, as Joel Barker
calls this 'paradigm paralysis', might <u>prevent you</u>
from <u>recognizing</u> future developments or
<u>possibilities</u>.

paradigm paralysis
limiting mindset

prevents
recognition of
possibilities

It is time to <u>look beyond</u> what we are used to, what
is familiar to us and <u>what has worked in the past</u>.
Only then will we be able to cope with the demands
of the future and actually <u>enjoy the change process</u>.

look beyond
what worked in the past

enjoy change process

4. The new paradigm of teaching and learning

As we have seen before, paradigms are sets of rules
which define boundaries and help us to behave so
that we are successful. Within these frameworks
we virtually do everything: learn, work, teach,
choose our partners, bring up our children; in short,
run our lives. As long as <u>paradigms are useful</u> and
really help us to perform better, feel better and
achieve what we want, <u>they are good for us</u>. But,
when existing frameworks do the opposite for us,
or <u>are even damaging</u>, particularly in education,

useful paradigms

are good for us

but when damaging

There can be no significant innovation
in education that does not
have at its centre
the attitudes of the teachers.
The beliefs, assumptions, feelings
of teachers are the air of
the learning environment; they determine the
quality of life with it.

Postman and Weingartner

Belief (Webster):
1) An acceptance of something true
2) Trust, confidence – (I have belief in her ability)
3) An opinion, expectation, judgement

we have to look for new ones which serve us better.
So, what are the new paradigms for teaching and
learning? They are really very simple but they also
contain provocations for traditionalists and those
who have a very limiting mindset.

we need new ones

contain provocations

For teaching, the new paradigm is: 'When students
cannot learn the way we teach them, we must learn
to teach them the way they CAN learn.' For human
learning the new paradigm is: 'Everyone CAN
learn but everyone learns in a different way.'

**new paradigms for
teaching and learning**

This whole notion of human diversity and learning
ability has its roots in recent brain research findings
about learning. The question everyone is asking is if
any of that will help us create better schools where
students will achieve more and better learning.
The answer has to be a sound 'Yes!' Why, might
we then ask, haven't we known about all that
before? There is a good reason: most of our present
understanding of the human brain dates back only
25 to 40 years, and most of it much less than that.
Neuroscientists have made great progress but much
helpful work has also been done by other disciplines,
such as cognitive science, biopsychology, brain
evolution, anthropology and computer science. Only
recently have facts, findings and concepts from these
fields come together and thrown some light on what
is considered the most complex structure in the
known universe.

create better schools

understanding the brain

most complex structure

Knowledge about the brain will change teaching and
learning for ever, and brain research applied to the
school environment is not a fad and is here to stay.
There is a simple reason for that: the brain is the
organ for learning because all learning occurs in the
brain and seems to be stored there. The brain not
only controls all body functions, but it also controls
all emotions, and as the 'executive' organ makes all
the decisions about our behaviour.

**brain research applied
to school environment**

For teachers it means that understanding learning
processes in the brain, accepting human diversity
and different learning needs will lead to better
teaching practices, to the use of new learning tools
and to new classroom management techniques.

understanding learning

**leads to
better teaching practices**

What's happening in

students' brains

may redefine teaching.

R. Nummela-Caine

For learners it means that <u>understanding one's own unique brain functions</u> and learning styles will lead to more confidence, greater achievement and <u>long-lasting learning success</u>. With brain-compatible methods students can learn faster and better, and the improvement can be up to 200 per cent or more. If this sounds incredible, read on.

understanding one's unique brain functions leads to long-lasting learning success

5. School learning will never be the same

Nearly 15 years ago two brain researchers-cum-educators already stated 'the most comprehensive learning includes an <u>absence of threat</u>, careful orchestration of <u>multidimensional teaching</u> strategies, <u>real-life experiences</u>, and an understanding of barriers to learning.' (3)

absence of threat multidimensional teaching real-life experiences

They also presented the following revelations of <u>brain research</u> relevant to teaching and learning:

brain research findings

- Learning involves all systems of the body.
- We process many functions simultaneously.
- The need to make sense of our experiences is innate.
- We learn what we experience and what we are told.
- Emotions cannot be separated from thinking and are crucial to memory.
- We absorb both peripheral and focused information.
- We learn better when we are challenged but unthreatened.
- All senses and basic emotions are integrated differently – we are unique.

Based on these insights which are now slowly <u>becoming common knowledge</u>, what are the <u>implications for learning styles</u> and applied brain research for educators so that school learning will never be the same?

common knowledge implications for learning styles

Among all the possible scenarios I consider the following as the most important ones because they beautifully describe a new set of paradigms for education in this new millennium.

THE MAGIC CLASSROOM
by Chris Mullane

This room is like no other, there is magic in the air
It seems kind of disorganized, and there's colour everywhere.

There are beanbags, cushions, couches,
some dividers and a screen.
And over on the other side, some tables can be seen.

Over there beside the window, the sun is shining bright.
But near the inside wall we see there is a lot less light.

In the background there is music for those who learn by sound.
And earmuffs are here for those who are the other way around.

On every wall there are pictures, each one a story tells;
there are also touchy, feely things and even pens with smells.

How anyone could use this room, I haven't got a notion.
It seems more like a recipe for some kind of magic potion!

Perhaps this room is magic and will cast a special spell,
so that everyone who enters here will learn so very well.

Be they tactile, auditory, or a visual kinesthetic.
An impulsive or a global or a reflective analytic.

No longer need they feel a sense of great frustration
when concentrating, processing, and retaining information!

*This poem was created during one of my seminars 'The Magic of Music'.
Chris is a corporate trainer and has integrated all the principles of
creative, accelerated learning in his training programmes.*

'Brain-friendly' teachers will:

- advise students how to use their learning style strengths independently to their own advantage in their studies at home, at school or at work;
- give visual, auditory, tactile and kinesthetic options routinely for activities;
- structure lesson plans and activities so that all students feel secure in the environment, are taught in their own styles most of the time but are also stretched in their flexibilities at other times;
- include both holistic/global and analytic brain processing styles for learning and self-expression;
- embed the teaching of new material in all the senses, emotions and concrete experiences;
- help students to understand their own learning styles and to recognize that all styles are normal, valid and equally valuable;
- teach appreciation for the complexity, the potential and the uniqueness of every human being.

brain-friendly teachers advise students

give V-A-T-K options

structure lesson plans

stretching their flexibilities

include holistic and analytic learning styles

embed material in senses, emotions, experiences understand own learning styles

appreciation for complexity potential and uniqueness

One can easily imagine what teaching in our classrooms would look and feel like if every educator had the knowledge about the brain and its role in the learning process, if every teacher had learned how to implement these approaches, and would truly respect every student as the unique human being he or she is. And how great it would be if that knowledge could be passed on to parents who then could support their children in learning in a very different way.

knowledge about brain

respect every student

knowledge passed on to parents – support their children differently

The exciting fact is that there are already thousands of teachers (and parents) worldwide who have begun to implement methods and techniques based on latest brain research, and I am pleased to say that through my work I am able to play a small part in the process of making a difference and changing traditional teaching methods for good.

making a difference

6. Pioneers at work – from New Zealand to Sweden, to the UK

The many schools in NZ, Sweden and lately the UK

Teachers Having Fun
Making Learning Style Tools

which have taken up the challenge and introduced learning styles to everyday teaching have done it mainly for two reasons:

1. Their leaders are true <u>pioneers,</u> <u>visionaries</u> and <u>risk-takers</u>; they know what they want for their school, have long-term plans with defined goals and are <u>daring enough</u> to take a calculated risk.

    **pioneers, visionaries
    risk-takers**

    daring

2. Their <u>staff</u> and everyone else involved (<u>parents,</u> <u>board members</u> and the <u>wider community</u>) have a particular interest in helping their children to become better learners and equip them with skills that will serve them a lifetime. They are <u>committed and dedicated</u> to making their school a better place for learning, to eliminate underachievement, and are prepared to <u>invest time and money</u> into improving their services to the young ones in our communities.

    **staff, parents, board
    members, community**

    committed and dedicated

    invest time and money

And the results speak for themselves. When I visit schools in Sweden, where the learning styles concept has been used since 1995, the results are very similar to the <u>changes</u> I am observing <u>in New Zealand schools</u>: <u>discipline has improved</u> (teachers say that there is a much more caring atmosphere since the introduction of learning styles); <u>academic performance has improved</u> (particularly of those students who struggled with learning and were underachieving); the atmosphere in the <u>staffroom</u> has changed (there is much <u>more</u> <u>co-operation</u>, more exchange of ideas and <u>better</u> <u>communication</u> among colleagues); and the school's standing in the community has changed because parents begin to understand that the school is now really working hard to help their children succeed in learning and therefore <u>parents become more</u> <u>interested</u> in their <u>children's schooling</u>.

**changes in NZ schools:
improved discipline**

**improved academic
performance**

**among staff
more co-operation
better communication**

**parents more interested in
their children's schooling**

7. Mike Scaddan – a principal's view on learning styles

Te Puna is a rural primary school situated 10km north of Tauranga in the North Island of New Zealand. It has a current roll of 450 pupils with 19 full-time and part-time teachers.

The illiterate of the year 2000

will not be the individual who

cannot read or write,

but the one who cannot learn,

unlearn and relearn.

Alvin Toffler

My interest in alternative learning processes came about after reading research as to how ineffective the majority of schools' in-service training was in bringing about <u>long-term change</u>.

long-term change

When I arrived at Te Puna in 1995, I instigated an in-service programme which included a series of 26 staff meetings dealing with principles in the *Learning Revolution* book by Gordon Dryden and Jeannette Vos, and the introduction of a <u>Thinking Programme</u>. All staff meetings included <u>games and activities</u> to reinforce learning about <u>brain functions</u>. What we did in effect with adults was to use good junior teaching practice, that is, short <u>bursts of activities</u> to improve concentration and a variety of reinforcements, especially kinesthetic activities. We worked for an extended period of time on this development in an effort to constantly reinforce and support <u>new classroom practice</u>.

Thinking Programme
games and activities
brain functions

bursts of activities

new classroom practice

This, however, was only the beginning. Any innovation is difficult to introduce as the risk of failure is high, and further support was needed to maintain enthusiasm for the proposed changes. I was lucky enough to attend a two-day Principals' Seminar conducted by Barbara Prashnig, and there I made the commitment that our next step was to enrol the whole school in the 'Diploma of Holistic Education' course. We began this at the end of 1995. Because of costing restraints the course was run during weekends and holidays, and I want to acknowledge the strong professional values of the staff in agreeing to this <u>huge time commitment</u>. All teaching staff, teacher aides, some parents and even our secretary participated.

huge time commitment

The value of Barbara and her associates coming in was that it reinforced much of what we had already covered, and she was also seen as an <u>outside expert</u> in the field and therefore 'must know what she is doing'.

outside expert

The diploma course modules followed similar lines to our staff meetings, involving learning games and activities to reinforce ideas. The courses were also extremely well planned and organized with a good flow.

There ain't no rules around here! We're trying to accomplish something.

Thomas Edison

What have the changes been <u>in the classroom</u>? Staff <u>awareness</u> of their own and their pupils' individual learning styles has led to the use of a raft of games and activities to reinforce learning. New ideas and learning tools are regularly shared and ideas exchanged during interval and lunchtime discussions. We have now employed a full-time <u>resource manager</u> whose sole job it is to make resources to support our programme. Lately we have also developed a specialization in producing learning tools especially for immersion Maori pupils. Learning tools are used in varying forms and curriculum areas from Year 1 to Year 8.

changes in the classroom
awareness

resource manager

All pupils aged six and above have completed the <u>Learning Style Analysis</u> survey, to find out their preferred learning styles and the conditions most favourable for their learning. Results have been shared and discussed with parents. <u>Classroom layout has changed</u> to include groups, pairs and single-unit seating, with a variety of high and low furniture, enabling children to choose an environment which suits their learning needs. By removing light bulbs we have created conditions of <u>varying light</u>, and our pupils who require low noise levels have found a use for broken headphones – they make great earmuffs.

Learning Style Analysis

classroom layout
has changed

varying light

All class teachers have multiple copies of <u>music</u> designed <u>to assist learning</u>, and manual or taped sound effects are also popular. We are now entering the phase of trying <u>suggestopedic learning concerts</u>.

music
to assist learning

suggestopedic concerts

<u>Games</u> to reinforce learning are an everyday part of class programmes. These mainly involve <u>cross-over exercises</u>, thinking skills or alternative methods to share information. The use of <u>Koosh ball circles</u> or similar exercises to start the day have become an integral part of our new Self-Esteem Programme. Children often need to be 'warmed up' for the school day and this is proving to be a successful method.

games
cross-over exercises

Koosh ball circles

Junior staff have noticed no significant changes in class with the new programme as children's individual learning needs have already been accommodated but the newly introduced <u>learning music</u> seems to be popular.

learning music

How Well Do You Listen?

1. Our listening and hearing usually become more acute when we don't have visual cues. In a safe part of your home (where you don't have to worry about tripping or falling), experiment for a half-hour by keeping your eyes closed and simply listening to the world around you. You may also use a blindfold, such as a scarf or towel wrapped around your eyes.

   You will in all likelihood begin to feel sound coming from different appliances. Can you differentiate among them? Is the hum of your refrigerator different from that of the air-conditioner or other appliances? Are you aware of birdsong or other sounds from outside your home?

2. Put this book down and list on a piece of paper the things you hear around you. Do this without concentrating too hard; the point is to be quick and casual.

   Then spend five minutes really listening. Close your eyes, exhale, and open the 'lens' of your ear.

   Jot down what you heard in those five minutes. How has the list changed? Do you hear dissonant sounds more clearly? Are you aware of the sound of the refrigerator, air-conditioner, space heater, or other 'background noise' in the room? Can you sense any sounds within your body? Your ears are like periscopes, able to focus on distant or near noise.

From: The Mozart Effect by Don Campbell (4)

Middle and senior class teachers' comments include: 'Koosh ball circles are really popular. A huge range of issues are now being discussed. Pupils are expressing their inner thoughts more and are less afraid to share opinions with others. There is more celebration of the positives. Pupils are enthusiastic about making and using learning tools. They love to manipulate them and share them with others. Knowledge retention appears to be improved. Whether this is the tools, the learning concepts or a combination, we are unsure. Learning is now being reinforced in many ways, like with raps, tools, mind maps and kinesthetic activities. Older children have become more selective about participating in learning activities, e.g. a group of visual learners chose not to take part in a kinesthetic maths tables activity. Children are settling more quickly after activity breaks and concentration appears to be better. They prefer baroque and classical music to no music at all. One child wrote that her teacher plays 'soothing' music. The tools have a real value as multi-testers. I feel more relaxed because pupils are in charge of their own learning.'

learning tools

knowledge retention is improved

concentration is better

teacher is more relaxed

It is difficult to judge at this stage any changes in the school tone. Presently we have a lot of construction going on and our ground space is really limited. There are, however, fewer pupils on detention and many games are being used on wet days. Teachers have more knowledge about their pupils through learning styles and Koosh circles, and the pupils appear to feel more valued. As we begin to formally evaluate the programmes, tone is one area which we will assess.

fewer pupils on detention

feel more valued

Our Board of Trustees were keen to involve parents in these developments, so I have begun a series of night classes which run for 10 hours. These have been so popular – 29 enrolments for the first series – that we are offering a rerun next term. Other schools have heard of our programmes and I have been sharing our ideas with them on a regular basis.

involve parents

sharing ideas

Where to now? This has always been viewed as a five-year programme and we have just successfully completed year two. The learning styles support our own Holistic Programme and we use them to

five-year programme

You can make a difference ...

In Maine they tell of an old man walking along the beach
with his grandson, who picked up each starfish they passed
and threw it back into the sea.
'If I left them up here,' the boy said,
'they would dry up and die. I'm saving their lives.'

'But,' protested the old man, 'the beach goes on for miles,
and there are millions of starfish.
What you are doing won't make any difference.'

The boy looked at the starfish in his hand,
gently threw it into the ocean, and answered:
'It makes a difference to this one.'

Past US President George Bush

reinforce thinking, self-esteem, goal setting and
recording all gathered data.

We do face the problem as a growing school with
the appointment of additional staff, therefore our
<u>professional development</u> in these areas will <u>need
to continue</u> in some form. I am now completing
my Master of Education degree in this topic and
have become an avid devourer of all 'Learning
Revolution' material; I am always on the lookout
for new materials which can further improve
our programme.

**professional development
needs to continue**

8. Students, parents and teachers say it in style

When I first heard about the <u>positive effects of
learning styles</u> on teachers, parents and students
in the USA, I naturally was very sceptical. I thought
these American teachers were exaggerating when
they reported enthusiastically about higher academic
achievements, <u>better attendance</u>, much <u>improved
discipline</u> and decreased behaviour problems.
Although I was convinced that the knowledge and
use of learning styles is one of the most potent
remedies to improve teaching and learning in our
schools, I had yet to see <u>results in New Zealand</u>
and in other countries where I had trained teachers
to incorporate learning styles in their daily work.

**positive effects of
learning styles**

**better attendance
improved discipline**

results in New Zealand

And results we got! It turned out that <u>learning styles</u>
is not only a wonderful '<u>quick fix</u>' <u>for under-
achievers</u> and those students who have difficulties
in some areas, but also, more importantly, it is a
<u>long-term remedy</u> for those who have <u>serious
learning problems</u>, who are in special needs groups
or had already been written off as hopeless cases.
It is heartwarming and often very emotional when
teachers tell stories about <u>incredible progress</u> in
their students, and parents rave about the <u>positive
changes in their children</u>, their <u>new attitudes
towards school and learning</u> and the impact this
has had on family life.

**learning styles: 'quick fix'
for underachievers**

**long-term remedy for
serious learning problems**

**incredible progress,
positive changes
in children, new attitudes
towards school and
learning**

Therefore I'd like to share with you, the reader,
some of the comments I have received over the
past few years which are representative of the

NOT BEING ABLE

TO SPEAK

IS NOT THE SAME AS

NOT HAVING ANYTHING

TO SAY.

positive reactions of thousands of people, young and old, of different races, countries and social groupings triggered by learning styles approaches.

First, let the <u>parents</u> speak:

parents

'It became apparent by the time our son was in Standard 2 that he was not settling into the "normal" education system. Despite bright prospects in the beginning, he was becoming increasingly adept at <u>avoiding</u> most aspects of <u>school work</u>. In the middle of his Standard 3 year he was diagnosed as having ADD (Attention Deficit Disorder) and prescribed low doses of Ritalin which greatly improved his work output. However, he still did not "slot in" and was <u>frustrated in class</u> and spent a lot of time on his own.

avoiding school work

frustrated in class

'Knowing Ms May's different approach to learning we were keen for him to be placed in her Standard 4 class and the <u>year was brilliant</u> for him. Through her whole-brain teaching style he has regained his <u>self-confidence</u>, made new friends, learned that it is <u>okay to be different</u> and, most importantly, found in Ms May a learning style that really suits him. Finding out that O learns kinesthetically and tactile-visually instead of auditorily has been a <u>major breakthrough</u> and we will constantly search for future teachers that embrace these four senses. The teacher's classroom techniques for our son, such as not insisting he sits at his desk while working, music in the form of accelerated learning tapes to help him relax and focus, and short bursts of Brain Gym® every hour, have all <u>enhanced</u> his <u>ability to learn</u>.

year was brilliant

self-confidence
okay to be different

major breakthrough

enhanced
ability to learn

'Although these methods may not be essential for every child to succeed, we feel that all the children in this class have benefited from them. Most importantly for us is that O, who was fast being lost into that percentage of students the education system does not cater for, is now heading in a much more positive direction.'

Sadly, Sheryl May, the teacher at <u>Frankton Primary</u> in Hamilton, New Zealand, who in March 1997 received an <u>Award for Excellence</u> in Education

Frankton Primary

Award for Excellence

Students Enjoying Their Learning Style Tools

Courtesy of Pilleval Skolan, Trelleborg, Sweden

Courtesy of J. Anderson-Johns, Intl School Manila, Philippines for successfully implementing a 'Holistic Learning Programme', has passed away but Principal Judy Dixon is very supportive and the whole staff went through the 'Diploma in Holistic Education'; the school has now become a leader in <u>whole-brain learning</u> in the area.

whole-brain learning

And here's what <u>students</u> say:

students

'I have found that working with Ms May this year has <u>improved all my learning skills</u>. It's neat to know that I can learn freely in a style that I am comfortable with. For example, I have discovered that I am a <u>very visual</u> person so I learn well by seeing things. Therefore, I usually don't learn as well as I could in the normal classroom structure where the teacher talks and the students have to listen. Also, we have not only learned the normal school subjects like reading and maths but have had different studies to <u>learn how our brains</u> actually <u>work</u> and what relaxation does for our learning. We even cut a brain up – very, very visual! Over the weeks I have found my <u>teacher</u> is not only my teacher but also <u>my friend</u>.'

improved learning skills

very visual

learn how brains work

teacher
my friend

'My <u>learning</u> in 1996 has been <u>very positive</u>. It has made me realize learning is for ever and I feel pretty <u>confident</u> about myself. I know I can and will be successful. I feel I am important and it is okay to feel like this.'

learning very positive

confident

Reflecting after five years at Frankton:
'The school is a <u>treasure for learning</u> – one of the best – and it's a <u>quality learning place</u>. Although it achieves good book work, that's not the only thing it teaches. It also teaches things on the inside (which counts). It teaches you to set your goals and go through with them, also known as walking your talk.'

treasure for learning
quality learning place

9. Implementing learning styles – an Action Plan

It's all right to read about schools which are already on the way to implementing learning styles and changing their school around but the question remains 'How can we do it so that it's not too painful?' Well,

Dare to Dream...

1. Write up elements of a successful education system.

2. Draw a mind map – brainstorm a successful education system.

3. Create a song/rap about the education system you'd like to see in the future.

here is a process which has been followed by many
schools successfully because it has been trialled,
allows the <u>accommodation of individual needs</u> and   **accommodation of**
integrates very well any school's own change   **individual needs**
programme. Once the decision to go ahead is made,
you can use the following <u>Action Plan</u> which is   **Action Plan**
also part of our in-service programme 'School of
the Future Based on Learning Styles'.

Ten steps to implement learning styles on a school-wide basis

1. <u>Teacher training</u> (Day 1) *Learning Styles and Classroom Management*
   including teachers' own personal LSA-Ad profiles

2. <u>Student assessments</u> with LSA questionnaires, production of computer-
   generated student profiles by the school itself

3. <u>Teacher training</u> (Day 2) *Learning Styles and Student Centred Teaching*
   focusing on Teaching Styles (TSA-Ed) for teachers and interpretation of student
   profiles with trained facilitator and production of learning style tools

4. <u>Observation period</u> carried out by teachers trained in learning styles

5. <u>Sharing results with students and parents</u>: interpretation of LSA profiles,
   homework and study strategies for students; parent evening

6. <u>Classroom redesign</u>: based on students' preferences and with students' input;
   school-wide co-operation is necessary to achieve the desired outcomes

7. <u>Creating and using learning style tools</u>, produced initially by teachers, later
   by students and/or parents/resource people

8. <u>Adaptation of classroom teaching</u> to suit analytic and holistic students – lesson
   preparation to accommodate L/R brain processing plus strategies for multisensory teaching to accommodate auditory, visual, tactile and kinesthetic needs

9. <u>Evaluation phase</u>: monitor students' progress and evaluate impact of programme
   on teachers, students, parents and the community at large

10. <u>Continuation</u>: incorporate new students, train new teachers and continue to
    build the 'School of the Future Based on Learning Styles' (see Chapter 12).

If you have any questions about this Action Plan,
or how we at <u>Creative Learning Co</u> can help your   **Creative Learning Co**
school, or for INSET training in the UK, contact
<u>Network Educational Press</u> (for address see   **Network Educational Press**
Appendix II).

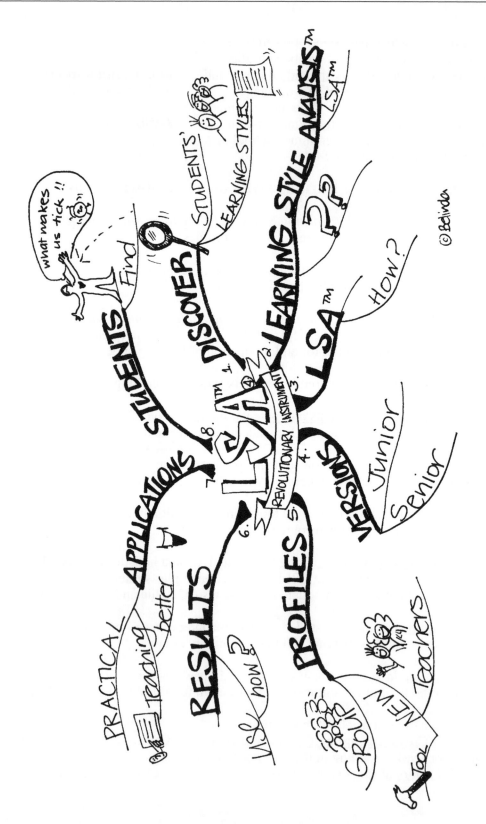

1. Discover your students' learning styles

For the <u>successful teachers</u> of the future it is vitally important to know what goes on in their students' heads, how they think, what makes them succeed or fail, and how they need to be treated to allow them to grow and develop their full learning potential.

successful teachers

Knowledge about learning styles helps teachers to create a multisensory learning environment which caters as much as possible for each student's <u>individual needs</u>. By utilizing the 'diversity concept' and accepting different styles, teachers will become more effective in their teaching strategies, and students will become more confident learners, being more satisfied with their own learning progress.

individual needs

How someone effectively <u>solves problems,</u> <u>learns and remembers</u> is the key to lifelong success. Even though everyone has the power to learn, few of us really use this power to the full. Why? Because everyone has his or her <u>own style</u> of learning, working and concentrating on something really difficult, yet very few people do it in a way that's best for them. Too often have we been <u>conditioned</u> to use a single style, an approach that is right for some, but not for all of us.

solve problems
learn and remember

own style

conditioned

Research on learning styles explains why certain children in the same family perform well at school whereas their siblings do not. It demonstrates the <u>differences in style</u> among members of the same class, culture, community, religion, or socio-economic group, but it also reveals the differences and <u>similarities</u> between groups. It shows style differences between teachers and their students, how boys' styles differ from girls', and reveals the reasons why some children learn to read easily and others obviously struggle.

differences in style

similarities

Although teachers claim to know their students quite well, research has also shown that they <u>cannot</u> <u>correctly identify</u> all the characteristics of their <u>students' learning styles</u>. Some aspects are just not observable and therefore we need assessment tools.

cannot correctly identify

students' learning styles

2. What is the Learning Style Analysis (LSA)?

After experimenting with creative, accelerated learning techniques, using brain-based teaching methods in my teacher-training programmes for many years, the development of the revolutionary 'diversity concept' for learning, training and working was the next step in an exciting journey. The first instrument, created together with Dr Ken Dunn of Queen's College in New York, was the Working Style Analysis. I have used it not only to build up my own business and to make my own staff more effective by utilizing their skills and drawing out their potential, but I have also helped thousands of teachers as well as people in business in New Zealand and overseas to achieve personal and professional success by understanding themselves and others.

'diversity concept'

drawing out potential

What is the Working Style Analysis (WSA)?

WSA

It is a new assessment instrument, completed in 1996 and derived from the original Dunn and Dunn learning style model which was created during the early 1970s in the USA. Expanded and improved, the WSA allows users to find out what their preferred working and learning conditions are. Research has proven that every individual prefers to learn, work and concentrate in a different way, and information intake is greatly enhanced when people can think, work or concentrate in their favoured conditions. Factors that determine someone's success are not only influenced by his or her intelligence or unique personality, but also by the physical space where someone works and concentrates, by the interaction with people, the time of day, their physical needs and their frame of mind. (1)

learn, work
in different ways

favoured conditions

unique personality

The widespread use, cross-cultural appeal and successful application of the WSA worldwide has led to an increased demand for a similar assessment tool for younger students and its use in school settings. Again, Dr Ken Dunn and I collaborated successfully in creating this new instrument – the Learning Style Analysis.

cross-cultural appeal

Learning Style Analysis

Biologically Based Elements

ANALYTIC ('Left')   HOLISTIC ('Right')

BRAIN DOMINANCE

BRAIN PROCESSING
sequential [░░░░░] [///////] simultaneous

THINKING STYLE
reflective [░░░░░] [░░░░░] impulsive

SENSORY MODALITIES

AUDITORY (hearing) [░░░░] listening
Auditory (external) [░░░░] talking/discussing
Auditory (internal) [░░░░] self-talk/inner dialogue
VISUAL (words) ———— reading
Visual (external) [░░░░] seeing/watching
Visual (internal) [░░░░] visualizing/imagination
TACTILE (touching) [████] manipulating/handling
KINESTHETIC (external) [░░░░] experiencing/doing
Kinesthetic (internal) [████] feeling/intuition

PHYSICAL NEEDS

MOBILITY
stationary ———— [///////] movement needed

INTAKE
not needed ———— [///////] needed

TIME OF DAY
early morning [░░░░] [///////] late morning
———— afternoon
████ evening

ENVIRONMENT

SOUND
quiet ████ ———— sound/noise/music

LIGHT
bright light [///////] ———— low light

TEMPERATURE
cool [░░░░] [///////] warm

STUDY AREA
formal ———— ████ informal/comfortable

KEY	████ = strong preference	[░░░] = flexibility	———— = non-preference
	[///] = preference		???? = inconsistency

It is the newest learning style assessment tool available on the market, based on the original instrument, the Working Style Analysis, and it comes in two versions: one for primary and one for secondary school students. For adult learners, however, the <u>LSA-Adult Version</u> is recommended as it also gives insight into style preferences of grown-up learners.

LSA-Adult Version

Like adult learners, younger students also prefer to learn, concentrate and process information in different ways and every child has a uniquely different learning style, but, contrary to style preferences in adults, <u>children's learning style features</u> change and <u>develop as they grow up</u>. Therefore it is correct to say that a learning style profile is a 'snapshot in time' revealing style elements which remain stable and others which can change, even daily.

children's learning styles develop as they grow up

The LSA assesses <u>49 individual elements</u> in the following <u>six basic areas</u> which are represented as layers of a pyramid. The first four of these layers seem to be <u>biologically or genetically</u> determined and the last two <u>conditioned or learned</u>:

49 individual elements
six basic areas

biological or genetic
conditioned or learned

1. LEFT/RIGHT BRAIN DOMINANCE
   showing <u>sequential</u> or <u>simultaneous</u> brain-processing strategies
   <u>reflective</u> or <u>impulsive</u> thinking styles
   and overall <u>analytic</u> or <u>holistic/global</u> learning styles

   sequential, simultaneous

   reflective, impulsive
   analytic, holistic/global

2. SENSORY MODALITIES
   including <u>auditory</u> (hearing, talking, inner dialogue)
   <u>visual</u> (reading, seeing, visualizing)
   <u>tactile</u> (manipulating, touching) and
   <u>kinesthetic</u> (doing, feeling) preferences

   auditory

   visual
   tactile
   kinesthetic

3. PHYSICAL NEEDS
   identifying needs for <u>mobility</u> (preferences for moving or being stationary)
   <u>intake</u> (eating, nibbling, drinking, chewing, smoking) and <u>time of day</u> preferences (personal biorhythm)

   mobility

   intake
   time of day

LSA - Sen

Conditioned/Learned Elements

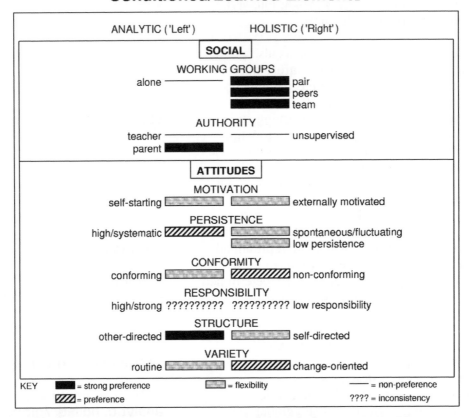

DIFFERENCES BETWEEN BIOLOGICAL AND LEARNED ELEMENTS:
The results on page 2 represent your biological needs when concentrating, reading a study text or learning something new and difficult. Preferences and non-preferences in these areas are usually hard to change and remain mostly stable over a life time. When they are mismatched over a longer period of time they will influence learning motivation, persistence and responsibility in a negative way. For lasting learning success, make sure that your strong preferences are being matched most of the time.
The results on page 3 reveal your conditioning, and show with whom you learn best and what your attitudes are when it comes to learning something new and difficult. These elements are not stable in your profile and can change quite rapidly. This usually happens when there are changes going on inside you or in the world around you. To be successful at school it is very important that you develop positive attitudes and always attempt the best you can do because your preferences become your strengths when you use them wisely.

4. ENVIRONMENT
   revealing preferences for <u>sound</u> (needing
   music/sound or wanting it quiet)

   sound

   <u>light</u> (needing bright or dim lighting)

   light

   <u>temperature</u> (needing a cool or warm
   learning environment) and

   temperature

   <u>work area</u> (wanting formal or informal/
   comfortable setting and furniture)

   work area

5. SOCIAL GROUPINGS
   including preferences for working <u>alone</u>,

   alone

   in a <u>pair</u>, with <u>peers</u>, or in a <u>team</u>, and

   pair, with peers, team

   <u>authority</u> (wanting to learn with a <u>teacher</u>

   authority

   and/or a <u>parent</u> or without them)

   teacher/parent

6. ATTITUDES
   showing <u>motivation</u> (internally or
   externally motivated for learning)

   motivation

   <u>persistence</u> (high, fluctuating or low)

   persistence

   <u>conformity</u> (conforming or non-conforming/
   rebellious)

   conformity

   <u>structure</u> (being self-directed or needing
   directions, guidance from others)

   structure

   <u>variety</u> (needing routine/consistency or being
   change-oriented/needing variety)

   variety

The Learning Style Analysis can accurately:

- <u>identify how students learn</u> in class or at home,
  how they think, concentrate, solve problems
  and can best master their learning activities;

  identify how students learn

- <u>assist teachers and parents</u> in creating the most
  appropriate learning or study environment for
  every child, either at school or at home;

  assist teachers and parents

- suggest how to <u>improve study skills</u> and
  enhance learning motivation;

  improve study skills

- <u>advise senior students</u> and their parents how to
  utilize personal preferences for future studies
  or <u>career planning</u>.

  advise senior students

  career planning

3. How the LSA works

By responding to a <u>questionnaire</u> which contains a
series of statements about themselves, students will
receive a computer-generated personal profile and

questionnaire

LSA - Sen   Sample five

Learning Style Tendencies

Compare this with your Left/Right Brain Dominance on page 2

ANALYTIC ('Left')		HOLISTIC ('Right')
quiet	████████ ————————	sound/noise/music
bright light	▨▨▨▨▨ ————————	low light
formal study area	———— ████████	informal work area
high persistence	▨▨▨▨▨▨ ░░░░░░░	low persistence
no/low intake	———— ▨▨▨▨▨▨	intake needed

Three or more of the following elements: preferring quiet, bright light, formal design/work area, high persistence (to complete tasks without interruptions) and low need for intake tends to suggest an ANALYTICAL (sequential) learning style. On the other hand, preferring sound, soft lighting, informal design, low persistence (completing tasks in bursts while working on multiple tasks simultaneously) and need for intake suggests a GLOBAL/HOLISTIC (simultaneous) learning style (Bruno, 1988; Dunn, Cavanaugh, Eberle, and Zenhausern, 1982).

Report Guidelines

FOR STUDENTS:
For really improving your study skills, follow the suggestions in your LSA™ Report and watch your own success. To achieve permanent improvement in learning and study situations please share and discuss this report with your teachers and your parents/guardians and make sure your learning needs are met.

FOR TEACHERS:
Please help your students to analyse their profiles, discuss their reports and their personal preferences; find out which areas of mismatch between the teaching styles used at your school and your students' learning needs could be the reason for frustration, poor learning motivation, stress or boredom, leading to learning difficulties or underachievement.

FOR PARENTS/GUARDIANS:
To help improve concentration, study skills, learning abilities, motivation and attitudes of this student, please follow the suggestions in this LSA™ Report closely, provide the necessary learning environment at home, accept their unique style and support their true learning needs.

report, allowing them to <u>identify their individual strengths</u> and personal preferences for learning, studying, reading and general information intake. Through this analysis they will also learn how to recognize and control the elements that can enhance their attempts to solve learning problems. The report helps them concentrate, learn, read and study more efficiently and with greater success and satisfaction. If personal <u>learning preferences are being matched</u> for students in the classroom and at home, these <u>become strengths</u> and will <u>improve their study skills</u>, concentration, consistency and quality of their school and homework as well as their academic performance.

identify strengths

learning preferences matched
become strengths
improve study skills

Apart from the computer-generated Personal Profiles the LSA Report gives a detailed explanation of all the <u>individual elements</u> of the LSA model plus advice on how best to utilize personal strengths for learning situations, counteract weaknesses and increase flexibilities.

individual elements

If the <u>recommendations are acted upon</u>, students will find that their overall academic performance, <u>behaviour and concentration improves</u> (to the delight of their teachers and parents). Learning abilities as well as problem-solving skills will be enhanced, <u>school-related stress will be reduced</u> and often learning satisfaction and self-esteem will increase dramatically. This, of course, is reflected in a noticeable <u>improvement in school discipline</u> wherever individual learning styles are the basis for teaching and learning.

if recommendations are acted upon, behaviour and concentration improves

school stress reduced

improvement in discipline

4. LSA Junior and Senior Versions

Both versions have been created to help students gain an insight into their true learning needs and to enable teachers and parents to help them learn in their best possible way.

- The <u>Learning Style Analysis Junior</u> is for students between six and twelve years of age.
- The <u>Learning Style Analysis Senior</u> is for students between twelve and sixteen/seventeen years of age.

LSA Junior

LSA Senior

The <u>reading skills</u> required for the questionnaires have deliberately been kept <u>at a very low level</u> so that administration of this instrument is easy and user-friendly. Although these are reading-based instruments, the reading itself should not be a barrier for students in obtaining useful results.

**reading skills
at very low level**

Sample questions LSA Junior Version

'I hardly ever think about eating or drinking when I learn.'
'I get more done when I have a friend to work with.'
'When the classroom is very quiet I can't concentrate.'

Sample questions LSA Senior Version

'I remember things better from the early morning classes.'
'When I am interested, no one has to remind me to finish something.'
'It's really difficult for me to sit still for a long time.'

Information about LSA software can be found in Appendix II. For adult students in education institutions the <u>LSA-Adult Version is used</u> (formerly WSA Education Version) and for people in the workforce the <u>WSA Corporate</u> is available. They all can be obtained individually or in large numbers from various <u>websites</u>.

LSA-Adult Version

WSA Corporate

websites

Now two other revolutionary instruments, the <u>Teaching Style Analysis (TSA-Ed)</u> and the <u>Training Style Analysis (TSA-Corp)</u>, allow teachers and trainers to assess their own styles so that they can compare it with their students' styles. The TSA-Ed instrument will, for the first time, make it possible to reveal <u>mismatches between teachers</u> and their <u>students</u> in a very factual, analytic way. It will help teachers to improve their teaching techniques and adjust to their students' true learning needs.

**TSA-Ed
TSA-Corp**

**mismatches between
teachers and students**

All instruments are freely available on the <u>internet</u>. They can be used individually, in businesses or educational institutions and in-depth training on applications is available through the Creative Learning Company, NZ, or through one of their international licensed distributors or accredited facilitators. (For details see Appendix II.)

internet

Learning Style Analysis™

Senior

prepared for:	Sample Group
7/06/01	Total number in group = 10

Group Percentages I (preferences)

Graph shows the % of people with preferences in the following areas:

BRAIN PROCESSING	sequential 10	60 simultaneous
THINKING STYLE	reflective 20	60 impulsive
SENSORY MODALITIES	AUDITORY (hearing)	20 listening
	Auditory (external)	10 talking/discussing
	Auditory (internal)	40 self-talk/inner dialogue
	VISUAL (words)	10 reading
	Visual (external)	40 seeing/watching
	Visual (internal)	30 visualizing/imagination
	TACTILE (touching)	70 manipulating/handling
	KINESTHETIC (external)	40 experiencing/doing
	Kinesthetic (internal)	60 feeling/intuition
MOBILITY	stationary 10	40 movement needed
INTAKE	not needed 0	40 needed
TIME OF DAY	early morning 10	20 late morning
		10 afternoon
		40 evening
SOUND	quiet 40	10 sound/noise/music
LIGHT	bright light 20	10 low light
TEMPERATURE	cool 20	40 warm
STUDY AREA	formal 20	50 informal/comfortable
WORKING GROUPS	alone 10	40 pair
		20 peers
		60 team
AUTHORITY	teacher 10	0 unsupervised
	parent 10	
MOTIVATION	self-starting 40	10 externally motivated
PERSISTENCE	high/systematic 40	0 spontaneous/fluctuating
		30 low persistence
CONFORMITY	conforming 0	40 non-conforming
RESPONSIBILITY	high/strong 50	10 low responsibility
STRUCTURE	other-directed 50	30 self-directed
VARIETY	routine 0	30 change-oriented
LS Tendencies	analytic 10	0 holistic/global

KEY ▮ = preferences

5. Group profiles – a new tool for classroom teachers

The software also generates several different
group profiles for unlimited numbers of students,
allowing teachers to gain a very good overview of
individual learning needs among their students.
Group profiles are very useful for finding out
similarities and differences among individuals or
groups, and can help to resolve discipline and
communication problems. They are also valuable
tools for preparing teaching programmes and
learning materials matching students' styles,
making any teaching much more effective and
more enjoyable for all participants – students
and teachers alike.

group profiles

similarities, differences

Multisensory learning kits can be produced
before the training (see page 146) and contain
the necessary learning tools for all the different
styles during information intake. With the help
of the group profile, teachers can prepare these
tools – often with the assistance of parents or
teacher aides – and orchestrate exercises according
to their students' preferences. Instead of
traditional uniform teaching programmes it is
now possible to have customized, accelerated
learning programmes for individuals within a
larger group of students.

multisensory kits

learning tools

**customized, accelerated
learning programmes**

6. How to use results from the LSA

These instruments help to identify a teacher's
individual teaching style or a student's unique
learning style, revealing personal features which
are applicable not only in the classroom but also
in the home environment because personal styles
influence whatever human beings do, and go well
beyond the classroom and the workplace.

**applicable in classroom
and home environment**

They are in fact the basis for our lifestyles, partner
choice as well as the reason for conflict or harmony
between parents and their children, as explained in
Chapters 9 and 10. Interpretation of results always
leads to a much better understanding of our human
diversity.

**basis for lifestyles
reason for conflict or
harmony**

LSA - Sen   Sample Group
                                                                           Members: 10

prepared for:	Sample Group
7/06/01	Total number in group = 10

Group Percentages II (non-preferences)

Graph shows the % of people with non-preferences in the following areas:

BRAIN PROCESSING	sequential 20 —	0	simultaneous
THINKING STYLE	reflective 40 ——	0	impulsive
SENSORY MODALITIES	AUDITORY (hearing)	— 20	listening
	Auditory (external)	0	talking/discussing
	Auditory (internal)	— 10	self-talk/inner dialogue
	VISUAL (words)	—— 30	reading
	Visual (external)	0	seeing/watching
	Visual (internal)	— 10	visualizing/imagination
	TACTILE (touching)	0	manipulating/handling
	KINESTHETIC (external)	— 10	experiencing/doing
	Kinesthetic (internal)	0	feeling/intuition
MOBILITY	stationary 30 ——	0	movement needed
INTAKE	not needed 50 ——	— 10	needed
TIME OF DAY	early morning 20 —	—— 30	late morning
		—— 50	afternoon
		— 10	evening
SOUND	quiet 30 ——	—— 30	sound/noise/music
LIGHT	bright light 20 —	—— 40	low light
TEMPERATURE	cool 20 —	— 20	warm
STUDY AREA	formal 50 ——	0	informal/comfortable
WORKING GROUPS	alone 40 ——	— 10	pair
		— 10	peers
		— 10	team
AUTHORITY	teacher 30 ——	— 30	unsupervised
	parent 30 ——		
MOTIVATION	self-starting 10 —	—— 50	externally motivated
PERSISTENCE	high/systematic 50 ——	— 10	spontaneous/fluctuating
		—— 40	low persistence
CONFORMITY	conforming 30 ——	0	non-conforming
RESPONSIBILITY	high/strong 30 ——	— 10	low responsibility
STRUCTURE	other-directed 10 —	— 10	self-directed
VARIETY	routine 40 ——	— 10	change-oriented
LS Tendencies	analytic 40 ——	0	holistic/global

KEY —— = non-preferences

Results can be used by students to: **results for students**

- gain important self-knowledge
- understand their strengths and weaknesses
  in learning, remembering and problem solving
- enhance study skills
- prevent misunderstandings between students
  and teachers or parents
- increase learning motivation
- raise self-esteem and confidence
- create a learning environment suited to their
  true style preferences
- be allowed to learn and study 'their way'
- plan their future career.

Although students usually benefit most from
knowing their learning style and how important
this is for school failure or school success, it is
also important for <u>teachers</u> to know their students' **teachers improve**
learning styles for <u>improving their teaching</u> **teaching practices**
<u>practices</u>. More information about LSA Profiles
can be found in LSA <u>Interpretation Manual</u> (p. 335). **Interpretation Manual**

Results can be used by teachers to:

- really understand human diversity in their classrooms
- become aware of learning differences between male and female students
- understand biological learning needs in students
- recognize the separate styles of underachievers, slow and 'gifted' learners
- improve communication with students and/or their parents
- help design classrooms better suited to students' individual learning needs
- carry out successful group-work in class
- improve the 'team spirit' of students working together on projects
- enhance student and teacher interaction
- be better capable of matching teaching and learning styles
- deal with at-risk students more successfully
- use time management techniques based on personal styles and biological needs
- reduce stress on a daily basis and in difficult classroom situations
- improve teaching performance and job satisfaction.

Results can be used by parents to:

- understand how different their children are in their learning needs
- support them more successfully in their learning efforts
- learn how to create a learning environment at home suitable to their children's style
- practise more tolerance with unusual style features of their children
- accept that their children have their own unique learning styles
- realize that they are not clones of themselves.

LSA - Sen

prepared for:	Sample Group
7/06/01	Total number in group = 10

Group Percentages III (flexibilities)

Graph shows the % of people with flexibilities in the following areas:

BRAIN PROCESSING	sequential 70	40	simultaneous
THINKING STYLE	reflective 40	40	impulsive
SENSORY MODALITIES	AUDITORY (hearing)	60	listening
	Auditory (external)	90	talking/discussing
	Auditory (internal)	50	self-talk/inner dialogue
	VISUAL (words)	60	reading
	Visual (external)	60	seeing/watching
	Visual (internal)	60	visualizing/imagination
	TACTILE (touching)	30	manipulating/handling
	KINESTHETIC (external)	50	experiencing/doing
	Kinesthetic (internal)	40	feeling/intuition
MOBILITY	stationary 50	50	movement needed
INTAKE	not needed 40	40	needed
TIME OF DAY	early morning 70	50	late morning
		40	afternoon
		50	evening
SOUND	quiet 30	60	sound/noise/music
LIGHT	bright light 50	40	low light
TEMPERATURE	cool 60	40	warm
STUDY AREA	formal 20	40	informal/comfortable
WORKING GROUPS	alone 40	40	pair
		70	peers
		30	team
AUTHORITY	teacher 20	20	unsupervised
	parent 20		
MOTIVATION	self-starting 40	30	externally motivated
PERSISTENCE	high/systematic 10	80	spontaneous/fluctuating
		20	low persistence
CONFORMITY	conforming 50	40	non-conforming
RESPONSIBILITY	high/strong 10	70	low responsibility
STRUCTURE	other-directed 40	60	self-directed
VARIETY	routine 50	50	change-oriented
LS Tendencies	analytic 40	90	holistic/global

KEY ▨ = flexibilities   ■ = preferences   — = non-preferences

7. Practical applications for better teaching

LSA profiles reveal which <u>type of instruction</u> a student, or group of students, needs to make information intake or <u>learning truly successful</u> and fun – through listening, talking, discussing, reading, watching, thinking, imagining, hands-on involvement, doing, experiencing or feeling. For many students, however, the traditional delivery of learning content through overheads and lecturing with little interaction is just not the best way to learn. Through our work with this instrument we have discovered that New Zealanders, young and old, are 'hands-on' people who learn best by doing, not by listening or only watching. For this reason, over the past few years, and with great success, we have been introducing various <u>interactive</u>, self-correcting <u>learning tools</u> to educators – always tailor-measured to a particular content or learning programme (see pages 145–146).

type of instruction

learning success

interactive learning tools

Teachers can also find out the kind of <u>environment</u> their students work best in (for example, light levels and temperatures they require, how much sound/ noise/music or quiet they need, and what kind of work area and furniture helps them to concentrate best). Particularly useful for high school teachers is knowledge about their students' <u>thinking styles</u>: whether they are analytical left-brain thinkers who focus on details and logic, or the more creative, right-brain thinkers who need the Big Picture for better understanding and like to have fun during the learning process, or those who are flexible in their thinking and can adjust easily.

environment

thinking styles

Maybe the most valuable information comes from two areas – <u>attitudes</u> and <u>social groupings</u> – particularly for teachers of teenage students. LSA profiles will clearly show the interconnectedness of attitudes like motivation (self-starting or externally motivated), persistence (high and systematic, spontaneous and fluctuating, or low), conformity or non-conformity, high or low responsibility, the need for structure (self- or other-directed) and variety (the preference for routine or changes). It is usually the <u>combination of these elements,</u>

attitudes/social groupings

combination of elements

LSA - Sen

Sample Group
Members: 10

Group Results

Group member code number	1	2	3	4	5	6	7	8	9	10	
BRAIN PROCESSING — sequential											sequential (analytic)
simultaneous											simultaneous (holistic)
THINKING STYLE — reflective											reflective
impulsive											impulsive
SENSES — AUDITORY (hearing)											listening
Auditory (external)											talking/discussing
Auditory (internal)											self-talk/inner dialogue
VISUAL (words)											reading
Visual (external)											seeing/watching
Visual (internal)											visualizing/imagination
TACTILE (touching)											manipulating/handling
KINESTHETIC (external)											experiencing/doing
Kinesthetic (internal)											feeling/intuition
MOBILITY — stationary											stationary
movement needed											movement needed
INTAKE — not needed											not needed
needed											needed
TIME OF DAY — early morning											early morning
late morning											late morning
afternoon											afternoon
evening											evening
SOUND — quiet											quiet
sound/noise/music											sound/noise/music
LIGHT — bright light											bright light
low light											low light
TEMPERATURE — cool											cool
warm											warm
STUDY AREA — formal											formal
informal/comfortable											informal/comfortable
WORKING GROUPS — alone											alone
pair											pair
peers											peers
team											team
AUTHORITY — teacher											teacher
unsupervised											unsupervised
parent											parent
MOTIVATION — self-starting											self-starting
externally motivated											externally motivated
PERSISTENCE — high/systematic											high/systematic
spontaneous/fluctuating											spontaneous/fluctuating
low persistence											low persistence
CONFORMITY — conforming											conforming
non-conforming											non-conforming
RESPONSIBILITY — high/strong											high/strong
low responsibility											low responsibility
STRUCTURE — other-directed											other-directed
self-directed											self-directed
VARIETY — routine											routine
change-oriented											change-oriented

KEY ■ strong preference   ▨ preference   — non-preference   ▦ flexibility   ? inconsistency the often intangible reasons for students' disruptive behaviour and their misunderstood or misinterpreted learning needs, which cause teachers frustration, anger or despair.

The Learning Style Analysis not only reveals to the teacher who in his or her class needs to move and who can sit still easily during the learning process, but also at which time of day or evening a student learns best. As an example of <u>mismatch between teachers' styles and students' styles</u> it is worth mentioning that we know from research from around the world that teachers generally work better in the early morning hours, yet the majority of students (during primary school years but particularly in high school) tend to be 'brain dead' until 11am. This means that they are only beginning to wake up when they come to school in the morning and find it very difficult to concentrate, let alone remember difficult information. A teacher, however, who is a morning person, expects every student to be bright and alert, ready to learn at that same time of day. This is a great fallacy, and <u>time mismatch</u> is actually one of the most widespread <u>reasons for underachievement</u> or learning problems.

mismatch between teachers' and students' styles

time mismatch one reason for underachievement

Equally important is information about how teachers <u>communicate</u> with their students. The way they interact with each other has considerable influence on the success or failure of someone's learning process. Results in the <u>social elements</u> of the LSA reveal how students work together and learn best: alone, in a pair, in peer groups or with a team, and it will become obvious how they respond to <u>authority</u> – whether they need supervision or not and how they accept a teacher or parent watching over their learning.

communicate

social elements

authority

8. Finding out what makes students tick

It is certainly pertinent to ask whether teachers and parents know which styles their students, their sons or daughters have, and how to <u>accommodate these style needs</u> on a daily basis. With the LSA we have – maybe for the first time – an assessment tool that goes far beyond psychological, cognitive and

accommodating style needs

*There is nothing more unequal
than the equal treatment
of unequals.*

Dr K. Dunn

THOSE WHO SUGGEST
THAT CHILDREN SHOULD ADAPT
TO THEIR TEACHER'S STYLE
DISREGARD THE BIOLOGICAL
NATURE OF STYLE.

DR R. DUNN

intellectual abilities of a student during the learning process. It gives profound and detailed insight into biological needs (like sound, light, temperature, work area, mobility, intake, time of day and sensory modalities) and how human brains seem to function when it comes to thinking, concentrating, problem solving, and absorbing and retaining new and difficult information. Beyond that, LSA reports show how conditioning or learned style elements (attitudes and social preferences) can influence the learning process to an extent that the student can become a success or failure at school.

biological needs

conditioning/learned style elements

school success or failure

Parents have known it for a long time and even teachers have realized that traditional and formal teaching methods do not excite the majority of students in our school systems any longer, that students are bored, that underachievement, negative attitudes and discipline problems are rapidly increasing and that the number of at-risk students and burnt-out teachers is on the rise.

There will not be much hope of leading students successfully in this new millennium, and creating lifelong learners, unless we are prepared to accept that human diversity exists in our classrooms but not only in a cultural, social and ethnic sense.

lifelong learners

It is time to realize that self-knowledge and a deep understanding of learning styles might be the only way out of the dilemma virtually every school system around the world finds itself in these days. It is no coincidence that requests for learning style assessment software and the accompanying learning styles training programmes have dramatically increased recently not only here in New Zealand but also overseas.

self-knowledge learning styles

Maybe learning styles IS the missing link between traditional mass education with its formal learning methods and the more humane individualized learning strategies of the future.

missing link

1. There are no learning disabilities – only teaching disabilities

When I first heard this statement – made by one of the <u>leading researchers</u> in the field of learning styles, Dr Rita Dunn of St John's University in New York, at a conference on accelerated learning in Minneapolis in 1992 – I was not only <u>provoked</u>, I was <u>offended</u> because I had been a teacher in many different educational institutions (from primary to secondary schools, to teachers' college and university) in different countries, and I knew I had always been <u>highly successful</u>. The results of my students spoke for themselves, didn't they? So how dare this woman tell me that *I am the one really responsible for my students' learning.*

leading researchers

provoked
offended

highly successful

Although most of my students always produced <u>good results</u>, there were also a few who did not make it, who remained way <u>below their abilities</u>, who were <u>not really interested</u> in learning or just dropped out. Still, my colleagues, with whom I discussed this problem, and I strongly believed we had done all we could for these students and it was really their, <u>not our, problem</u> when they couldn't learn, thank you very much.

good results
below their abilities
not interested

not our problem

But the more I thought about Rita Dunn's words the more I had to <u>question general beliefs</u> about <u>education and learning</u>. What if she was right? I began to look into the research and statistics on <u>learning styles</u>, going back over a quarter of a century, and I had to admit, the statement which <u>provoked</u> me and had hurt my professional pride so much in the beginning became more and more the truth for me the longer I reflected on it.

question general beliefs
education and learning

learning styles

provoked

All these experiences have caused me to <u>rethink traditional teaching methods</u> and common learning practices and have set me on a crusade, literally around the world, to have <u>diversity accepted</u> in the classroom, <u>different styles recognized</u> in any workplace or educational setting, and the need acknowledged to <u>blend</u> them with <u>creative, accelerated learning techniques</u>.

rethink traditional teaching methods

**diversity accepted,
different styles
recognized,
blended with creative,
accelerated learning**

Whenever I speak to teachers about learning styles

A provocation

is awkward in the

beginning

but

gets easier

over time.

Edward de Bono

these days, I quote Rita Dunn's statement and
often get similar reactions to the ones I had
when I heard it first: disbelief, confusion or
ridicule on the mild side, anger, cynicism and
often outrage or even hostility, particularly from
educators in high schools and tertiary institutions,
and more from males than from females!

**reactions of
disbelief – confusion
ridicule – anger – cynicism
outrage – hostility**

more from males

Negative reactions are less common from people
in business education – they are amazed to find
such diversity among their trainees and then
are very eager to try anything which will make
their training more effective. Observing these
diverse reactions made me wonder a lot about
teachers and their attitudes towards their students
and learning in general!

**less common from people
in business education**

**eager to try anything
training more effective**

**teachers and their
attitudes**

No matter what educationalists think about this
new approach, research continues to prove it,
teachers who are using learning styles swear by it,
and I know it from individuals and groups I have
introduced to the notion of learning and working
styles. Individualized instruction does work and
I am now convinced that there are no learning
disabilities, only teaching disabilities.

**individualized instruction
works**

If educators continue to disregard human diversity
in their classrooms and are not prepared to teach
to groups with individual styles, too many students
will continue to underachieve and many more will
believe they are learning failures.

disregard human diversity

**underachievers
learning failures**

2. Underachievement – the unnecessary disease in our schools

Over the years, studies on learning styles have
revealed that the learning styles of underachievers
and drop-outs are significantly different from
those students who remain in school and finish
their education successfully. Another sad aspect
of this widespread 'disease' in our schools is
that underachievement is often the first step
to becoming an at-risk student, and dropping out
of school is the final unhappy solution for many.

**underachievers
significantly different**

**dropping out
unhappy solution**

The significance of these findings lies in the
necessity to understand that learning style is

learning style

If any learner

leaves your instruction

with a decreased desire

towards your subject

or learning in general,

then you are guilty of

EDUCATIONAL MALPRACTICE

Nikos Kazantsakis

a <u>biologically and developmentally imposed</u> <u>set of characteristics</u> every human being possesses. This provides an important insight into the ways students take information in during the learning process. It is the <u>individual difference</u> in personal styles that makes the same teaching method wonderful for some and terrible for others – even when the children come from the same family.

The annoying insight for all concerned is that these underachieving students, sometimes called 'reluctant learners', '<u>could do much better</u>' as we have all heard over and over again from teachers at parent evenings, read in school reports and thought for ourselves if they would just put <u>more effort</u> into their school or homework. We as parents look at these children with despair because we know they are <u>not dumb</u>, they are actually <u>very smart kids</u> and we know they CAN do good work, they often ARE motivated and CAN concentrate ... <u>IF</u> ... they are <u>interested in the learning task</u>.

Teachers, on the other hand, cannot comprehend why these students can be very <u>successful in some</u> <u>subjects</u> (often sports, craft, drama, woodwork, home economics, computers or special interest projects) where they show all the necessary positive attitudes: high interest and motivation, persistence, enthusiasm and the will to achieve their goals. And teachers always are at a loss to explain why these same students often <u>fail dismally in academic</u> <u>subjects</u>, don't do their homework and find school boring and a waste of time. It is quite obvious that, <u>despite</u> their often <u>high abilities</u>, these students do not actively participate in the learning process, are unwilling to put extra effort into their work and only do what's necessary for 'getting by'. Often teachers get very angry when they realize these students often <u>waste their learning potential</u>.

No one seems to understand what's going on here but everyone agrees that they could succeed more if they were better motivated or just knew how. Read on to find out what makes them tick and how all the affected parties can be helped by simply gaining <u>knowledge about the style features</u> which underachievers share worldwide in our systems.

biological/developmental set of characteristics

individual difference

could do much better

more effort

not dumb but smart kids

if
interested in learning

successful in some subjects

fail in academic subjects

despite high abilities

waste learning potential

knowing style features

All learning styles are OK.

There are no good or bad styles.

3. Learning styles of underachievers

According to the Dunn and Dunn learning style model and the research which has been carried out over the years, <u>underachievers</u> and highly at-risk students have <u>eight statistically different style elements</u> compared to students who are successful at school. Such students, however, are <u>not</u>, as the Dunns put it, '<u>learning disabled</u>' as often diagnosed by their teachers. They are simply, but rather inconveniently for traditional educators, <u>learning different</u> (as 'special needs' teachers well know) and generally have strong needs for:

**underachievers have
8 different style elements**

**not
'learning disabled'**

learning different

1. <u>Mobility</u> at frequent intervals
2. <u>Variety</u> of learning tools, resources and teaching methods
3. <u>Informal seating arrangement</u> in their learning environment because of their inability to sit on hard chairs for more than 10 to 15 minutes
4. <u>Low light</u> because their brains seem to get overstimulated, especially by fluorescent light, which often leads to agitated behaviour
5. <u>Tactile/kinesthetic</u> learning tools and resource materials to introduce new and difficult material through their preferred modalities because they are usually not highly visual or auditory
6. <u>Late morning or afternoon</u> for difficult subjects rather than early morning classes
7. <u>Non-authoritative teachers</u> who treat these students collegially and know how to respect their non-conformist thinking
8. <u>Recognition of their high motivation</u> despite their obvious problems which are more often than not caused by inappropriate teaching methods. (1)

mobility
variety

informal seating

low light

tactile/kinesthetic

late morning/afternoon

non-authority teacher

**recognition of
high motivation**

When I first heard about these <u>style combinations</u> and how relatively easy it would be to switch these students on to learning, I thought it can't be that simple. My academically trained mind wanted to make me believe that the reasons for under-achievement must be found in much deeper-rooted psychological problems, socio-economic conditions,

style combinations

Subject						Comment
FRENCH P. BROADHURST	C+	A				Sigrun has undoubted ability and can produce very good work. She has yet to overcome her tendency to "wander off" & remaining on-task for the full hour is still a problem at times. She is, however, gaining in confidence, and her exam result was excellent.
Social St A L Fong	B+	A				Sigrun has the ability to do even better than what she has produced in this subject. Her assignments, test and her final exam demonstrates total commitment to organisation and research. Polite and very 'clued up' (Top mark in Soc. St. 73½%) Sometimes a little too talkative
English D McCarthy	C	B2 54%				The School Certificate Examination. Sigrun had an awkward start to the term and did not quite overcome some disorganisation. She is confident orally though she needs to focus cleanly on detailing her written work to show her understanding. A competent writer, but she really needs to spend time at home and at school thinking through the ideas she expresses in writing.
SCIENCE	B	72	21=	30	75	Sigrun is settling down and achieving well, but she must try not to chat in class. JRM

Form Teacher's Comments: It is evident that while Sigrun is attaining a high level of achievement in some areas, in others she could benefit from a more organised approach to her work. She is always a vivacious, outgoing student who brings to her studies a delightful, original flair. M.V. McDougall Form Teacher

Dean's Comments: Sigrun should aim to develop more consistent work habits. She needs to learn her work and revise thoroughly. Some results are most pleasing. R. J. MacCormick Dean

Ruth Jones MA Dip Ed Headmistress

| PHYSICAL
EDUCATION | C+ | | | | | Sigrun is energetic, enthusiastic and obviously enjoys all the activities. JL |
| 6 Biology
E Bowater | C+ | 4-6 | | | | Throughout the year Sigrun's assessment results have been somewhat variable. Some show excellent understanding of biological ideas, but some of the homework-type assignments have a rushed, disorganised air about them. Better attentiveness in class, and better organisation will ensure future success in Biology. |

lack of motivation and parental support, poor study skills, and so on. But then I began to think about <u>my own daughter</u> and all the <u>learning problems</u> she had, particularly during her <u>high school years</u> in New Zealand schools. I knew she didn't have psychological problems, we lived in very healthy socio-economic conditions, she wanted to learn and there was no lack of parental support. Quite the contrary, we often overdid it. And on top of that we also had proof about her <u>high intelligence</u>, her <u>many talents</u> and her high <u>learning abilities</u>. So, 'what was wrong with her?' we began to ask ourselves as we got more and more desperate over the years.

my daughter's learning problems during high school years

high intelligence many talents and abilities

Despite all our efforts her <u>school reports</u> kept stating the same facts over and over again as you can see on the opposite page. (I do have her permission to reveal extracts of her school reports.) We all dreaded these reports, knowing what would be in them, feeling the <u>disappointment</u>, discussing the results, seeing the <u>tears and desperation</u>, hearing the repeated <u>promises</u> and not knowing what to do. She was average or below, slowly giving herself up as a learner in formal education. And here I was, a caring parent, an educator with all my years of training and yet I had <u>no clue how to help her</u>, how to make her high school years more successful (socially she was very successful but learning was a near disaster) and how to <u>unlock her true learning potential</u>.

school reports

disappointment tears and desperation promises

no clue how to help

unlock true potential

If you have experienced a similar situation in your own family, you will share with me the <u>sorrow and agony</u> about an underachieving child, the deep <u>frustration and helplessness</u> and ultimately the <u>final resignation</u> that nothing much can be done.

sorrow and agony

frustration and helplessness final resignation

Fortunately enough we did not experience any other related problems like drug and alcohol abuse or suicidal tendencies, as often occurs in under-achieving students during their teenage years. We thought we would just have to put up with a strange phenomenon no one could explain and a 'disease' for which there was obviously no cure.

And then I found out about learning styles ...

What you bring forth

out of yourself from the inside

will save you.

What you do not bring forth

out of yourself from the inside

will destroy you.

Gospel of Thomas

We had our daughter assessed with the old, original Dunn and Dunn LSA instrument, and for the first time in my life I physically <u>began to understand</u> her <u>true learning style needs</u> when I saw them printed on paper.

understand
true learning style needs

I wish I had known about <u>style differences</u> long ago as it became one of the biggest eye-openers for me and my whole family. All of a sudden it dawned on me how different we all were in our learning needs (as you will see in Chapter 10) and what this child of mine I thought I knew so well needed when it came to learning. At that time she was already in her final year and <u>teachers</u> at her local high school unfortunately were <u>not interested</u> <u>in learning styles</u> because they 'knew what they were doing' and kept telling me that my daughter could 'do much better' (here we go again) if she just studied harder and put more effort into her work. They had made up their minds about underachievers and so had I: from now on I would fight for <u>more</u> <u>understanding</u> of these students' styles and <u>better</u> <u>teaching practices</u> in our schools.

style differences

teachers
not interested
in learning styles

more understanding
better
teaching practices

Regrettably nothing much could be done at her old school (and is still not being done for under-achievers there) but at least my daughter now knew her style, her <u>learning needs</u> and that there was nothing wrong with her. The following year, with <u>appropriate study techniques</u>, she – probably for the first time as an adolescent student – experienced true <u>learning success</u> when she graduated with honours from a self-chosen veterinary nursing course. I had never seen her happier because she had finally done the <u>studying HER way</u>!

learning needs

appropriate study
techniques
learning success

study her way

I had to share this personal experience with you because I see similar problems in many families, not only in New Zealand but also in other countries, causing a lot of <u>unnecessary heartache</u> for all concerned, often ending in tragedy. Therefore I will not give up my quest to have learning styles concepts firmly established in education systems around the world and to help classroom teachers understand human diversity in learning.

unnecessary heartache

To learn without doing

is like making love

without touching.

As long as teaching methods are not individualized and teachers continue to use <u>identical teaching strategies</u> for everyone, knowing they are only effective for some, they <u>will not reach students</u> who need them most, and will keep losing their students in the learning process and, what's even worse, lose them as lifelong learners.

identical teaching strategies
do not reach students

That's why <u>lip service is not enough</u>. Nothing will change as long as teachers say – and I hear it all the time – 'Oh yes, we always tell our students about learning styles' or 'We would love to use learning styles, but we have too many students in our classes', or 'It's a great idea, but we don't have the money to introduce it', and so on. All it takes is the doing, and even <u>small beginnings</u> with a <u>pilot group</u> are better than just talking about it. Part of the knowledge about learning styles is the insight into how the <u>human brain</u> seems to process information and how <u>thinking processes</u> work. However, it goes further.

lip service not enough

small beginnings
pilot group

human brain
thinking processes

While step-by-step instruction and rote learning are still favoured methods in traditional education, they are inferior to other learning techniques which <u>activate the right brain</u> and encourage <u>dual-brain thinking</u>. How differently students respond to the same teaching method and why underachieving students clash with so many teachers but get on very well with a few will be explained towards the end of this chapter.

activate right brain
dual-brain thinking

4. School is hell for touch-dominant/tactile students

In learning styles, language tactile (tactual) means that sensory information intake happens through <u>touching and manipulating</u> objects. All sensory modalities play an important role in the learning process as described in detail at the beginning of Chapter 6, and people with a tactile preference learn and remember best through <u>hands-on activities</u>. As most young students and many teenagers have strong tactile preferences, it is quite obvious that our traditional school system, with formal instructions mainly based on reading and writing, does not cater for the tactile needs of these students, particularly not

touching and manipulating

hands-on activities

CREATIVE VISUALIZATION

For touch dominant people

Here are three sets of instructions used to show how the imagery technique can be adapted for the touch dominant. All have been thoroughly tested, and even people totally convinced that they 'can't DO that!' find that they can do these with ease. The instructions are brief and the user should feel free to add many more details, from any of the sensory systems; the more details they contain, the more vivid they are.

1. You are walking a tightrope between two trees, about six inches off the ground (so there's no need to be afraid of falling). Feel your feet on the rope as you move along. Each time you set a foot down or lift it up, be aware of the sensation(s) you feel in the foot and the adjustments your body has to make to stay balanced. Go back and forth as many times as you like.

2. You're swimming – having a wonderful time – through a substance that you find pleasing: warm or cool water; blackberry jam; baby powder; sand; your choice. You don't have to worry about breathing or effort, you just swim along through it easily and gracefully. Put your attention firmly on the way the substance you chose for your 'sea' feels on your skin, all over your body, as you swim.

3. You are a broad ribbon of velvet, draped over the back of your favourite chair (or a limb of your favourite tree, or any other support that pleases you). You are absolutely relaxed and absolutely safe and totally comfortable ...

From *Try To Feel It My Way* by Suzette Haden Elgin

at high school level. Despite the huge amount of information which over the years has been written about learning styles, there is not much literature available about this particular group of learners.

However, I was pleased to find *Try To Feel It My Way: New Help for Touch Dominant People and Those Who Care About Them* (1996) by Suzette H. Elgin. The book makes fascinating reading and although I do not agree with everything discussed in there, this is at least one of the few publications describing the problems highly <u>tactile or touch dominant</u> children and adults have. In particular I do not agree with Elgin's unclear distinction between kinesthetic and tactile preferences because, based on my experiences with learning styles, it is very important to <u>distinguish between learners</u> who are highly <u>tactile</u> and those who are highly <u>kinesthetic</u>, preferring whole-body experiences and physical activities during the learning process. It is also not appropriate to call all the 'doing-learners' touch dominant. But that aside, Elgin's book contains a wealth of dialogues, practical hints and exercises to recognize touch dominant children or adults and helps us to communicate better with them.

tactile/touch dominant

distinguish between tactile and kinesthetic learners

The questions now are: Why do these people have problems with communication and why is <u>school so difficult for tactile students</u>? The reason seems to lie in the fact that our Western societies have developed more towards visual (seeing) and auditory (hearing) based information intake and stimulation. We don't know why but, as Elgin says, it may be that in our '<u>Don't touch!' culture</u> more of us *learn* to prefer our eyes and ears. Most likely, it's a combination of the two. (2)

school is difficult for tactile students

'Don't touch!' culture

Not only is our society putting more emphasis on sight and hearing plus rewarding these abilities, but nearly all of our presently used <u>teaching methods</u> rely heavily on <u>visual and auditory</u> skills of teachers and students alike. For young children and primary school pupils it is very much acceptable that they involve their hands a lot, have large amounts of learning materials and they are allowed to 'play' with things during the learning process. But as

teaching methods visual and auditory

Koosh balls

soon as they enter <u>high school</u>, their <u>tactile stimulation</u> during classes is <u>drastically reduced</u> to handwriting (which they don't like anyway) and to computer work (which many of them love); and any other activity with their hands (doodling, fiddling, playing with pens, and so on) is outright <u>forbidden and often punished</u>. Despite all the warnings and reprimands, these highly tactile students – more often boys than girls – will not stop their finger movements, particularly <u>when</u> they are <u>bored</u> or have to <u>listen or concentrate hard</u>.

**in high school
tactile stimulation
is drastically reduced**

forbidden or punished

**when bored,
listen or concentrate hard**

Therefore it is so important for teachers to really understand that manipulating and <u>using their fingers helps</u> tactile students <u>to concentrate</u>, even <u>listen better</u>. The more they are told not to do that, the stronger the need grows and the more they have to suppress it. And that means they concentrate on what NOT to do instead of concentrating on the learning content.

**using fingers
helps to concentrate,
listen better**

But there's more which adds to the misery of touch dominant students – the way they are told to study and the instruction methods teachers use for them. Instead of being allowed to learn with <u>manipulatives</u> (that is, learning tools from a learning style kitset), <u>hands-on activities</u> and <u>movement</u>, they are <u>forced to sit still, listen, read and write</u>. They can do all that but they have to work harder than their visual and auditory classmates because their sensory preferences lie in a different area. That's the reason why <u>such students lose interest</u>, <u>get bored</u>, don't quite understand, <u>fall behind</u>, and finally <u>give up participating</u> because there is nothing in it for them. If you are a highly tactile person and you can't use your hands and fingers or are constantly reprimanded, even a class period of 45 minutes can be hell!

**need manipulatives,
hands-on activities,
movement; when forced
to sit still/listen/read/write**

**students lose interest,
get bored, fall behind,
give up participating**

I wish teachers would understand better what these tactile students really need and learn how to teach them. Being highly <u>tactile AND kinesthetic</u> (which is a very common style combination) was one of the reasons for my daughter's learning problems during high school because these two senses were just not stimulated enough in theoretical subjects and that contributed to her being bored, switching off and falling behind. Had I just known this then!

tactile and kinesthetic

When I was young and free and
imagination had no limits,
I dreamed of changing the world.

As I grew older and wiser,
I discovered the world would not change,
So I shortened my sights somewhat and decided
To change only my country.
But it seemed too immovable.

As I grew into my twilight years,
In one last desperate attempt,
I settled for changing my family,
Those closest to me, but alas,
They would have none of it.

And now, as I lie on my deathbed,
I suddenly realize:
If only I had changed myself,
Then by example I might have changed my family.
From their inspiration and encouragement
I would have been able to better my country, and who knows,

I may have changed the world.

Written on the tomb of an Anglican bishop,
Westminster Abbey in AD 1100

5. Dropout candidates – highly kinesthetic students

It's bad enough for highly tactile students not to be allowed to learn predominantly through their hands, but for the truly kinesthetic students, those who need body involvement and physical experiences to understand the learning content, it's even worse. Sitting in classrooms where there is nothing to do, where moving around is not allowed and where the teacher just talks and talks is not only hell for these students, it actually becomes unbearable. It's no wonder that after a few years of unsuccessfully trying to listen, read and write like most other students, they give up participating and behaving as it is expected of them. They begin to 'play up', they become discipline problems, get together with like-minded (equally kinesthetic) classmates and can create hell for teachers. These boys are usually taller and stronger than their fellow students, and kinesthetic girls are often described as 'tomboys', never growing out of their rough and tumble behaviour, never becoming 'ladylike'.

body involvement
physical experiences

kinesthetic boys are
tall and strong
kinesthetic girls are
'tomboys'

Due to their very physical style needs which are not matched at all in academic, theoretical subjects, there is not much which interests these students other than practical subjects and sports activities where they are usually very good and successful. They come to the conclusion – often fuelled by their teachers' and parents' beliefs – that they are not the 'learning types', that school is not for them, and over time their learning motivation disappears, school progress diminishes, and being out in the streets or doing sports only becomes much more desirable. First they become underachievers, then discipline problems, then truants and finally school dropouts with a profound dislike, often hate for school and anything which has anything to do with formal learning or education.

practical subjects and sports
very good and successful

underachievers
discipline problems,
truants, then dropouts
dislike/hate school

In the past these early school leavers could easily go into manual jobs, work hard and, particularly in New Zealand, be compensated for their lack of formal education through their great practical skills and abilities and were able to build a successful life for themselves. But all that has changed now; there

practical skills

'Consider:
As a sensory system
the skin is much the most
important organ system of the body.
A human being can spend his life
blind and deaf and completely
lacking the senses of smell and taste,
but he cannot survive at all
without functions performed
by the skin ...
Among all the senses,
TOUCH
stands paramount.'

Montagu 1986

are hardly any manual jobs left, they are poorly paid and the first to go when companies do 'downsizing' exercises. There is nowhere to go, nothing much to do and no great future prospects for these highly kinesthetic students. Out of this desperation, often paired with social problems, we now see a growing number of young people dropping out of school, with no formal qualification, unemployed and unemployable, taking comfort in alcohol, sex, drugs, gang activities and crime.

dropping out of school

Maybe, if teachers, parents and decision makers in education knew more about learning styles and diversity, and understood and acted upon them, then we might even see fewer teenage pregnancies and suicides in New Zealand, but certainly many more students who want to learn and choose to stay at school instead of giving up.

want to learn
stay at school

6. Misfits, slow learners and school failures

Now we have investigated underachievement, tactile and kinesthetic learners and their problems in traditional education settings, we can easily understand why so many students become misfits and school failures. Matching learning and teaching styles, better classroom management and creative learning techniques will certainly help all these students to draw out their potential and become more successful at school.

matching learning and teaching styles

There is, however, one group of students who, in addition to their difficult combination of style elements (similar to underachievers yet overall different), do have various other problems like failing health, poor hearing or eyesight, severe social or psychological problems, often slight malfunctions of the brain, or physical handicaps. They are the school failures, the true 'special needs' kids, for whom learning styles and creative learning techniques will not be enough to remedy the problems. They are the slow and poor learners and need help from specialists and all the support they can get. But even here a knowledge of style differences can make life much easier for teachers, parents and students concerned.

other problems

'special needs' kids

slow and poor learners

DEALING WITH PROCRASTINATION

For each item below rate yourself from 1 to 5 in the space provided:

1 = Never a problem   **2** = Rarely a problem   **3** = Sometimes
4 = Often a problem   **5** = Very frequently a problem

_____ 1. I delay until the last minute before starting important projects.

_____ 2. I fail to return phone calls promptly.

_____ 3. I pay my bills late.

_____ 4. I say I will do a particular task,
              but then don't get around to it for a long time.

_____ 5. I show up late for appointments.

_____ 6. I collect materials to use on a project and then delay doing the project.

_____ 7. I avoid situations where I believe I won't be very successful.

_____ 8. I delay answering correspondence.

_____ 9. I feel as though there is just one crisis after another in my life.

_____10. I tell myself that tomorrow I will begin.

Add up your responses and see how you rate. The higher your result the more you are prone to procrastination.

What is the impact of these problems on your daily life, at work or at home?

Can you think of areas in which these affect your colleagues, students or family?

Based on a handout by Educational Research and Advisory Unit, University of Canterbury

Generally so called 'slow and poor' learners have the following combination of style features:

slow and poor learners

1. Right-brain dominance: need the Big Picture first, find it hard to think analytically

   right-brain dominance

2. Tactile-kinesthetic preferences: are usually not visual and rarely auditory, but strongly feeling-based

   tactile/kinesthetic

3. Mobility: find it hard to sit still, often fidget

   mobility

4. Late morning or afternoon: have difficulties in early morning classes

   late morning/afternoon

5. Sound: find it harder to concentrate when it's quiet, music enhances their learning

   sound

6. Low light: seem to get overstimulated by fluorescent light, show agitated behaviour

   low light

7. Informal work area: find it difficult to sit on hard chairs for more than 10 to 15 minutes, need comfortable learning environment

   informal work area

8. Pair/peers/team: don't work well alone, need other students with similar styles to work with

   pair/peers/team

9. Authority: are often afraid of teachers but need them to organize learning tasks

   authority

10. Low motivation: find learning hard, fail frequently, become passive, uninvolved

    low motivation

11. No persistence: give up easily, frequently used phrase: 'I can't'

    no persistence

12. Need structure: cannot do learning tasks without guidance; when left alone, nothing gets done

    need structure

13. Dislike variety: need consistency and routine; change is threatening.

    dislike variety

This complex picture explains why slow and poor learners struggle with school, have very low self-esteem and need all the support they can get from their teachers and care givers who need to know about their style features, their strengths and not only about their obvious weaknesses. Many successful applications of learning styles in the USA have helped these students to become accomplished learners despite their other problems (3) and in New Zealand we are beginning to see similar results.

struggle with school
low self-esteem

Very different from this category of learners are the so called 'gifted' students who differ dramatically in their style features even from average students as international research findings have shown.

'gifted' students
differ dramatically
from average students

Success is

attainment, achievement, accomplishment of

goals

when failure is possible.

Paul Messier

Most people
are addicted
to feeling bad.

L. Machado

7. 'Gifted' students have significantly different learning styles

When talking about 'giftedness' we need to clarify what the criteria are, and I have chosen a very good definition by Dr Donald Treffinger, an American specialist in giftedness. He states: 'Giftedness refers to a person's creative accomplishments, over a sustained period of time (that may be years or even decades), in a domain that matters intensely to that person.' (4)

'giftedness'

creative accomplishments

Traditionally, 'gifted' students have been identified by meeting specific criteria, often heavily dependent on rigorous assessments and IQ tests, and then put into so-called programmes for gifted students. With the knowledge about learning styles, many different activities and services should be offered to these students, not just a single, fixed programme, and Treffinger maintains schools should be concerned with the following:

so-called programmes for gifted

- individualized basic instruction
- appropriate enrichment
- effective acceleration
- independence and self-direction
- personal growth and social development
- career perspectives with a futuristic orientation.

Based on those he urges schools to consider what additional support (people, time, materials) may be needed to expand, extend or enhance the regular programme. (5)

additional support

Various studies on gifted adolescents have revealed that their styles vary significantly from average or even high-achieving students. If you are a teacher, compare the following list of style preferences with the styles your 'gifted' students display, and if you are a parent, this information might give you valuable information on how to support your gifted child because often we don't quite know what to do with these (sometimes 'weird') young people. High IQ and talented students dropping out of school may be highly gifted young people who become unmotivated because conventional schooling does not complement their learning styles.

gifted adolescents

talented students drop out of school

ASSESSMENT of HEMISPHERIC RELATED STRATEGIES (6)

The Mighty Right and the Brain That's Left

i. Read each statement. Score each statement according to how much it is true for you, from 1 to 10 (with 1 being the lowest).

   e.g. 10 = I am 100% like that; that describes me to a T.

     5 = I am like that sometimes/I'm not sure/or it depends.

     1 = No way!

ii. Try to write your first reaction; it is more likely to really describe you than if you think it over for too long.

iii. Write your score for each statement in the column provided.

iv. Be honest with yourself!

                                                                  Score

1   I base decisions on objective facts rather than feelings.

2   I am psychic.

3   I like using symbols or images in solving problems.

4   I am artistically or musically creative.

5   I am logical.

6   I am good at solving crossword puzzles.

7   I can read quickly.

8   My daydreams are vivid.

9   I can think of synonyms for words easily.

10 I can remember dreams.

11 My dreams are vivid.

12 I am fluent in using words.

13 I am good at using images in remembering and thinking.

14 I use a playful approach to problem solving.

15 I use a serious, all-business approach to problem solving.

16 I like to keep experiences planned and structured.

17 I like to read and think while sitting upright.

18 My thinking consists of words.

19 My thinking consists of mental imagery.

20 I like to explain something using a visual presentation.

SCORING: Left nos: 1, 5, 6, 7, 9, 12, 15, 16, 17, 18 ☐

                   Right nos: 2, 3, 4, 8, 10, 11, 13, 14, 19, 20 ☐

Add up the scores for Left and Right. Write them in the boxes above. Subtract the smaller number from the larger, and divide that result by 10: e.g. 74 (left) – 48 (right) = 26; 26/10 = 2.6 (left). The higher score indicates the hemisphere-related strategies you prefer. The larger the number, the greater the preference for that hemisphere. As a rule of thumb, a final score of 0.7 or higher indicates a preference.

The following combination of preferences sets gifted learners apart from the rest of the student population yet often causes problems at school and at home:

gifted learners

1. Left/right-brain integration: can be highly analytical or holistic but can also integrate extremely well

   left/right-brain integration

2. Multisensory abilities: learn easily through several senses but prefer tactile/kinesthetic

   multisensory abilities

3. Early morning or evening preferences: do well at these times

   early morning/evening

4. Sound: analytics prefer quiet environments, but if strongly right-brained, they like music in the background

   sound/quiet

5. Low/bright light: depending on their brain dominance

   low/bright light

6. Work area: depending on their brain dominance, but show a tendency towards formal learning environment

   formal work area

7. Social: prefer to work alone, only accept true peers to work with

   alone/true peers

8. Authority: do not accept it, make their own rules, don't want to be supervised

   no authority

9. High motivation: internally motivated, thirst for knowledge, often learn for the learning's sake

   high motivation

10. Extreme persistence: never give up, can be stubborn in pursuing learning goals

    extreme persistence

11. Non-conformity: dislike rules, don't mind to be told what has to be done but not HOW, always want to do it their way, can get frustrated and walk out

    non-conformity

12. Responsibility: usually only interested in their own projects, can show low social responsibility

    responsibility

13. Don't need structure: always know how to go about their learning tasks, don't like interference from teachers or parents.

    low structure

They often feel isolated or misunderstood and in contrast to 'average' students they are very intuitive. They will often go by their feeling in decision making, when they follow personal criteria and consider values and relationships. Again, a sound knowledge of their learning styles can help to understand and support them better.

isolated/misunderstood
very intuitive
go by feeling

What Analytic Learners Expect From A Teacher

- To focus on tasks and details.
- To provide information in a sequentially organized format.
- To provide outlines and specifics.
- To be tested on details and facts.
- To be left undisturbed and uninterrupted in their thinking process.

What Holistic Learners Expect From A Teacher

- To focus on personal needs and feelings.
- To provide overviews and the Big Picture.
- To provide guidance and personal interaction.
- To be tested on general concepts and effort.
- To be allowed to socialize during the learning process.

Recognizing What Analytics Say

- Does spelling count?
- Should I use pen or a pencil?
- Will this be on the test?
- Please check my work before I hand it in.
- I need to know what comes first? What second?
- Why can't we do one thing at a time?

Recognizing What Holistics Say

- Why do we have to do this?
- Not now! I'll do it later.
- Is it important? Does it really matter?
- Don't touch the piles on my desk, I'll find it!
- Why do we have to do it now? It will still be here later.
- I can't sit any longer, I need a break.

Based on: *A Curriculum Companion, a Visual Staff Training Resource to Teach Global and Analytic Strategies.* Rita Dunn, St John's University, 1993

8. Analytic and holistic students exist worlds apart

When I began to reshape the <u>WSA Model</u> – now in the <u>form of a pyramid</u> – I asked myself if there might be a hierarchy of elements, and by going through the literature on learning styles it became quite obvious: learning styles begin with left- and right-brain dominance, thinking style and brain processing. For that reason these elements had to go at the top of the pyramid because the way a <u>brain processes information</u> influences all the other <u>style elements</u> of a person.

**WSA Model
in pyramid form**

**brain processing influences
style elements**

As we have seen in Chapter 2, the left/right brain metaphor is a very simple one to explain preferences in brain processing styles but there is more to this useful distinction. <u>Hemisphericity</u> – another term for <u>left- or right-brain dominance</u> – manifests itself not only in information intake preferences but also in typical <u>style combinations</u> and <u>resulting behaviour</u>. We therefore need to know what the differences are between left-brain dominant (analytic) students and their right-brain dominant (holistic/global) colleagues. And yet again, research on learning styles and practical experience with the WSA and LSA instruments provide the answers.

**hemisphericity
left/right-brain dominance**

**style combinations
resulting behaviour**

The difference between <u>analytic and holistic styles</u> is like day and night and, one can say, students with these strong preferences are worlds apart. The first divide occurs in the <u>five basic areas</u> where students have the exact <u>opposite needs</u> (in the following list **A** stands for 'Analytics' and **H** stands for 'Holistics'): (7)

analytic/holistic styles

**five basic areas
opposite needs**

1. <u>Sound</u>
    A: prefer quiet while learning
    H: need sound/music/noise
2. <u>Light</u>
    A: need bright light
    H: prefer low light when learning
3. <u>Work area</u>
    A: prefer formal furniture, hard chairs, like to sit upright when learning
    H: prefer informal arrangements, soft chairs, lying or sitting on the floor or on a bed

sound

light

work area

Right-Brain Dominant Profile

 LSA - Jun   Natasha

Graph 3. Learning Style Tendencies

Compare this result with your Left/Right Brain Dominance graph on page 2

ANALYTIC ('Left')   HOLISTIC ('Right')
quiet //////// ——————— sound/noise/music
bright light ——————— //////// low light
formal study area ——————— //////// informal study area
high persistence ——————— //////// low persistence
no/low intake ——————— //////// intake needed

Left-Brain Dominant Profile

al no 1011222S/v7.3

Working Style Analysis™ - Corp
Dunn & Prashnig

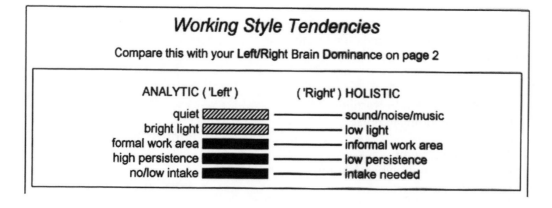

Working Style Tendencies

Compare this with your Left/Right Brain Dominance on page 2

ANALYTIC ('Left')   ('Right') HOLISTIC
quiet //////// ——————— sound/noise/music
bright light //////// ——————— low light
formal work area ████████ ——————— informal work area
high persistence ████████ ——————— low persistence
no/low intake ████████ ——————— intake needed

4. Persistence

persistence

   A: prefer to work on single tasks without interruption until they are finished, have high persistence

   H: like to work simultaneously on several tasks, need frequent breaks, procrastinate, have low persistence

5. Intake

intake

   A: do not eat, drink, chew or nibble when learning, find it distracting, do it when task is completed

   H: work better when snacking, chewing, drinking, becomes part of the learning process

Beyond those there are many more features which set these groups of students apart although most people are a complex mix of analytic and holistic features. However, approximately 5 to 10 per cent of any population are strongly one way or the other and find it hard to flex.

people are a complex mix

General characteristics of ANALYTIC students: they are obedient, controlled, quiet, verbally oriented, reflective, logical, detail oriented, sit upright, respect authority, work well alone, need structure, read a lot and participate in discussions, are conforming, self-motivated and highly responsible, bright and alert in the morning – in short, they are the 'ideal students'.

analytic students

'ideal students'

Do you know such students and how do you react to them when they say, 'Will this be on the test?' or 'Does spelling count?' and 'Please check my work before I hand it in.' Depending on your own style preferences and your flexibility, you will either be on the 'same wavelength' and accept such comments or find them baffling and senseless.

There is, however, an ever-growing group of students who have style features most teachers find hard to handle and would certainly describe as distracting from real learning, even destructive.

growing student group style features

distracting from learning

General characteristics of HOLISTIC students: they are likely to 'play up', are extroverted, noisy, impulsive risk takers, scatterbrained, hate details, slouch in their chairs, chat and socialize a lot, can't

holistic students

General
Style Differences between

Analytics

don't like to talk
pack days before trip
plan/prepare
compulsive/accurate
obsessively organized
on task/on time
perfectionists
blame others
competitive
outlines/lists/graphs
decision making
don't trust, need proof
worrying/stressed
step by step, details
love/need detailed instructions
follow recipes when cooking
wardrobe – things straightened out
single-minded on tasks
logical/reflective
serious/earnest
specialists

Holistics

communicative, motormouths
last-minute packing
dislike planning/carefree
flexible/laid back
sloppy/disorganized
distracted/usually late
not 100%, 'good as gold'
could always be improved
often cruising
mind mapping/summaries/overviews
undecided/oscillating
socialize/many friends
easygoing, less stressed
overview, Big Picture
prefer general directions
creative cooks/alter recipes
wardrobe – untidy, mess
multiplicity in doing things
intuitive/spontaneous
fun loving/forgetful
generalists

Exercise: check which features you combine in your personal style, compare with your partner.

sit still, often rough and tumble, good at sports, are night owls and usually 'brain-dead' in the morning, show low responsibility and learning motivation, just getting by, are <u>hands-on kids</u> with a very <u>practical sense</u>, strong non-conformists and tend to stay away from teachers.

**hands-on kids
practical sense**

Such students are definitely <u>not the favourites</u> in our classes and often they are labelled LD (learning disabled), ADD (attention deficit disorder), discipline problems, underachievers, at-risk students, school failures, truants or dropout candidates.

not the favourites

It is amazing that a simple difference in L/R brain dominance and preference for <u>analytic or holistic styles</u> should be the reason for such vastly different behaviours and <u>achievements at school</u>. And that's exactly what it is: different brain styles lead to different learning styles which in turn lead to different school performance. Like it or not, these partly <u>biologically influenced style combinations</u> determine success or failure for students because our education <u>systems</u> still <u>reward analytic styles</u>, not true potential and learning abilities. Students who don't fit 'the norm' have very little chance of success in our present system, and unless teachers and decision makers <u>accept diversity</u> in the classroom and fully <u>introduce learning style programmes</u>, conditions will get worse.

analytic/holistic styles

school achievements

**biologically influenced style combinations
systems reward analytic styles**

**accept diversity
introduce learning styles**

We have just explored the profound differences between analytic and holistic students and I hope this has given you, as a concerned teacher or parent, a new insight into human diversity. Now we have to investigate where teachers fit into this scenario.

9. And teachers live in a world of their own!

Given the <u>historic development</u> of the <u>teaching profession</u> and the problems education is facing worldwide, we have to ask ourselves a few questions:

**historic development
of teaching profession**

Who were the people in the past who formally educated the young generations? Wasn't it always the 'learned' men, the clergy and academia? Didn't they determine the teaching methods? Wasn't it

Left-Brain
Analytic

Right-Brain
Global

mainly 'chalk and talk'? And what kind of brain processing styles did these men have? Right, it was the <u>analytical, logic, left-brain, scientific</u> approach which still dominates formal education to this day, despite a world which would need more people using their 'whole brain' and utilizing their creative right-brain skills better.

analytical, logic, left-brain, scientific

Whoever went into the <u>teaching profession</u>, liked it and stayed on (often died on the job), had no real problems accepting the <u>existing standards</u>, procedures and expectations – and they were all, and still are, guided by logic, left-brain, analytic styles. All those who had the same style features fitted in nicely, were comfortable and passed on their way of thinking and being through teaching methods based on <u>analytic preferences</u>. For centuries in education there was always a near <u>perfect match</u> between a mainly elitist student population and their analytic teachers. They quickly and eagerly grew into the <u>formal ways of learning</u> practised in schools. Many of the strongly held views about the 'right' teaching and learning methods date back to these times, have not yet been eradicated and are still flourishing, particularly in university education but also in senior high school settings.

teaching profession

existing standards

analytic preferences in the past perfect match

formal ways of learning

Education had always attracted more <u>left-brain oriented professionals</u> who fitted the system nicely and perfected their formal, analytic teaching styles. It was a simple and quite <u>successful formula</u>: *analytic teachers* (lecturers) taught *analytic subjects* (like the sciences) to *analytic students* (who had learned to think analytically in high school) through *analytic methods* (by lecturing and reading/writing assignments).

left-brain professionals

successful formula: analytic teachers analytic subjects analytic students analytic methods

But then <u>mass education</u> came along and with it large numbers of students who did not fit the picture of the 'traditional' student, who struggled with traditional teaching methods but spared no effort to make it through formal education. Initially it was not so bad because those who were <u>not</u> <u>'academically minded'</u> left school early, found <u>manual jobs</u> and only those with matching (analytic) styles stayed on and completed their studies. So <u>analytic teachers</u> were still at ease and successful

mass education

not academically minded found manual jobs

analytic teachers

Different authors have used different terms to describe the two
basic differences in brain processing styles.

ANALYTICAL	HOLISTIC
left hemisphere	right hemisphere (R. Sperry)
reflective/analytic	impulsive/global (Dunn and Dunn)
sequential	simultaneous (Dunn and Prashnig)
introvert	extrovert (R. Ornstein)
high gainers	low gainers (R. Ornstein)
deliberator	liberated (R. Ornstein)
single track	multi track (A. Gore)
masculine	feminine (J. Nicholson)
logical left-brain	intuitive right-brain (H. Alder)
box and triangle	circle and squiggle (S. Dellinger)
High S and C	High D and I (DISC profiles)
academic parts	creative activities (G. Dryden)

with the remaining students. Since the early 1960s, however, <u>more students stayed longer in formal education</u> and that was the time when all the problems started. All of a sudden, there were vast numbers of students in formal education who would and could not learn the way they were being taught, for whom analytic teaching methods did not make sense and who would have needed very <u>different</u> approaches and <u>learning techniques</u>. But teachers were not and still are not trained for a vastly different and hugely diverse student population with very different expectations, aspirations and ambitions compared to one generation ago. The <u>mismatch between teaching and learning styles</u> is particularly obvious in <u>high schools</u>, vocational institutions and <u>universities</u>. The <u>situation</u> is much <u>better in primary schools</u> where student-centred teaching methods have been practised for many years and learning style techniques are being accepted more readily.

students stay longer in formal education

different learning techniques

mismatch between teaching and learning styles, high schools and universities situation better in primary schools

Traditional, analytic teaching methods are still OK for a small number of students, but the majority would need more integrated, flexible, brain-friendly approaches. Unfortunately most <u>teachers</u> cannot deliver because they <u>have never been trained</u> in these <u>new methods</u>. Many are oblivious, uncertain, reluctant, often cynical about learning styles and creative, accelerated learning, particularly in higher education. Despite student complaints about bad and inadequate teaching practices, most teachers remain stuck in delivery methods they have learned at teacher training colleges many years ago (from very analytical lecturers) and are not even willing to contemplate more user-friendly methods.

teachers have never been trained in new methods

This attitude really alienates traditional teachers from an ever-growing <u>student body demanding modern teaching practices</u>, appropriate for the fast-changing world we live in. Although this is a broad generalization as there are plenty of good and progressive teachers (often frustrated with the system), it seems that many teachers have built a world of their own, which is their comfort zone and which they are not prepared to leave. As I am an optimist, I know that these conditions will change, albeit slowly, and therefore I will continue to work tirelessly for <u>bringing about changes</u>.

students demand modern teaching practices

bringing about changes

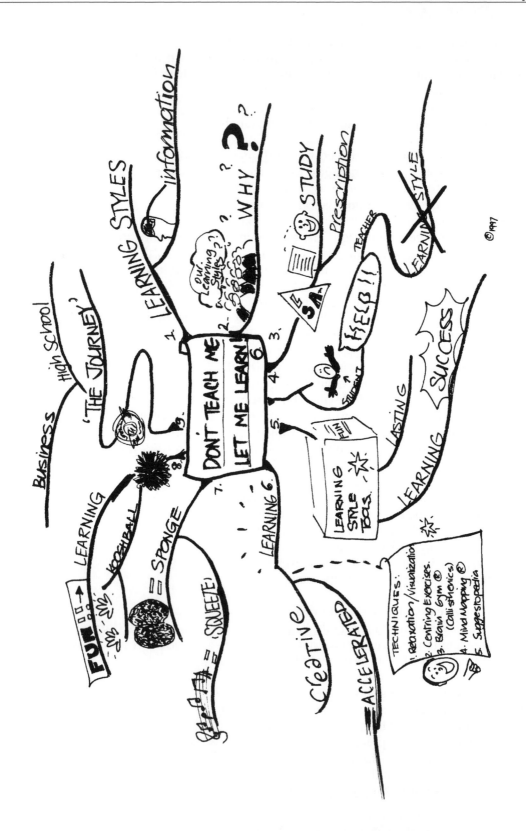

1. Learning styles and information intake

As we have already seen, information intake is strongly dependent on the way people go about it, and that has far-reaching consequences for their success in learning and training. By instructing students through their personal learning style strengths an immediate behavioural change is noticeable and the failure rate in schools can effectively be brought down to zero. The effects, particularly on underachieving students, are instant because insight into their own learning abilities leads to ongoing performance improvement in class when they begin to understand their own style.

behavioural change
failure rate
zero

performance improvement
understand own style

The research for underpinning these claims goes back over twenty years in the USA and is rapidly growing worldwide. (1)

Among all the elements which make up a person's overall style, four of our six senses (seeing, hearing, touching and feeling) are the ones which most influence information intake, memory and learning. Translated into more technical terms they can be described as visual, auditory, tactile and kinesthetic sensory modalities or perceptual preferences (see page 130).

senses
seeing, hearing
touching, feeling
information intake

sensory modalities
perceptual preferences

Centres for processing sensory information are spread all over the brain and develop at their own pace in each human being. Children first begin learning and remembering difficult things by experiencing them kinesthetically (**K**), which means they need to involve their whole body for information intake and acquiring basic skills. The second modality to develop is tactile (**T**); that's why young children have to touch everything that interests them – they are learning through manipulation and interaction with objects and people. Around age eight, some children begin to develop strong visual (**V**) preferences which allow them to take information in more through observing and watching what's going on around them. Seeing becomes a very important learning tool. Around eleven years of age many begin to become more auditory (**A**),

develop at own pace

kinesthetic (K)

tactile (T)

visual (V)

auditory (A)

SENSORY MODALITIES
and submodalities

VISUAL
- reading
- seeing/watching
- visualizing/imagination

AUDITORY
- listening
- talking/discussing
- self-talk/inner dialogue

TACTILE
- manipulating/handling

KINESTHETIC
- experience/doing
- feeling/intuition

which means they can now learn well mainly by listening and can easily remember complex information they hear. (2)

However, the <u>majority of school-aged children</u> remain <u>kinesthetic/tactile</u> throughout their primary school years; <u>far fewer students</u> than teachers ever imagined are <u>highly auditory</u> or <u>strongly visual</u>. We found the same results among New Zealand adults (from executives, managers and workers, to polytechnic, university or business school students) by applying our new Working Style Analysis instrument.

**most school children
kinesthetic/tactile
few students
highly auditory or
strongly visual**

Yet, traditional university and <u>adult education</u> and formal training are still strongly based on <u>auditory/ visual information intake</u>. Hands-on, so-called 'doing learning', or experiential training, is still seen as an add-on to 'serious' or academic learning. Educators seem to be unaware that learning by <u>listening</u> is the <u>least preferred</u> and hardest way for most students to remember complex or difficult information. <u>Auditory learners</u> can remember approximately 75 per cent of what they hear, but <u>less than 30 per cent of the school-aged population</u> in the USA is auditory (3) and the same figure is true for adult learners in New Zealand.

**adult education
auditory/visual
information intake**

**listening
least preferred
auditory learners**

**less than 30 per cent of
school children**

Therefore, when students and adults do not do the things they have been told or <u>can't remember</u> what they were told, it is usually because they find it very difficult to absorb and remember <u>spoken instructions</u> and <u>explanations</u>, particularly if they are given in a series of directives. As we will see in Chapter 9 there also seem to be <u>sex differences</u> which might account for different preferences, styles and behaviour in males and females as well as for <u>misunderstandings</u> and miscommunication between the sexes.

can't remember

**spoken instructions
explanations**

sex differences

misunderstandings

When it comes to <u>visual preferences</u>, <u>only 40 per cent of the school-aged population</u> in the USA is visual – able to remember approximately two-fifths of what they have read or seen. Figures from New Zealand show an even lower number of visual learners (30 per cent), particularly among adults, but the situation is more complex than that.

**visual preferences
40 per cent of
US school children**

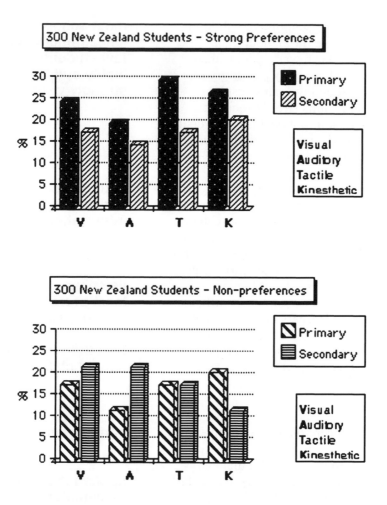

Note that most students display <u>multiple</u> preferences,
and many students are flexible with no preferences,
therefore these figures can exceed 100%.

Visual analytics (people with left-brain, sequential and reflective thinking style) seem to remember words and numbers better; their counterparts, visual holistics (people with right-brain, creative, random thinking style), tend to remember pictures, illustrations, graphs and symbols much better.

visual analytics

words and numbers
visual holistics
pictures, illustrations, graphs and symbols

If children and grown-ups don't remember a great deal of what they hear and see, how do they remember? They remember what they touch, feel, handle and/or manipulate. These are the tactile (**T**) learners who make up the largest group of children in New Zealand. However, we also found that information intake through their hands is the preferred style of over 30 per cent of adult learners.

touch, feel,
handle, manipulate
tactile learners – T

over 30 per cent of adults

Another large group are kinesthetic (**K**) learners – those who need to experience what they learn. The majority of young children, and many students and grown-ups, learn most effectively and remember best when they do something – play, take a trip, build, cook, create, experience, visit, meet and interact with others. They are able to learn most easily and remember best through whole-body activities (K-external) and an international study has revealed that even gifted and highly talented adolescents are strongly tactile and kinesthetic. That's why we have introduced the use of Koosh balls as a highly effective learning tool, as we will see later.

kinesthetic learners – K
experience

do something

whole-body activities
K-external

Koosh balls
learning tool

By using our Working Style Analysis we discovered that there are also many adult learners who need to feel good about what they are doing (K-internal); it has to make sense to them, otherwise they find it very hard to remember. Unless it feels good they are not even interested or willing to begin a learning experience, and it is nearly impossible to motivate them to do more than the absolute minimum.

feel good
K-internal, make sense
hard to remember
not interested

So far we have considered information intake through the different modalities but for successful learning, working and problem solving we also need to consider how humans process, store and retrieve or access pieces of information.

information intake

process, store,
retrieve/access information

Learning Style Classrooms

Courtesy of St Georges Preparatory School, Wanganui, NZ

Courtesy of Rosegarden Skolan, Västeras, Sweden

It seems that the information intake process does not always equal the information output process. This means that people might well prefer to take in information through their visual sense, which triggers feelings, which in turn help to process, connect and store this bit of information; but when it comes to retrieving it, they might then use a physical movement or touch, combined with a feeling to remember.

information output

As every brain works best through multisensory input (which means involving more than two modalities), imagine a situation where people can take information in through listening only – like in a long telephone conversation. What would they do to remember the content? Depending on their sensory style they might move around, doodle or fiddle to enhance their listening if they are not auditory learners and then, for processing, they might transform what they hear into internal pictures or feelings. Later, when they need to recall the telephone conversation, they might look at something – maybe their doodles – or move or touch something and remember what they heard. Observe how these processes work for you and how you can enhance them.

multisensory input

The more you are aware of your intake and processing styles, the more you will be able to utilize your brain skills, which in the sensory areas seem to be genetically predetermined, particularly in the visual system of the brain. With these experience-independent processes sensory signals are selected and categorized. (4)

aware of your intake and processing styles
utilize your brain skills
genetically predetermined

Knowledge about the range of information intake preferences, the importance of modalities, and how strong they are in each individual, not only helps parents to understand their children's true learning needs better but also permanently changes teachers' and trainers' beliefs about how human beings are supposed to learn. It can give them vital information for preparing teaching programmes and training materials and how to conduct their work with students, accommodating all their modalities. Multisensory learning and training kitsets, as pictured on page 146, are an

preparing programmes and training materials

multisensory learning and training kitsets

As Individuals

we are all DiffeRent

but as Crowds

we are all the SAME.

Ben Elton

ideal combination of learning tools suitable for any age group and for all possible <u>combinations of modalities</u> in students. More on these kitsets – how to produce and use them – is described later in this chapter or can be found in the Dunn and Dunn books on learning styles (see Bibliography and Further Reading).

combinations of modalities

2. Why students need to know their learning styles

Imagine you are walking through heavy fog, not sure where to go, with no equipment to show you the way and no one to ask. That's how students must feel, I imagine, if they have <u>no clue about their own learning style</u>, being lost in the fog of learning where everything becomes a blur because they don't know what goes on in their brain during the learning process. They don't know consciously which strategies they are using, so they can't repeat them next time, even if they have been successful before. <u>Learning</u> actually becomes <u>a trial-and-error process</u>, costing a lot of energy. The result is <u>frustration</u>, <u>stress</u> and <u>disappointment</u>, mixed with occasional <u>elation</u> when things go well. What a roller coaster! Under these conditions even successes don't mean much because the price was too high.

no clue about their own learning style

learning a trial-and-error process frustration and stress disappointment, elation

As you might guess, knowing their personal learning style, actually receiving/touching their LSA Profile and <u>seeing</u> their <u>learning style strengths</u> black on white, can be a huge turn-around, especially for students with <u>low self-esteem</u> due to previous learning failures. In my work with teachers and students I have seen the <u>relief</u>, the <u>astonishment</u> and the <u>pride</u> in their faces when they realize that there is nothing wrong with them, that they don't need to feel awkward because they know they are different. I have heard children say, 'Now I will prove to my teacher that I CAN learn, that I am not dumb.'

seeing learning style strengths improve low self-esteem

relief, astonishment, pride

My request therefore is, <u>every two years</u> have your students' <u>learning styles assessed</u>, discuss their profiles and allow them to learn 'their way'.

every two years learning styles assessed

LEARNING

is a matter of

ATTITUDE

not

Aptitude.

Dr Georgi Lozanov

3. The Learning Style Analysis (LSA) – a study prescription

When students have responded to one of the LSA questionnaires, their data has been entered into the computer, and their LSA Profile and Report (see pages 72, 74 and 76) has been printed, a unique document will be available, describing <u>style preferences</u>, <u>dislikes and flexibilities</u>, containing also detailed recommendations for how this student can learn best. Teachers, parents and students themselves will get more than just a description of someone's learning style but a true study prescription, which will, if acted upon, certainly <u>improve academic performance</u> and make life easier for those with so-called learning difficulties.

style preferences, dislikes and flexibilities

improve academic performance

<u>Every single element</u> of the Learning Style Pyramid (see page 78) is <u>described</u> in a separate paragraph in the LSA Report. Following are a few examples of a student's printout (note that the reading level of the text passages is not too high but also not targeted at the students only, as are the questionnaires):

every single element described

LSA Report samples printout:

NEED FOR INTAKE: (from LSA Senior)
You usually use some kind of intake – eating, nibbling, drinking, chewing – when concentrating or learning something new and difficult, but also when you are bored, frustrated or impatient. You find it hard to go for long periods without something to eat or drink and you might chew your pens, pencils or fingernails instead. You should give yourself frequent opportunities to eat nutritious foods or have drinks of water and healthy snacks during thinking processes, reading or studying. Just watch out how much you eat or drink because, particularly under stress, you might not be aware of the amounts you take in! (Attention: If you are already smoking, or have tried smoking, you might be in danger of getting addicted to this potentially lethal habit due to your preference for intake!)

AUTHORITY: (from LSA Senior)
You definitely prefer to learn unsupervised or without an authority figure present. You will often do the opposite of whatever a teacher/coach/team leader or parent suggests. However, you can learn with people in authority, but only if they have a collegial approach. It is most important for your study success that you are not under constant control, that you trust the people who are in charge, and that they understand your strong need to study without being controlled all the time. However, you need to prove to your superiors that you have self-discipline in learning, and can produce better results without supervision. If you are about to leave or finish school, you need to take that into account for your future career planning.

If we think of the great teachers in history – Socrates, Jesus, Montessori – did they spend five hours a night on lesson plans? No. They were great teachers because they were learned people, because they learned through reflection, long walks, reading, solitude and writing.

Calkins

PERSISTENCE: (from LSA Senior)
Most of the time following through with your school or homework is up and down, and whether you complete what you start always depends on your interest in the learning task or study assignment. As soon as you lose interest or get bored with your learning you tend to abandon it and do something else. Often the overall situation is much more important for you than the learning task itself. But when you are really excited about a job, your persistence can increase dramatically and you then become very systematic in your approach.

TACTILE (**touching**): (from LSA Junior)
You are a hands-on learner! When you study, read or concentrate you really like to involve your hands. You probably play with pens, tap your fingers, fiddle and/or doodle a lot – especially when you have to listen for a long time. This increases when you are impatient, bored, frustrated or stressed out in class. To enhance your listening skills and for better memory, always involve your hands. Use Koosh balls for hand stimulation, mind maps for note taking, hands-on learning and models or real objects when you learn something new and difficult. Learning tools you can manipulate are particularly good for you. Involving your hands and fingers when you read helps you to understand and remember better. Your teachers and parents need to know that you learn much better when you use your hands.

MOBILITY: (from LSA Junior)
You find it very difficult to sit still for long periods of time. Having to sit still and listen to the teacher can be deadly for you. Your concentration improves and your brain works better when you can move your body. You change your body posture frequently, often tapping your feet and fidgeting. You really like to move around while studying, concentrating, listening, even reading. When you are bored, frustrated, or under stress, you can become very restless, often agitated – even more so when you have to listen for long periods of time. That's why teachers will often say you are 'hyperactive'. To improve your concentration, make sure that you are allowed to stand up and stretch regularly, walk around, take a break, and then return to your learning task. Moving while you are learning something new and difficult helps you concentrate. Physical learning activities and games are good for your understanding of something new. It is very important that your teachers and parents understand your strong need for mobility. Despite your preference for mobility, be aware that not everyone likes to move around as much as you do! There are people who don't want to be disturbed when they learn, they need peace and quiet. Be considerate.

From these examples you can see that even if you are not familiar with learning styles and diversity, these underlined reports will certainly give you a good understanding about the learning needs of a young person and will help you help them. But of course I do recommend that you learn more about this fascinating concept, particularly when you are a principal, teacher or parent of teenagers.

detailed reports
learning needs

teenagers

If as a student you are

not being taught in

your learning style,

you are being handicapped.

J. Ingham

4. Help, my teacher doesn't understand my learning style!

We have heard this exclamation from students whose parents had arranged for them to get their learning style assessed and who began to understand what enhances their learning and what puts them off. Armed with that knowledge, increased awareness and self-esteem they go back to school and find their teachers are not interested or don't want to know! It's a sad state of affairs, often found in high schools where teachers are too burdened by the curriculum, too stressed out to consider yet another fad (?) and just want to get on with their regular programme. Unfortunately they do not, or do not *want* to consider how a knowledge of learning styles might actually help them to reduce stress, manage their classroom better and equip them with instructional methods useful to all types of learners.

enhances learning

teachers not interested

often in high schools

**learning styles knowledge
reduce stress**

Similar reports come from parents who went to see their children's teachers, presented them with their daughter's or son's LSA profile and wanted them to take their learning style needs into account but teachers brushed their requests aside, discarding them as unimportant or inappropriate. Sometimes they got defensive, saying it is all nonsense. When such a situation prevails, it is most unfortunate, not only for communication between parents and school but also for the progress of the student, because existing learning problems will not go away and strategies prescribed by the school often do not work for the simple reason that they do not take into account style differences. However, if teachers refuse to be part of a learning styles concept there are only two choices parents have: either transfer the child to another school where learning styles are accommodated, or provide all the support they can give at home, create the learning environment their child needs and teach them study skills based on their learning style they can use in class.

parents

learning style needs

unimportant/inappropriate

learning problems

**two choices: transfer child
to other school
provide support**

teach them study skills

In any case, a knowledge of learning styles should always be the basis for student–teacher interaction, for understanding and supporting students in their learning needs and in helping them become more flexible too.

**learning styles
basis for student–teacher
interaction**

INGREDIENTS
OF
CREATIVE, ACCELERATED LEARNING

LEARNING/WORKING STYLES
SELF-KNOWLEDGE
HOW THE BRAIN WORKS
(LEFT/RIGHT BRAIN, ALPHA STATE)
RELAXATION AND VISUALIZATION
CENTRING EXERCISES
BRAIN GYM® (EDUCATIONAL KINESIOLOGY)
WATER
PROPER BRAIN FOOD
BREATHING
MEMORY TECHNIQUES
MIND MAPPING
USE OF MUSIC
KOOSH BALLS
MENTAL STATE OF LEARNER
PHYSICAL STATE OF LEARNER
POSTURE
LEARNING ENVIRONMENT
INDIVIDUALIZED INSTRUCTION
SUGGESTOPEDIA
VISION AND PURPOSE OF LEARNING
GOAL SETTING
ENJOYMENT, FUN AND MOTIVATION
LEARNER'S SELF-IMAGE
ART AND CREATIVITY
MOVEMENT AND DANCE
ACCELERATION OF INFORMATION INTAKE

5. Learning style tools for lasting learning success

One of the main aspects of student-centred teaching and <u>individualized instruction</u> based on learning styles is to create <u>resources and learning materials</u> which are <u>reusable</u> and can be utilized by ALL students at different times and for very different purposes. For some they will be learning enhancers but for others these tools will be the main activity to learn new and difficult concepts.

individualized instruction reusable resources and learning materials

Who are the students <u>who benefit most</u> from the use of learning style tools? You may have already guessed – it's the <u>hands-on, highly tactile learners</u> who also have <u>v</u>isual and <u>k</u>inesthetic <u>preferences</u> who learn best with <u>manipulatives</u>, have a short attention span, low learning motivation and persistence, are more holistic in their brain processing style and who <u>need variety</u> and <u>multisensory stimulation</u>.

who benefits most?

hands-on, highly tactile learners, V/K preferences manipulatives

need variety and multisensory stimulation

As you can see on pages 64 and 134, such tools are being used by students in various countries and have helped them to understand difficult information much better than just by reading or only talking about it.

All these tools are <u>self-correcting</u> and easy to make; the <u>most popular</u> ones are:

most popular, self-correcting learning tools

- Task cards/puzzles
- Learning circles
- Wrap-arounds
- Flip chutes/flip boxes
- Electro boards
- Pic-a-holes
- Board and floor games.

Initially, making those tools takes a lot of time but once techniques are known, older <u>students</u> can <u>make their own tools</u>, and in many schools a <u>resource person</u> or <u>teacher aide</u> is helping to create these resources. From our experience with working with schools we also know that <u>parents</u> are often willing to <u>contribute time</u> and <u>materials</u>, particularly in primary schools.

students make their own tools resource person or teacher aide parents contribute time and materials

Learning Style Kitsets

Courtesy of Creative Learning Co., Auckland

When put together in a box containing a set of tools about the same learning content you have a 'MIP' (Multisensory Instructional Package) or Learning Style Kitset, as pictured opposite, which is especially appropriate for learners who require structure. The step-by-step procedures provide clear, sequenced directions that are repeated in a variety of ways until success is achieved.

put together

Learning Style Kitset

structure

If you are interested in creating these tools please consult one of the excellent Dunn and Dunn books on learning styles (see Bibliography and Further Reading) or come to one of our practical workshops on learning styles where you will actually make these tools and then take them away with you (for training dates see www.networkpress.co.uk for Europe or www.creativelearningcentre.com for New Zealand).

make these tools

6. Techniques to achieve creative, accelerated learning

From what has been explained in this chapter so far, it is obvious that more knowledge about styles, diversity and brain functioning will definitely enhance any learning process. However, to make information intake even more successful there are further techniques which, combined with the above, will result in creative, accelerated learning. The following can only be a short introduction to these learning techniques and is meant to be just an 'appetizer' for an extensive 'smorgasbord' of truly revolutionary educational methods available these days. Practitioners who are interested to learn more about this subject will find a comprehensive selection of books in the Bibliography and Further Reading.

further techniques

introduction
'appetizer'
'smorgasbord'

According to the Bulgarian psychiatrist and educator Dr Georgi Lozanov (often referred to as the 'father' of accelerated learning), human learning is the most basic and natural function – easier than breathing or walking. By birthright, learning is an easy, joyful process. Unfortunately, the prevailing, Western educational world view denies that human beings are capable of unlimited learning. Lozanov proved that learning is accelerated by 'desuggesting' limiting beliefs in the learner,

learning – natural function

easy, joyful process

desuggesting

CENTRING EXERCISE

Find a comfortable position,
uncross your arms and legs …
take in a deep breath – hold it – and exhale …
And with another deep breath
tense your whole body
from your toes to your head …
… and let go …
Take another deep breath …
… and exhale.
Now let your breathing establish a
comfortable rhythm …

As you are sitting here …
getting more and more relaxed …
think back how you came here this morning (evening) …
Think back how the day began for you.
How did you get up? …
Where were you? What did you do?
Were you relaxed or in a hurry?…
Did you have breakfast? …
Who was with you … or were you on your own?
How did you get here?
Did you drive or walk?
Were you alone or with someone else?
What were your thoughts
when you came up to this building? …
And when you entered this room …
how did you feel? …
what did you say?

… And as you are getting more and more relaxed,
think of all the **problems**
you are carrying around with you right now …
you **don't need them for today** …

constantly affirming at <u>conscious and/or</u>
<u>subconscious levels</u> that they can learn quickly,
easily and pleasantly. An ever-growing body
of research results reveals that the <u>link between</u>
<u>brain theory</u> and <u>learning practices</u> is crucial
for improving mental powers and learning ability.

**conscious and/or
subconscious levels**

**link between brain theory
and learning practices**

The term 'Accelerated Learning', which I prefer to
broaden into 'Creative, Accelerated Learning', is
now widely used for learning techniques based on
understanding <u>how the brain works</u>. They can be
applied in any field where <u>information intake</u> is
crucial: general education, language learning,
vocational and business training, parenting,
sports performance, military instructions, self-
improvement and management training. The list
on page 144 contains <u>methods and techniques</u>
which, <u>combined in the right way</u> for every
individual learner, can bring astonishing results
and drastically <u>improve their learning</u>.

**how the brain works
information intake**

**methods and techniques
rightly combined**

improve learning

Many of these components are of course used on
a daily basis in many situations outside learning
settings, and the more we apply and combine them
the more we are successful in handling problems
and <u>mastering difficulties</u>. For the purpose of
taking in the information contained in this book,
the following <u>techniques will be very useful</u> and
you are invited to try them out when going
through the individual chapters.

master difficulties

useful techniques

Relaxation/Visualization
Before we can even think of getting into any
learning or concentration process you need to
<u>prepare your body and your mind</u> accordingly.

relaxation/visualization

prepare body and mind

With any gadget we use we readily accept that it
has to be prepared for its use (it has to be set up,
plugged in or switched on). To reach and maintain
an <u>optimal learning state</u> and to deal with stress or
anxiety successfully, relaxation and visualization
are essential starting points. Lozanov calls this
mental state '<u>pseudo activity</u>' where the person
experiences relaxed concentration, like in a
classical concert – <u>physically relaxed</u> but
<u>mentally alert</u>. Although most people can relax in

optimal learning state

'pseudo activity'

**physically relaxed
mentally alert**

CENTRING EXERCISE CONTINUED

Imagine, there is a really nice **bag**
standing right in front of you …
What does it look like?
Do you recognize it, is it old, is it new? …
Now **open the bag** and notice
that it is **empty** …
I want you to put all your **worries** and **sorrows**,
all your problems into this bag …
one by one …
Whatever bothers you, put it in!

To show me that you are really filling up
your bag, give me a nod with your head … good.
Have you found another worry? Put it in …
Is your bag already full?…
When you have put in your last problem or worry
close your bag … **and lift it up** …
Is it heavy, is it light? …
Now **carry your bag out of this room** …
round the corner …
down the stairs (hallway) …
… and put all your bags in one place …
Pile them up, stack them …

Take a last look at your bag …
see all the other bags, they are safe there.
If you wish, you can pick up your bag later,
when you go home …
but you can also **leave it there**,
it's safe, no one will carry your problems away …

Now **turn around** and **come back into this room**,
feeling light, excited, and ready to learn …

So, wriggle your fingers and toes,
open your eyes wide, look around,
feel relaxed and **alert** – stretch, and **smile**!

non-stressful situations, they find it impossible
to get into a peaceful state of mind when they are
frustrated, under pressure or stressed out,
especially in learning or work situations. Without
a relaxed body and a relaxed mind it is impossible
to access higher brain functions or draw on
the powers of the right brain, thus limiting
memory input and storage.

access higher functions
right-brain powers

The use of music and/or a combination of
relaxation and visualization techniques is the
quickest way to change brainwave patterns
naturally from Beta to Alpha state (see page 166),
to slow down breathing and heartbeat rate, and
to achieve the best state for learning – relaxed
alertness. It is impossible to calm the mind
without relaxing the body.

change brainwaves

slow down breathing and
heartbeat rate
relaxed alertness

For this simple reason relaxation exercises should
always start with a physical relaxation, including
breathing, then have a mental relaxation part and
finish with a positive, creative visualization.
Such exercises should be done regularly
before you start a learning session and need to be
learned and practised like any other skill.

physical relaxation
mental relaxation
creative visualization

before a learning session

The centring exercise on pages 148 and 150 is
an example of combined relaxation/visualization
which I have been using with great success in
my seminars over many years. I invite you to
follow the given instructions carefully, practise
the exercise a few times and discover whether
it has the desired effect of relaxing you. If you
don't like this particular exercise, try others –
there are many tapes on the market but be careful
that you choose exercises which also contain
positive learning affirmations. Used always
in combination with relaxation and visualization,
they are powerful tools to accelerate your learning
and guarantee success. You must have the patience
and persistence to find out what's best for you.

centring exercise

desired relaxing effect

positive affirmations

accelerate your learning

what's best for you

Centring exercises

centring exercises

When learners have trained themselves into being
more relaxed before they begin learning activities
and have been using the suggested exercises on a
regular basis (either in a group or by themselves),

more relaxed

NZ School Children Preparing for Learning in Koosh Circles

there is one more way of <u>focusing one's attention on the learning process</u>. Especially in groups these 'centring' exercises have proven to be extremely effective for learners of all ages. They can also be used to <u>start classes</u> and precede discussions or group projects. The main purpose is to focus students' attention on the task at hand without jumping into the matter right away to help them relax, <u>make them feel welcome</u> and <u>comfortable</u>; to give them time to <u>mentally prepare</u> themselves; to <u>'switch on'</u> their brains.

focusing attention on learning

start classes

welcome and comfortable
mentally prepare
'switch on' brains

Although you can do these exercises quietly by yourself, focusing on what you have to do, it is recommended to do it with <u>groups</u> of children or adults who are about to learn, concentrate or work on something. Ask all the participants to <u>sit in a full circle</u> so that they face each other, either sitting on the floor or on chairs (if the group is large, it will have to be broken up into two or more circles of approximately 10 to 15 people). Then the group leader starts the process that will <u>become a ritual</u> over time: he or she holds a <u>'speaking token'</u> to signal to everyone that it is their turn to speak. We find that <u>Koosh balls</u> (see page 106) are very inspirational for this exercise, especially for <u>tactile/visual learners</u> who can control their nervousness by holding them. The leader chooses a phrase like 'I feel like saying ...' or 'Today/right now/this morning I ...' and says what's on his or her mind – either related to the learning session or totally unrelated but necessary to share with the group because it's bothering them and would otherwise interfere with the learning process.

groups

sit in full circle

ritual
'speaking token'
Koosh balls

tactile/visual learners

Each student should only say a <u>few sentences</u> unless something really important comes up and has to be cleared. Then the speaking token is passed on until everyone has had their say. If some children <u>do not want to speak</u>, that's OK, <u>don't force them</u>; maybe at the end they will be ready to contribute. You must always <u>respect</u> their reasons for not wanting to participate yet. When everyone has had their turn, the teacher continues with the set programme. If, however, the group is <u>still not ready for learning</u> after the

few sentences

not wanting to speak
don't force them
respect

not ready for learning

Brain Gym ®

is the registered trademark of the Educational Kinesiology Foundation.

CROSS-OVERS

With your right hand touch your left knee, & vice versa.
Do these movements in quick succession to upbeat music. Do the similar crossover behind your body: with your right hand touch your left heel & vice versa.

Grasp shoulder and look over it, pulling shoulder blades towards each other & breathing deeply...

Turn smoothly to look over other shoulder while breathing out with a 'whooo' sound. Change shoulders.

stretching

Cross legs and balance. Glide crossed arms downwards while breathing out and lift to horizontal while breathing in. This can be done seated.

centring exercise, it might be necessary then to
add on a relaxation/visualization exercise. This
usually happens in groups where students are very
stressed out and teachers have to work harder
to get them relaxed. Don't forget: it always
depends on the group leader how well he or she
prepares the whole group for learning!

add relaxation/visualization

if stressed out

**prepare group for
learning**

Brain Gym® (callisthenics)
Paul Dennison, a pioneer in the field of applied
brain research, discovered that a certain sequence
of arm and leg movements signals the brain to
balance the activities of the left and right
brain hemispheres, helping to enhance integration
and communication between them. The terms
he created were Educational Kinesiology, Edu-K
and Brain Gym®, which all mean 'draw out
through motion'. Dennison combined traditional
body movements (callisthenics) with others he
invented, and practitioners over the past fifteen years
have successfully introduced these exercises
on a large scale in schools worldwide.

Brain Gym®

**arm and leg movements
left/right brain hemispheres**

**Educational
Kinesiology**

Whenever you need to concentrate better or your
energy gets low during studying or concentrating,
try any of the cross-over exercises opposite and
experience how these simple and fun movements
(particularly when exercised with upbeat music)
can rebalance your brain functions and actually
re-energize you. Practised on a regular basis
you might also notice that your co-ordination
will get better and your memory will improve.
An important add-on to all Brain Gym® exercises
is to drink plenty of water. The reason is that
not only physical but also mental activities, like
learning and concentrating, use up body fluids
and they need to be replaced regularly. This is
particularly crucial during periods of high stress
when the water intake should be doubled.

low energy

**with upbeat music
rebalance**

**co-ordination better
memory improve**

**drink plenty of water
mental activities
use up body fluids**

**high stress
double water intake**

The exercises described so far for accelerating
learning and enhancing concentration should either
be done before or during learning sessions.
The following technique is useful for speeding up
information intake and enhancing memory at any
time during the learning process.

exercises

before or during learning

enhancing memory

HOW TO CREATE A MIND MAP

FOUR STEPS

1. *Topic in the centre*
2. *Add branches*
3. *Write cue words*
4. *Personalize (add colour, symbols, pictures, and so on)*

Mind Mapping®

This note-taking technique has become very
popular among students over the last few years.
Originally created by Michael Gelb, the method has
been popularized by Tony Buzan, who called these
structures 'mind maps' and registered the name. It
was then put into practical applications by Nancy
Margulies, Colin Rose and Eric Jensen (see the
section Bibliography and Further Reading).

Mind Mapping®
note-taking technique

Why is it so effective for so many people, young
and old? When considering different learning
styles, this technique is particularly helpful for
holistic thinkers, who need the big overview
and who have visual and tactile preferences in their
information intake. Analytical thinkers, however,
needing a step-by-step approach, and learners who
are not highly visual, often experience mind or
memory maps as disjointed structures that don't
make sense to them. Therefore it is very important
for your own learning success to find out your style
first so that you can choose the appropriate method
for your needs.

effective

holistic: big overview
visual, tactile
analytical: step-by-step
approach

find out your style first
choose appropriate method

If you are a right-brain oriented person, you will
find that by using mind maps instead of linear
note taking you will improve your memory,
save time, get more things done and will be much
more creative. The technique can also be used
for brainstorming, generating ideas, planning
and problem solving. Instead of full sentences, in
learning maps we use pictures, symbols, structure,
colour and keywords only. For many learners
it is much less stressful than traditional note taking
and much more fun to do!

right-brain oriented
mind maps
improve memory
save time
more creative
brainstorming/planning
problem solving

less stressful

If you want to try out this technique or improve
your already existing mind-mapping skills, follow
the instructions on the opposite page and create
your own personal mind map similar to the one
on page 176 about the different topics of Chapter 7
or any topic of your choice. Prepare what you need,
begin it now and have fun!

try out, improve
mind-mapping skills

Suggestopedia

For over thirty years, <u>Bulgarian psychiatrist</u> and professor of education <u>Dr Georgi Lozanov</u> has been studying perception and learning. He was the first scientist to systematically research the phenomenon of <u>rapid learning</u>. He called his teaching system 'Suggestopedy', based on 'Suggestology', the science of suggestion in all its different aspects.

Suggestopedia
Bulgarian psychiatrist
Dr Georgi Lozanov

rapid learning
Suggestopedy
Suggestology

The words he coined refer to the fact that 'suggestion' is used to speed up learning by <u>tapping into human reserve capacities</u>. Suggestopedic teachers <u>organize and orchestrate</u> the <u>learning environment</u> and practise pedagogy based on the use of positive suggestions. (5)

tap reserve capacities
organize and orchestrate
learning environment

According to Don Schuster, professor at Iowa State University, this revolutionary teaching system clearly <u>accelerates learning</u> by:
a. using advertising-like suggestions to bypass common barriers against rapid learning
b. relaxing students and making learning fun
c. presenting lessons dramatically to help students make vivid imagery
d. reviewing lessons calmly with slow, rhythmic baroque music. (6)

accelerates learning

Lozanov's system blends exceptionally well with the individualized learning style approach. After personal training with the 'Great Master', studying suggestopedic methods, and working intensively with our LSA model but particularly with teachers on the LSA model, classroom management and lesson planning, I have come to the conclusion that these two <u>holistic models complement</u> each other perfectly because <u>learning styles individualize</u> Lozanov's uniform approach and <u>Suggestopedia adds the larger framework</u> to learning styles teaching.

models complement
styles individualize,
Suggestopedia adds
larger framework

The methods he developed and mainly used for <u>teaching foreign languages</u> the fast way are the historic basis for what is presently known as 'Superlearning', 'Whole-Brain Learning' or 'Creative, Accelerated Learning'.

foreign language teaching

Sample of suggestopedic text presentation

	Scene 2 In the National Gallery	**Szene 2** **In der Nationalgalerie**
	They get off the bus at Potsdamer Brücke, and the National Gallery is directly in front of them.	**Sie steigen an der Potsdamer Brücke aus, und die Nationalgalerie liegt direkt vor ihnen.**
Peter	I would like to see pictures by the expressionists.	**Ich würde gern Bilder von den Expressionisten sehen.**
Hilde	Oh, how intelligent you are! So you know the painters belonging to the 'Brücke' and 'Blauer Reiter' group. Good. Let's go and see the expressionist paintings first and afterwards whatever interests you.	**Ah, was du nicht alles weißt! Du kennst also die Malergruppe 'Brücke' und 'Blauer Reiter'! Gut! Da schauen wir uns zuerst den Expressionismus an und dann, was dich sonst noch interessiert.**
Erzähler	They spent a good two hours at the exhibition and saw pictures by Kandinsky, Franz Marc, by Macke, Beckmann and Schmidt-Rotluff. Peter was very impressed by their strong colours and the enormous size of their canvases.	**Sie verbrachten gut zwei Stunden in der Ausstellung und sahen Bilder von Kandinsky, Franz Marc, von Macke, Beckmann und Schmidt-Rotluff. Peter war sehr beeindruckt von den kräftigen Farben und den großen Flächen.**
Hilde	These paintings give the best effect when you don't stand too close to them. Seen at a very close range, they look very different.	**Diese Bilder wirken am besten, wenn man nicht zu nah davor steht. Von der Nähe gesehen, wirken sie ganz anders.**

From: *Accelerated German Language Course*, by Colin Rose

Among the many learning enhancing techniques
of the Lozanov method described explicitly by
two of the top European trainers in Suggestopedia,
Tony Stockwell and Lonny Gold, there is one
aspect I find extremely useful for accelerated
information intake – the suggestopedic text. It is **suggestopedic text**
based on the ability of the human brain to take in
a certain amount of information at once and store it
in its short-term memory bank. For text layout **short-term memory**
this means 10 to 12 syllables grouped in
semantically meaningful clusters (for foreign
language texts only 7 to 9 syllables). Similar to
newspaper columns, this layout allows the reader **newspaper columns**
to go over text passages quite fast without a lot
of eye movement to the left or right. Skimming **skimming**
down the text passages with the help of two or
three fingers can bring the reader close to real
speed reading. That is the reason why I have **speed reading**
chosen the suggestopedic text presentation for
this book.

Peripheral vision, another powerful tool for **peripheral vision**
fast learning, is also utilized in this type of layout.
Certain keywords, selected from the text and **keywords**
underlined, are repeated in bold on the right-hand **repeated in bold**
side of each text column. The effect is that these
keywords, even without reading them fully **without reading them**
consciously, will be stored in the reader's memory **fully consciously**
and enhance information intake. This style of text
presentation is my own further development **further development**
of Lozanov's original suggestopedic text layout
used for foreign language learning as you can see
on the opposite page. (7)

7. The mind is a sponge and music is the squeeze

Music has always played, and still does play,
a central role in the cultures of the world, and
the effects of music on society and on
an individual's emotions, body and mind
have been well documented throughout the ages.

So it is no surprise that, among all the creative,
accelerated learning tools, music is definitely **music**
the favourite. Once educators have learned how
to use it appropriately and have experienced

The Magic of Music

how it makes the <u>learning process</u> so <u>much more pleasurable</u>, they and their students do not want to be without it. Even if there are students in the group who need absolute quiet and get distracted by background music, there are ways of using music for them as well.

**learning process
more pleasurable**

Many books about the <u>use of music in learning</u> have been published in recent years, each containing a wealth of information about this topic. The best ones are listed in the Bibliography and Further Reading. It would go way beyond the intentions of this book to try and give a comprehensive account of the use of <u>music as a learning tool</u> but I feel it is necessary to present at least an <u>introductory overview</u>. This, I hope, will make readers interested enough to learn more about the magic of music and investigate more deeply this whole new world of possibilities.

music in learning

**music as a learning tool
introductory overview**

What is so fascinating about the use of music in learning is that certain styles or <u>types of music</u>, particularly <u>baroque music</u> with its 60 beats per minute, when used as the <u>background</u> to a spoken presentation (known as 'concert reading'), acts as a carrier signal within the brain, activating right-hemisphere functions.

**types of music
baroque music
background**

In their book, *Accelerated Learning with Music – A Trainer's Manual* (8) – one of the best available on the use of music for learning – Doug and Terry Webb describe <u>music</u> as the '<u>interstate highway to the memory system</u>'. Both Webbs trained with Dr Lozanov and share their vast knowledge about music with their readers, helping them 'achieve success in learning through the <u>strategic use of music</u>'.

**music
interstate highway
to the memory system**

strategic use of music

As far as the use of music in learning goes, the historic, <u>revolutionary contribution</u> by <u>Bulgarian psychiatrist</u> and educator <u>Dr Georgi Lozanov</u> can no longer be disregarded. His discoveries are the foundation of the educational science known as '<u>Suggestopedia</u>' (explained more fully in this chapter, beginning on page 159).

**revolutionary contribution
by Bulgarian psychiatrist
Dr Georgi Lozanov**

Suggestopedia

For hundreds of years music has been used to assist in healing the aches and pains of the mind

MUSIC SELECTION I

Baroque and Pre-classical Music

Slow tempo: 40–60 beats/minute:

A. Albinoni   –   Adagio for Strings in G Minor
J. S. Bach   –   Fantasy for Organ in G Major
                     –   Prelude and Fugue in G Major
                     –   Brandenburg Concertos
A. Corelli   –   Concerti Grossi, op. 6, No. 2–12
G. F. Händel   –   Water Music, Concerto Grosso op. 3
J. Pachelbel   –   Canon in D
A. Vivaldi   –   Concerto for Viola d'amore
                     –   Concertos for Flute and Chamber Orchestra
                     –   Four Seasons (Spring, Summer, Autumn, Winter)
LIND tapes, CDs   –   Largo and Adagio

Classical and Romantic Music

Medium tempo: 60–80 beats/minute:

L. V. Beethoven   –   Concerto for Piano and Orchestra No. 5 in B Flat
                           Major op. 73
                     –   Concerto for Violin and Orchestra in D Major
J. Brahms   –   Concerto for Violin and Orchestra in D Major, op. 77
F. Chopin   –   Waltzes
J. Haydn   –   Symphony in C Major, No. 101, in G Major, No. 94
                     –   Concertos No. 1 and 2 in C Major for Violins and
                           Orchestra
N. Rimsky-Korsakov   –   Symphonic Suite for Thousand and One Nights,
                           op. 35
W. A. Mozart   –   Symphony in G Minor, No. 40
P. I. Tchaikovsky   –   Concerto No. 1 in B Flat Minor for Piano and
                           Orchestra
Rondo Veneziano   –   Mozart, Vivaldi, Venice 2000
LIND tapes, CDs   –   Andante and Allegro, Pianissimo

and body. Current research shows us how to improve memory, reduce stress and modify our abilities to heal. One of the latest fascinating findings about the use of music as a learning-enhancing tool has been named the 'Mozart Effect'. Researchers at the Centre for Neurobiology of Learning and Memory at the University of California, Irvine, have for several years been conducting experiments that associate musical phenomena with brain functions. Startling results were announced in 1993: after only ten minutes of listening to the Sonata for Two Pianos in D, K 448 by W. A. Mozart, 36 students were able to perform on an average of 8–9 per cent better on intelligence tests. (9) The scientists are also in no doubt that Mozart should be played to children because they found that preschoolers score up to 80 per cent better on tests of spatial and temporal reasoning after a year of daily musical sessions.

'Mozart Effect'

association of musical phenomena and brain functions

students perform better on intelligence tests Mozart played to children, score better on tests of spatial and temporal reasoning

The UC Irvine has established the Music and the Brain Information Centre (MBIC) to function as a free source of information on research in music and behaviour. (10)

Don Campbell, one of the great masters in using music for learning enhancement, has now written a book *The Mozart Effect*™ which describes all the different aspects of research findings in this area and to which effect music can be used. It describes the general uses of music to reduce stress, the specialized uses of music to improve memory, awareness and the integration of learning styles, and the experimental uses of music and sound to improve listening disorders, dyslexia, attention deficit disorder and autism. It also explains the therapeutic use of music for mental and physical disorders and injuries.

music for learning enhancement

therapeutic use of music

Don Campbell uses 'The Mozart Effect' as an inclusive term signifying the transformational powers of music in health, education and well-being.

But there is more: over the last fifteen years modern music has also been used to help students remember difficult concepts in any subject. By creating songs,

modern music

songs, rhymes, raps

MUSIC SELECTION II

Uplifting and High-energy Music

Fast tempo: 80–120 beats/minute:

A. Khatchaturian	–	Sabre Dance
M. Ravel	–	Bolero
R. Wagner	–	Ride of the Valkyries
J. Sibelius	–	Alla Marcha (from Karelia Suite)
J. Strauss	–	Radetsky March, Die Fledermaus Overture
J. Fucic	–	Florentine March
W. A. Mozart	–	Overtures Don Giovanni, Magic Flute
L. V. Beethoven	–	Egmont Overture
F. Liszt	–	Hungarian Rhapsodies
J. Rodrigo	–	Concierto Aranjuez
G. Verdi	–	Triumph March from Aïda
G. Rossini	–	William Tell, Overture
G. Holst	–	The Planets
A. Fiedler	–	Anthology of Marches by Boston Pops
O. Liebert	–	Nouveau Flamenco
Rondo Veneziano	–	Venice in Peril, The Best of Rondo Veneziano

Modern upbeat music, movie soundtracks

Brainwave patterns

Beta

When wide awake – the conscious mind: 13–25 cycles per second

Alpha

Ideal learning state of 'relaxed alertness': 8–12 cycles per second rhymes, raps and even academic musicals, it is possible for any learner to be more involved in the learning process and retain the content much longer. Putting difficult concepts to music is an invaluable tool for fast information intake and long-term storage for learners of any age.

academic musicals

retain content

fast information intake
long-term storage

Considering learning and working styles, the old belief that students learn more and workers perform better in an absolutely quiet environment no longer holds, because research shows that many students (adults as well as children) and people in the workforce think and remember better with music in the background.

quiet environment

students/people at work
think and remember better
with music in background

It is also true that a small minority of students (more high school than primary school students and more girls than boys) need absolute quiet while concentrating or taking in new and difficult information. Teachers, educators and parents must respect that need for quiet by setting up classrooms, learning environments and home study areas accordingly. However, even these students can and should be using music for revision and reinforcement of already learned material.

absolute quiet

music for revision and
reinforcement

That sounds great, you think, and might want to jump into using music right away – but be warned!

A little knowledge is dangerous and the wrong use of music in a learning environment will achieve the opposite effect. Inappropriate application or wrong timing will certainly create resistance and switch off students' attention.

wrong use of music
opposite effect

resistance

The type of music used has to be chosen carefully because sceptical adults and teenagers, particularly those who are used to listening to modern, upbeat music, will resent it. Only with proper information, and careful introduction by a knowledgeable teacher or instructor, will learners accept the type of music which truly enhances and speeds up information intake processes.

choose music carefully
sceptical adults
and teenagers

careful introduction

speed up information
intake processes

After having experienced various versions of unprofessional use of music in learning and training environments, my advice to educators

Text for an 'Active Concert' used for a Parent Group

By Mike Scaddan

Music, man's used for thousands of years,
It's entertaining, soothing and calming of fears.
It can uplift an army who move into battle,
Or surround us in adverts with 'buy us now' prattle.

But this is only a fraction of what *music* can do,
It's importance in *learning* has been discovered too.
Music activates electrical neurotransmissions,
To dendrites enabling more associations.

The more stimulation, the more connections are formed,
To make more associations with knowledge that's stored.
Music then triggers our right-brain *memory*,
And makes learning as simple as A, B and C.

Our brainwaves are made up of *Alpha* and *Beta*,
With *Theta* and *Delta* completing the picture.
Beta is active and used every day,
But for high-level thinking, Alpha's the way.

By relaxing our moods and slowing the waves,
Music stimulates Alpha's creativity phase.
Baroque music's amazing as it matches the rhythms,
Allowing insight and deep thought associations.

So *music* stimulates creativity thoughts,
By altering mood and reducing brain stress.
This *relaxed alertness* is an essential state,
To help us all learn at incredible rates.

in all educational settings is the following: if you
want to be serious about the <u>use of music</u>
in your classroom, <u>learn it professionally</u>.

**learn use of music
professionally**

Learn it from the masters in this field,
<u>introduce it slowly</u>, and begin to feel the
magic of music during the learning process.
Finally, <u>enjoy the relaxation</u> music brings, and
<u>celebrate the results</u> with your students and
trainees.

introduce it slowly

**enjoy the relaxation
celebrate the results**

8. Want to have a ball in learning? Use a Koosh ball!

To round off the smorgasbord of learning tools,
methods and techniques, I'd like to describe one
<u>educational tool</u> which has fascinated me ever
since I encountered it. It was on the first day of a
course on Rapid Learning at Houston University,
Texas, some years ago. The teachers there were
using brightly coloured <u>rubber pompoms</u>, called
<u>Koosh balls</u>, for various exercises. We experienced
the <u>positive effects</u> they had on our learning as we
passed them on to fellow students while giving
answers to questions, threw them at different
targets during some learning games, or just fiddled
with them while we were listening.

educational tool

**rubber pompoms
Koosh balls
positive effects**

Although I was not too sure about the reasons
why Koosh balls <u>helped the learning process,</u>
I found them so useful that I introduced them to
New Zealand educators. They, too, found them
very useful in enhancing the learning process
of their students and a real Koosh ball craze
started which is not over by far. In the meantime
it has even spread into corporate training rooms
and offices!

helped learning

It wasn't until I knew more about learning styles
and the <u>different needs</u> people have during
information intake that it finally dawned on me:
Koosh balls are the ideal learning enhancement tool
for <u>tactile learners</u>! These are the people – young
and old – who always need to <u>fiddle</u>, <u>doodle</u>
or constantly <u>manipulate something</u>, especially
when they take in new or difficult information,
concentrate hard or are experiencing stress.

different needs

**tactile learners
fiddle, doodle,
manipulate something**

Text for an 'Active Concert' used for a Parent Group continued

Soft *music* as background while learning and thinking,
Or *sound effec*ts to promote wider memory linking.
Music's also helpful with our rhythmic fitness,
But needs to be *calmer* for non-physical business.

BUT before you use music, here is a caution,
The *wrong music* destroys a learning situation.
Music with *lyrics* or heavy rock beat,
Will hamper your learning as you tap your feet.

Plant roots wither on a diet of rock,
It *hinders* the brain if it's played quite a lot.
Rock *doesn't* help learning, an indisputable fact,
But convincing a teenager's not as easy as that.

Instead try *Mozart's* 'Eine Kleine Nachtmusik',
or *Vivaldi's* 'Four Seasons', another good pick.
Pachelbel's 'Canon in D' will also be helpful,
As will others I'll tell you after this recital.

This *Active Concert* that you're taking part in,
Is followed by passive to promote retention.
It's the story of music and an explanation,
And the role it should play in all education.

Combined with a <u>high need for intake</u> (when people need to eat, nibble or drink continuously) you have the <u>perfect profile of a smoker</u> as we have seen in many smokers' profiles. However, when these people can fiddle with a Koosh ball *and* have something to nibble or drink most of the time, their <u>craving for a cigarette</u> generally seems to <u>diminish</u>. On many occasions I have observed that they either <u>smoke much less</u> or not at all when they can <u>play with a Koosh ball</u>!

high need for intake

perfect profile of a smoker

craving for cigarettes diminishes, smoke less when playing with a Koosh ball

We have also seen <u>remarkable improvements</u> in shy children, in nervous adults under stress and in people who usually fiddle a lot. They quickly <u>calm down</u>, their listening skills improve, their attention span is prolonged and they are <u>less fearful</u> speaking in front of groups.

remarkable improvements

calm down

less fearful

But I wanted to know more: who are the people <u>using Koosh balls</u> most during these activities? Results gained from the analysis of our WSA and LSA instruments clearly defined the following groups: <u>primary school children</u>, <u>high school students</u> (in this particular group <u>more boys than girls</u>) and, not surprisingly, <u>far more men than women</u> in the adult group.

who uses Koosh balls?

primary school children, high school students, more boys than girls, more men than women

That explained why I had seen so many men from all walks of life not letting go of a Koosh ball, once they had begun using it during a training seminar. Then they kept using it back in their own work environment! And the many stories teachers tell me about the success they have with using <u>Koosh balls in class</u> – how these little gadgets have helped boys to participate more in group discussions, to show <u>better discipline</u> and to <u>improve their concentration</u>. Even parents have come to appreciate the magic of these balls for their highly tactile children and know they are not just like any other ball.

Koosh balls in class

better discipline improve concentration

So Koosh balls are not just a fancy toy, they <u>stimulate brain activity</u> and learning processes in tactile/visual learners, they <u>relax or activate</u> and are above all a <u>lot of fun</u> to use! If you can't get hold of Koosh balls, allow them to use squish balls, play dough or small soft toys.

stimulate brain activity relax or activate a lot of fun

COURSE CONTENT

DAY 1

UNIT 1: OVERVIEW

The Journey	p 1
Introduction	p 2
Creative Accelerated Learning	p 3

UNIT 2: KNOW YOURSELF & OTHERS

The Control Room	p 4
That's Me (Working Style Analysis)	p 5
WSA Description	p 6

UNIT 3: GETTING READY FOR THE JOURNEY

The Big Shift in Organizations	p 7
Take Control	p 8
Who's on Board	p 9
My Personal Team Profile (DISC)	p 10
Team Roles	p 11
The All Star Crew	p 12

DAY 2

UNIT 4: CHANGE—CHANGE—CHANGE

Changes Everywhere	p 13
Values	p 14
Our Company's Values	p 15
Vision	p 16
Vision & Mission Statement	p 17
Leadership	p 18
Leadership—Case Study	p 19

UNIT 5: MAKING THE JOURNEY SUCCESSFUL

Great Teamwork	p 20
Empowered Teams—Successful Business	p 21
Market Place	p 22
Sales & Marketing	p 23
Money—Risk—Investment	p 24
Sample Budget 1	p 25
Sample Budget 2	p 26
New Zealand Business Success Story	p 27

DAY 3

UNIT 6: WHAT KEEPS US GOING?

Technology Serving People	p 28
Crisis Vs Opportunity	p 29
Life & Business Stages	p 30

UNIT 7: ON THE ROAD AGAIN

Presentation Skills	p 31
Team Presentation Check List	p 32
My Personal Action Plan	p 33
Reading List	p 34

9. 'The Journey' – a business course for high school students

It was during an educational conference in 1993 in Auckland with the intriguing title 'Successful Schools – Successful Business' that I heard several prominent business leaders talk about the necessity for schools to teach successful learning strategies, to expose students to good business practices and help them acquire positive attitudes towards work and business in general. The simple reason is that when students leave school, they sooner or later will be part of this ever-changing business world. Various examples of successful co-operation between schools and individual companies were presented and it all sounded interesting and really well meant.

business leaders

good business practices
positive work attitudes

successful co-operation
schools and companies

I realized that these honourable efforts, often with substantial amounts of sponsorship dollars and great time effort, were often directed at individual students or at those who were particularly interested in certain business aspects and/or how the economy works. Despite obvious successes, such projects were certainly not reaching a wide enough student population fast enough.

substantial sponsorship
great time effort
for individual students

My idea was to create a leading-edge business school programme for large groups of high school students, combining good business practices with learning/working styles and fully integrating creative learning techniques so that even those could be reached who have never shown interest in business at all.

business school programme
for large student groups

learning/working styles
creative learning

With nothing but a dream I set out to find a suitable basic content, fitting well into the new economics curriculum for senior high school students, to put a small working group together and to secure corporate sponsorship. It all came together very nicely and for a whole year we worked on the development of 'The Journey – Business, Life and Everything'. Initially sponsored by Pepsi NZ and the Lion Nathan Education Foundation, its content is based on the book *The All Star Company* by Nick Marsh and using creative teaching methods to deliver the content in an interactive way.

for a whole year
'The Journey' was developed

delivered interactively

'The Journey' feedback

'I would like to take the opportunity to thank you all for the contribution you made to the learning experience of our 80 young men. The Lion Nathan School of Business "The Journey" was a special experience for all involved. I thank you and indeed the Creative Learning Company for all you did in this regard.'

'I look forward to working with you again in the near future, and again thank you for the wonderful opportunity that you provided to 80 young men of Rotorua Boys' High School.'

'I am grateful for the Lion Nathan's commitment to sponsoring this programme in the college as I believe it is having a powerful impact upon the young people concerned. Several of the students who were participants in "The Journey" last year are now at university taking programmes in the commerce faculty. They are young people for whom business held no particular fascination prior to taking the course. Now career decisions have altered as a consequence of their participation.'

'While it is sometimes difficult to establish clear causal connections between these events, the students themselves make reference to the programme as being the turning point in their knowledge of themselves and in the society in which they live.'

'They liked such things as the team-building experience, meeting new people, learning about how business operates, learning styles, "thinking outside the square", style of learning, positive presenters and free drinks!'

'Some skills and information they gained: teamwork, how to communicate within the business, financial and presentation skills, business knowledge, "things to help me succeed in school", onfidence, information about themselves, working under pressure, tolerance and stepping outside their comfort zone. So it sounds like they got the right message from "The Journey" as well as having a great time.'

This three-day programme for a group of 80 senior high school students is facilitated by two presenters and one logistics person. The overall aim is to give students, through <u>simulation games</u>, an in-depth understanding of <u>how organizations work</u> and how they are adapting to present-day challenges. The programme introduces students to the concepts of <u>leadership</u>, vision and mission, <u>company values</u>, management styles, <u>teamwork</u>, the market place, modern technology, <u>financial planning</u>, risk and investment, as well as to the principles of setting up and running a company, and creating and <u>marketing a product</u>.

simulation games
how organizations work

leadership, company values, teamwork, financial planning

marketing a product

The end result is a <u>short business presentation</u> by each participating team using a wide variety of audio-visual technologies to a group of 'real life' <u>senior managers</u> who are invited to function as <u>a panel of judges</u> assessing the students' work.

business presentation

to senior managers as judges

Above all, the concepts of <u>self-knowledge</u>, true <u>co-operation</u> in difficult situations and <u>working in teams</u> to achieve a positive end result are the main objectives to create the longest lasting impact. In all student evaluations teamwork has always ranked highest as one of the most valuable concepts learned during the course, equally impressing teachers who witnessed the evolving process: 'the programme introduced students to the concept of teamwork when so often in learning environments it is one against the rest to get the top mark.'

self-knowledge
co-operation
teamwork

From its first trial run '<u>The Journey</u>' was an <u>instant success</u> and has received overwhelmingly positive reviews from students and educators alike. It ran in about 30 New Zealand high schools for over three years, made possible through substantial <u>sponsorship</u> by the Lion Nathan Education Partnership. As the financial support came to an end in early 1998, the programme became open to individual companies who were willing to continue sponsoring the course.

'The Journey'
instant success

sponsorship

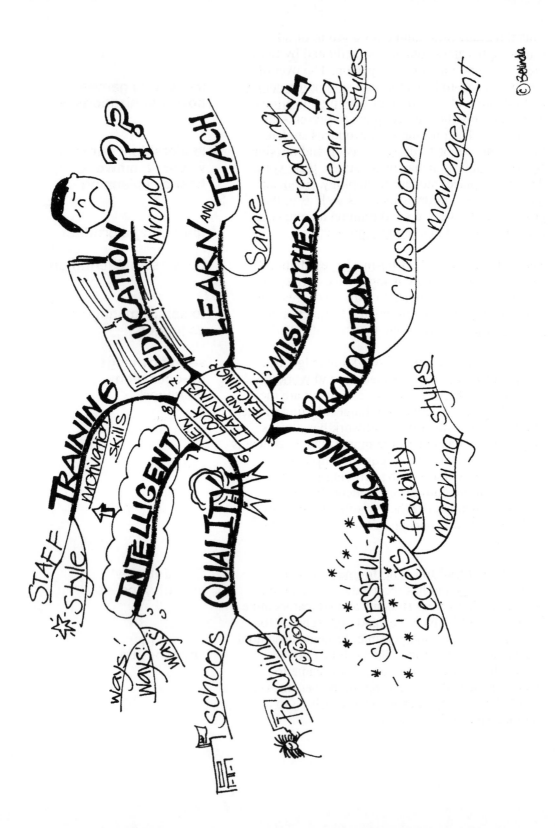

© Belinda

1. What has gone wrong in education?

The term 'educational crisis' is now being used
in literally every country around the world; it's
headlines in daily news and problems of education
are being discussed and debated everywhere.
But the underlying issue is not education, it is
learning. How we have come to regard the role
of learning in our societies, families, the workplace
and in the world at large is the real issue.

educational crisis

learning

the real issue

In the past, value has been placed solely on what
people KNOW, but presently, and even more so
in the future, value will be placed on how people
can LEARN. This in itself represents another
paradigm shift – from *knower to learner*.
The comparison on page 178 makes very clear
how profound the difference is between these two
and how extremely important this new paradigm
of human beings as *learners* is. It values not only
'what we know', it values 'how we know' and
allows us to gain a new attitude towards our own
learning ability which has profound implications
for our mental health from an early age.

**paradigm shift:
from knower to learner**

Let's consider formal education and ask a few
questions: how many thousands of hours do
students sit in classrooms experiencing lectures or
activities which bore them to death, which stifle
their curiosity and their spontaneously emerging
interest? What happens when a child experiences
uncertainty about details of the presentation? How
many hundreds of hours do they spend reading
books? And again, what can students do when they
encounter something they do not understand or
evokes their curiosity? Will they raise their hands
and ask? Only those who are not easily intimidated.
The majority of students, however, learn to ignore
all but their most powerful urges. Slowly but surely
their experiences at school result in a deadening of
their inner sensitivity.

formal education

**lectures, deadly boring
activities**

reading books

**school experiences kill
inner sensitivity**

Unlike the way children learn informally before and
outside school, the entire educational system dis-
courages them from 'tuning' into their own inner
learning processes. They become conditioned to

KNOWER

- Learning is something kids do in school.

- Teachers know and teach and students learn.

- The goal of education is a knower with a particular corpus of knowledge, a particular range of skills and a particular way of behaving.

- Learning is a process used to acquire knowledge, facts, skills and experience.

- Remembering information and patterns in knowledge leads to passing examinations.

- Relevancy is an external association in information and knowledge.

- Uncertainty is a sign of insufficiency and causes discomfort.

- Overall value is WHAT we know.

LEARNER

- Learning is something we all do every instant of our lives.

- Facilitators of learning learn with and, at the same time, about learners.

- The goal of education is a learner who understands how to relate to and learn from knowledge, other human beings and his or her self.

- Knowledge, facts, skills and experience are used to enrich, extend and exercise our capacities for learning.

- Realizing the relationships among meanings forms the basis for 'transference' in learning.

- Relevancy is the process of building meaning into the flow of an individual's attention.

- Self-honesty about uncertainty is a key to developing 'critical thinking'. Uncertainty is illuminative and leads to deeper understandings and insights.

- Main value is HOW we know.

Based on: 'Learning Insights' conference handout 1991

disregard their own meaning, their learning needs, their style and individuality in favour of acquiring machine-like behaviours and uniform outcomes favoured by the system and those who represent it. Consider the following: before children go into formal education, they learn miraculously by developing an inner sensitivity for their learning processes which is their day-to-day experience for years. When they go to school, in the process of being taught various subjects, the message they receive now is: what goes on inside your head is meaningless, pay attention and do as we tell you!

disregard own meaning

uniform outcomes

children learn by developing inner sensitivity

at school

pay attention do as you are told

This whole dilemma has nothing to do with teachers' intentions; this is not the issue. The problem is not WHAT is being taught but HOW it is done. The formal environment and traditional teaching methods continually discourage children from remaining sensitive to their own most essential capacities for learning. It's the overall education experience which turns, almost as a rule, highly energized, curious, eager and alive children into mainly tired, uninterested, uneasy, bored and frustrated students. This is true for schools in every country I have visited so far, from Finland to Hong Kong, from New Zealand to Sweden, from the USA to Denmark. And what's even more alarming, this unfortunate development can be seen everywhere – despite the school, the teacher, even the socio-economic family status of the student.

education experience turns curious, eager, alive children into bored, frustrated students

It is little wonder that years of negative experiences at school lead to disappointment, learning problems, underachievement, discipline problems, despair, social problems, drug and alcohol abuse, isolation, giving up on oneself and, like currently in New Zealand, to ever-increasing numbers of teenage suicides and violence in schools.

negative experiences at school

The following recollection, given to me by Daniela Cassinelli, a teacher from Argentina, says it all:

recollection

'When I started school I had to learn to speak another language. It was not so easy or natural as my mother tongue. I was told not to move, not to touch, not to dance or sing or even play and pretend! Simple grammar, past tense, auxiliary, and so on. Sit and write. Use your brain, your logical one. What about knowing intuitively, words coming out just naturally, because we sang them in that unforgettable song or heard them in a funny

If you are in a teaching/coaching role,

or in any sense a facilitator

of learning processes,

always bear in mind

that your own thinking style

probably dominates

your approach to teaching,

perhaps much more strongly

than you realize.

We tend to teach in the same way

we like to learn.

Karl Albrecht

rhyme or had to read them to make those ginger cookies? Why did we have to make this switch from natural, right-brain learning to merely logical left-brain learning? Didn't we all learn to speak a language only naturally and yet successfully? I don't remember mums in the park talking among themselves about having 'learning disabled' children who could not talk. We all could!

Now, at school, not all of us learn the way teachers ask us to. Some of my friends are finding it difficult to sit and copy. I heard my teacher talking about slow learners. My friends heard it too! Now they are worried. They think they are different. But teachers say we are all different and that differences are good. Why can't we learn differently, then? Two of my friends told me that when they are given a test, they feel stressed and that a new feeling of helplessness has started to grow inside themselves and those inner words 'I can't, I won't' are being repeated again and again. How strange, when I was in kindergarten I had this feeling of power, of well-being; the certainty that everything was possible!

Yesterday I heard the teacher telling Mum that my problem was low self-esteem. Mum wonders how I lost it. She remembers me as a clever, inquisitive child, never afraid to try out new things. And then these words: 'disabled learner' and 'low self-esteem'. I see Mum is worried. She doesn't know how to help me and I don't know what to do. I try to remember when it was that I started to feel insecure at school. Maybe the day I was told there were too many mistakes in my paper, or when I saw a number on it and the teacher explained to me it meant 'failed'. Or that day they gave me a long test and they told me to keep my eyes on the paper and to try hard. Yes, I remember my hands were wet and I don't know why. Or maybe the day I wanted to stand and sing; I would have loved to perform the part of the hero in the story I had to read, but there was no time. I was told to read it and to answer the questions in long form. Instead I wanted to stand and act it out.

And then I began to feel bored. I lost interest. I thought: 'This is not fun!' And those low figures in my papers appeared more and more often. I knew I was good at singing, acting, creating, imagining, but there were no figures for those things. I don't know why. We did not do these fun things very often either. I would have loved them too! I was good at them and I felt great about myself when I did them. Sometimes our teacher still talks about respecting differences. I wonder what she means.

2. The way you learn is the way you teach

As we have mainly dealt with learning, information intake, retention and academic achievement of students, it is now time to consider the people who 'deliver' the learning methods – <u>teachers and educators</u>. We have to ask the question whether the personal <u>learning styles</u> of these professionals <u>influence the way they teach</u>, interact with their students and shape the expectations they have of their students' performance. From my work

teachers and educators

their learning styles influence their teaching

Teaching Style Analysis – Education

Teaching Style Analysis™ - Questionnaire Part I

Name:_____ School:_____

Answer the following questions according to the FREQUENCY of their occurrence in your teaching. (Circle one number only for each answer)

Please rate yourself:
5 – Almost always	2 – Occasionally
4 – Frequently	1 – Hardly ever
3 – Sometimes	0 – It depends/undecided

1. Do you use background music during your classes?_____ 5 4 3 2 1 0
2. Do you keep your classroom quiet (except during discussions)?_____ 5 4 3 2 1 0
3. Are there computers and other electronic media available in your classroom? _ 5 4 3 2 1 0
4. Do you expect your students to work at their desks?_____ 5 4 3 2 1 0
5. Do you allow students to sit on the floor, cushions or soft furniture in class?___ 5 4 3 2 1 0
6. Is it uncomfortable for you if there is not enough artificial light in your
    classroom? _____ 5 4 3 2 1 0
7. Do you provide the opportunity for students to work in low-light areas?_____ 5 4 3 2 1 0
8. Are you aware that temperature can influence your students' concentration? __ 5 4 3 2 1 0
9. Do you allow your students to wear warm comfortable clothes in class?_____ 5 4 3 2 1 0
10. Do you instruct your students to work by themselves in your classes? _____ 5 4 3 2 1 0
11. Do you allow your students to work with a friend during classes? _____ 5 4 3 2 1 0
12. Do you provide learning tasks for small groups of students?_____ 5 4 3 2 1 0
13. Are there possibilities for your students to work within team projects in class? _ 5 4 3 2 1 0
14. Are you closely controlling your students' school or classwork? _____ 5 4 3 2 1 0
15. Do you tend to step back and become the facilitator of your students'
    learning? _____ 5 4 3 2 1 0
16. Are your students required to sit still during the learning process? _____ 5 4 3 2 1 0
17. Do you allow your students to stand up, stretch or move around while they
    are listening to you or learning something difficult? _____ 5 4 3 2 1 0
18. Do you do energizing exercises (like Brain Gym® or cross-overs) with your
    students in class to help them concentrate better? _____ 5 4 3 2 1 0
19. Are your students generally allowed to eat, nibble or drink water during class?_ 5 4 3 2 1 0
20. Do you get annoyed when your students chew on pens, pencils and other
    things while you teach?_____ 5 4 3 2 1 0
21. Do you suggest that students should have their 'most difficult' subjects during
    morning hours while they are fresh? _____ 5 4 3 2 1 0
22. Are you aware that your students' learning ability is influenced by their bio-
    rhythm (their best time of day)?_____ 5 4 3 2 1 0

with thousands of teachers over the past ten years and the data collection from their LSA and TSA results it is quite obvious that virtually <u>everybody teaches through their own learning style</u> because this is the only way they know how and their brain feels comfortable with it.

everybody teaches through own learning style

Whether teachers like it or not, the fact is the way you learn is the way you teach because what makes sense in your own brain must make sense to everyone else, particularly students, you think. Unfortunately that is not so. Although there are quite a few students whose learning styles match their teachers' learning/teaching styles, there are <u>many more students</u> whose style needs are <u>totally different from their teachers' styles</u> and that's where the trouble begins, as we have already seen in Chapter 5 and will see even more clearly soon.

many students have totally different styles from their teachers

It is also not hard to understand that <u>learning styles equal teaching styles</u> because the strategies which made students successful in their learning during their own studies are of course later being used when these students become teachers. It is very interesting to note that most people who choose teaching as their profession do it for the simple reason that they love learning, have usually been successful learners and love to pass on knowledge to the next generation – in their own way. We all know how these mechanisms can work brilliantly between pupil and teacher (between master and student in the old days) when there is a <u>style match</u> or when the <u>teacher knows</u> about <u>style differences</u> and is capable of being <u>flexible</u> in the teaching methods used. We probably all have fond memories of our <u>favourite teachers</u> which last a lifetime. Whenever such a situation occurs, learning just happens naturally; it is joyful, highly satisfactory and always leads to success for both sides.

learning styles equal teaching styles

style match, or teacher knows style differences or is flexible

favourite teachers

One might think this is the way learning and teaching in our system should always happen, but we all know how often these processes can be disastrous for everyone concerned, and how much despair, frustration, stress and ill feelings are involved when teaching goes wrong. The main reasons are given in the next section.

TSA-Ed Model

3. Mismatches between teaching and learning styles

More and more educators are becoming aware that instructional methods of the past are no longer appropriate because they make it impossible for many students to develop their full learning potential. During the past 30 years, research has shown how it is possible to teach students of all ages either by <u>matching their individual styles</u> or by teaching them to teach themselves by <u>finding out their preferences</u> and capitalizing on their <u>personal learning style strengths</u>.

matching individual styles
finding their preferences
personal strengths

This simple concept explains why some children perform well in school and others – often from the same family – do not, or fail altogether. Research also explains how boys' and girls' learning styles differ and why some children learn to read early and very well, and others do not.

Results from schools in New Zealand, Switzerland and Sweden show very clearly a <u>mismatch</u> between <u>teaching methods</u> based on teachers' styles and <u>students' learning needs</u> as the group profiles reveal on pages 80, 82, 84 and 86. The biggest mismatches are generally in the areas of <u>kinesthetic and tactile</u> preferences, as well as the need for <u>mobility</u> which teachers often do not share, particularly with their younger students. Another striking mismatch is the need for <u>sound in students</u>, particularly among male teenagers, and the need for a <u>quiet</u> learning and teaching <u>environment among teachers</u>. The same is true for <u>low light levels</u> which many <u>students</u> prefer, and <u>brightly lit classrooms</u> which <u>teachers</u> prefer. An expected and, through American research, well-documented mismatch is the fact that teachers are much <u>more auditory than their students</u>, which has led to the age-old complaint by teachers that their students just don't listen! There is of course a widespread difference in attitudes between teachers and their many students, particularly among under-achievers. Results show that <u>adolescent students</u> these days are much <u>more non-conforming</u>, show <u>less persistence</u> when it comes to difficult learning tasks, and are of course <u>less responsible</u> than their teachers. However, highly successful students

mismatch between
teaching methods
students' learning needs

kinesthetic and tactile
mobility

sound for students,
quiet environment
for teachers
students: low light
teachers: bright light

teachers more auditory
than students

adolescent students
more non-conforming
less persistence
less responsible

TSA-Education
Personal Profile

 TSA - Ed   Sample five

Graph 1: Teaching Style

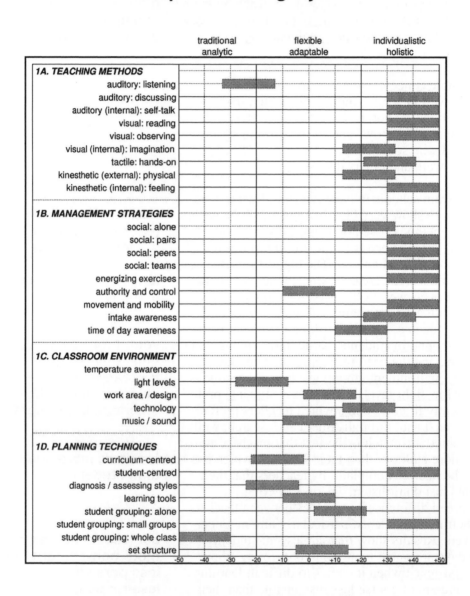

show a much greater match in their learning style features with their teachers, and that's probably one of the reasons why they do so much better at school.

In addition to all the above mentioned mismatches between teaching and learning styles there is one which causes endless frustration, conflict, and often serious trauma, resulting in loss of motivation, low self-esteem and finally the inability to learn with success. It is the profound difference between analytic, left-brain oriented teachers and holistic, right-brain oriented students, and all the related style features described in Chapter 5 and explained in detail from page 119 onwards. For positive attitudes towards school and lifelong learning strategies such a mismatch can prove fatal because we now know beyond the shadow of a doubt that young children, primary school pupils and under-achievers are much more holistic in their thinking than their teachers or their older and/or successful fellow students. Analytic, step-by-step teaching based on logic and consistency is confusing for holistic students – who need to know WHY they have to learn things, who need to see the Big Picture, and for whom feeling good is the most important aspect about learning.

analytic, L/B teachers holistic, R/B students

fatal mismatch

young children, pupils and underachievers – holistic

analytic teaching, logic and consistency is confusing for holistic students

feeling good – most important in learning

Whenever we get results from assessing teachers' working/learning styles and compare them with their students' learning style needs it saddens me to see how strongly analytic most teachers are in their thinking (and teaching), not only at university level where we have also seen grave mismatches between the styles of lecturers and their students, but particularly in primary schools where these analytic teachers really struggle to teach their highly holistic pupils – pupils who need variety, movement and an informal work area, whereas teachers try to instill routine, have them sit quietly in rows of desks, and cut out individuality as much as possible. A similar scenario can be observed in high schools where teachers have long given up on underachievers. But teachers cannot be blamed solely for this unsatisfactory situation. I believe they all do their best with the knowledge and the means they have and they all have been trained, like me, in a system that requires uniformity,

most teachers strongly analytic thinkers

highly holistic pupils

underachievers

system ~ uniformity

TSA-Education
Personal Profile

 TSA - Ed _____ **Sample five**

Graph 2: Brain Dominance

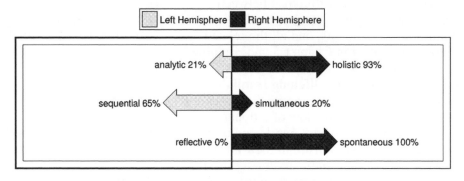

| Left Hemisphere | Right Hemisphere |

analytic 21% ⇦ ➡ holistic 93%

sequential 65% ⇦ ➡ simultaneous 20%

reflective 0% ➡ spontaneous 100%

Graph 3: Professional Characteristics

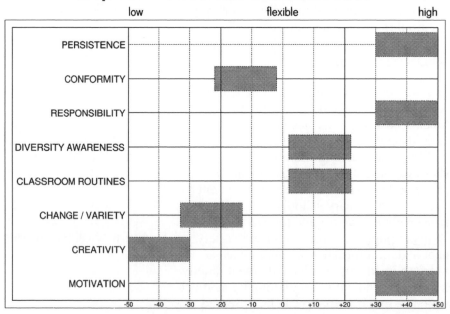

low   flexible   high

PERSISTENCE

CONFORMITY

RESPONSIBILITY

DIVERSITY AWARENESS

CLASSROOM ROUTINES

CHANGE / VARIETY

CREATIVITY

MOTIVATION

-50 -40 -30 -20 -10 0 +10 +20 +30 +40 +50

**Please note: the graph above shows elements that can be influenced or changed. If the score is
in the FLEXIBILE area, it means that attitudes can change according to the situation.**

rewards formal teaching methods and expects conformity. They have never really been trained to recognize individual learning needs, to accept individuality and capitalize on diversity in the classroom. The main thrust of all Western education systems has been, and still is, uniformity in class, information dissemination and assessing/recording results. Learning outcomes, goals and objectives are still more important than the learning process.

rewards formal teaching expects conformity

learning outcomes still more important than the learning process

That's why I am working so avidly to spread the word with the help of so many teachers who are already experiencing the magic of learning styles, who now know there is a better way and who are achieving incredible results never thought possible. How do they do it? All it takes is some professional training, some goodwill, a lot of practice and a skilful combination to experience teaching success.

4. More provocations for better classroom management

Traditional teaching methods and educational practices made Western school systems strong and successful over the first half of the twentieth century, but the same systems in this century have to service vastly diversegroups of students like never before. Over the past 25 years virtually every teacher in every country has been experiencing problems in class unheard of in the past and most teachers are ill-equipped to handle situations for which they have not been trained. This unsatisfactory status quo, stress and severe burnout among educators, plus the insight that old teaching practices just don't work any longer, have led to a search for new and more appropriate methods to educate the young.

problems in class unheard of in the past

search for new and more appropriate methods

Contemporary wisdom tells us that unless we succeed in educating every single child AND its parents, whole societies suffer. School failure and drop-out students put our whole society at risk by what they do to us, to our children, to our property and to our social and welfare systems.

school failures and drop-out students put society at risk

Discipline problems in class, negative attitudes towards school in general and so-called learning disabilities can be eradicated, if teaching methods

discipline problems and learning disabilities can be eradicated

TSA-Education

Results and Action Plan from TSA Profile

 TSA - Ed

1B. MANAGEMENT STRATEGIES

This graph describes your management strategies in the classroom which are often based on your personal experiences during your own schooling. It reveals how you manage the physical and social learning needs of your students.

YOUR PERSONAL SCORE

> Your current management strategies seem to be already very individualistic/holistic and you are acutely aware of your students' individual learning needs in class. Congratulations! Given your high awareness in this area combined with learner-centred management techniques you tend to use in your classroom, it should be easy for you to notice changes in your students' energy levels, alertness, responsibility and learning motivation. You have already developed a variety of approaches and know when to use them and for whom. Please keep up the good work!

A few questions worth considering:
Do you allow your students to work in groups, with a friend, or do they mostly learn alone?
Do you build in energizing exercises when you notice your students are tired?
Are you the ultimate authority in the classroom and do you look over their shoulders, or do you allow your students to learn in their own way?
Can you accept that some of your students can concentrate better while they move around and that not everyone can sit still for lengthy periods of time?
Do you allow them to drink water or nibble on something healthy while you are teaching them?
Are you aware that students have different time preferences for learning new and difficult content and that the morning hours are not the best time for many students to concentrate on new and difficult learning content?

MY SELF-ENHANCEMENT ACTION PLAN 1B:

1.   **WHAT** can I do to improve my Classroom Management Strategies? (my **GOAL**)
2.   **HOW** will I do this? (my **ACTION**)
3.   **WHEN** will I take concrete action to move closer to matching my students' learning needs with my teaching strategies? (my **TIME FRAME**)

IN CLASS:
1.   WHAT?_____
    _____

2.   HOW?_____
    _____

3.   WHEN?_____
    _____

IN PLANNING:
1.   WHAT?_____
    _____

2.   HOW?_____
    _____

3.   WHEN?_____
    _____

are used to reach young people and make them more responsive. These <u>student-centred methods</u> are <u>based on learning styles</u>, and are particularly useful for students who cannot learn and retain information in ways traditional education provides.

student-centred methods based on learning styles

With the information about learning styles so far described in the previous chapters and the insights gained from this new knowledge, we now have to investigate popular but <u>outdated beliefs</u> about <u>learning and teaching</u> which, particularly in high schools, are still the basis for handling students in class but are far removed from effective and successful classroom management. If you read the following statements as a teacher, you might feel <u>provoked, even offended</u>, and you might think it is impossible to manage classrooms in the suggested way. I can only tell you that thousands of teachers in many countries around the world are <u>practising</u> these <u>new management techniques</u>, and on a daily basis experience <u>greater success</u> with their students and <u>more job satisfaction</u>. If you are a parent reading these fallacies, please accept that school <u>teaching IS different</u> from the time you went to school and requires different methods to equip our children with the necessary knowledge, skills and learning attitudes.

outdated beliefs about learning and teaching

provoked, even offended

practising new management techniques greater success more job satisfaction

teaching is different

Here are the <u>10 false beliefs about learning</u> which <u>cause high stress and burnout in teachers</u> and often <u>inability to learn</u> in students:

10 false beliefs high stress and burnout inability to learn

Fallacy 1: *Students learn best when <u>seated upright</u> at desk or table.*

seated upright

Research shows that many human beings perform better in an <u>informal environment</u>. Making students sit upright on their chairs does not necessarily make them more responsive to learning. Studies on high school students in the USA have shown significant improvement in maths and English when taught and tested while the students were seated on cushions, lounge chairs and rugs, if informal design was their preference. Our own work with learning styles has resulted in much happier teachers and students after <u>rearranging their classroom</u> and establishing informal work areas for those who need them.

informal environment

rearranging classrooms

Traditional Education

– confines body to limited territory

– confines energy to limited activity

– limits stimulation of senses

– limits social interaction

– limits experiences to the classroom

– subordinates initiative to others

– assumes ignorance

Norm Ericson, IBM

Fallacy 2: *Students learn best in <u>well-illuminated areas</u> and damage their eyes when they read and work in low light.*

students learn better in well-illuminated areas

Research shows many students perform significantly better in <u>low-light environments</u>; bright light makes them restless, fidgety and hyperactive. Low light calms them down and helps them relax and think clearly. The <u>younger children</u> are, the <u>less light</u> they seem to need! They only need the amount of light for reading in which they feel comfortable, but their need for light seems to increase every five years. Teachers who permit students with low-light needs to work in low-light corners are always surprised by their <u>improved behaviour</u>, attention and better grades within six weeks. Low light is particularly good for underachievers!

low-light environments

young children need less light

improved behaviour

Fallacy 3: *Students learn more and perform better in an <u>absolutely quiet environment</u>.*

quiet environments

Research findings show that <u>many adults</u> think and remember best when <u>studying with music</u>, many primary school children <u>read better with sound</u>, even noise present, and a high number of adolescent students, especially boys and <u>underachievers</u>, learn much better with very <u>loud music</u> or <u>background noise</u>. When students who need sound have to work in quiet environments, they lose concentration very quickly and they will make their own sounds, like finger drumming, pencil clicking, humming and tapping their feet. Despite countless teacher warnings these distracting noises never stop. The right learning music in the background alleviates this problem. As there are always a few students in each class who need absolute silence while they are learning, <u>each classroom should have quiet sections</u> for those who cannot concentrate with noise, and should also have areas where students can learn with music. Although most <u>teachers prefer quiet</u> learning environments themselves, they need to accept that different brains work differently and that what's good for some is not good for all.

many adults
study with music
read better with sound

underachievers
loud music or
background noise

classrooms should have quiet sections

teachers prefer quiet

Fallacy 4: *Students learn difficult subjects best in the <u>early morning</u> when they are <u>most alert</u>.*

most alert early morning

It is <u>not</u> the child who bears

the responsibility for learning,

it is the <u>teacher</u> who bears responsibility

for identifying each child's learning style strengths

and for matching those with

responsive environments and approaches.

Dr Rita Dunn

This is only true for those we call 'early birds' – but what about the 'night owls' and 'afternoon learners' of the student population? Research has shown that when students are allowed to learn difficult concepts at their preferred time of the day, their behaviour, motivation and achievements improve. The same goes for test results.

**'night owls'
afternoon learners**

Fallacy 5: *Students who do not sit still are not ready to learn.*

**sitting still –
ready to learn**

Many students need to move when they learn. One American study revealed that half of one school's seventh grade students needed extensive mobility while learning, and when they were allowed to move from one learning area to another while taking new information in, they achieved statistically better than when they had to remain seated in their chairs. Most students who are actively involved are likely to learn more, pay closer attention and achieve higher test marks than when they just sit and listen.

**need movement
when learning**

**when actively involved
learn more, pay attention**

Fallacy 6: *Eating should not be permitted in classrooms during lessons.*

no eating in class

Many students concentrate better when they can have something to eat, nibble, chew or drink while learning, and many teachers will have observed that a number of students chew on whatever they can get hold of during classes, particularly when they have to listen for a while, when they are bored or nervous. It seems that mouth stimulation helps them concentrate, and as the brain dehydrates during thinking processes, it is essential that students are allowed to have drinks of water whenever needed. Students with a high need for intake should be allowed to have healthy snacks, and with good management techniques there will be no mess in class. Thousands of teachers who have successfully introduced a 'healthy nibbles policy' are proof that it works, and discipline, together with student performance, improves significantly.

**concentrate better when
eat, nibble, chew, drink**

**mouth stimulation helps
concentrating**

drinks of water

healthy snacks

Fallacy 7: *Effective teaching requires clearly stated objectives followed by detailed, step-by-step, sequential explanations until students understand what's being taught.*

**detailed, step-by-step,
sequential explanations**

A uniform way
of teaching and testing
is patently unsatisfactory
when everyone
is so different.

Howard Gardner

While <u>holistic, right-brain dominant learners</u> tend to <u>grasp large concepts first</u> and then deal with the related facts and details, <u>analytic, left-brain dominant learners</u> pay attention to the <u>facts first</u> and use them for building up the whole concept. Only these are the ones who work well with step-by-step teaching. Many, probably most, teachers use analytic styles and a few teach only holistically, using a lot of creativity. Every teacher should (and successful teachers always do) include <u>elements of both styles</u> in their <u>teaching</u>.

holistic, R/B learners grasp concepts first; analytic, L/B learners need facts first

elements of both styles in teaching

Fallacy 8: <u>*Whole-group instruction*</u> *is the* <u>*best way to teach*</u>.

whole-group instruction best way to teach

Some students work well in teams or groups, but many <u>prefer to work in pairs</u>, and others cannot concentrate well with other students around them. <u>Gifted students</u> tend to prefer to work <u>by themselves</u> and some students prefer to work with adults rather than with classmates; others may work well with media rather than with people. The best way to teach is to allow for a <u>variation of social preferences</u> among the students in class.

prefer working in pairs

gifted students work by themselves

variation of social preferences

Fallacy 9: *Generally, the* <u>*older students*</u> *are, the easier it is for them to* <u>*adapt to the teacher's style*</u>.

older students adapt easier to teacher's style

While older students require less teacher supervision and <u>less structure</u>, they continue to learn differently from one another, and still have <u>varying learning needs</u>. They do tend to need more independence as they grow older, so giving them <u>options and choices</u> about their own learning is appropriate. This also gives them a chance to develop their responsibility.

less structure varying learning needs

options and choices

Fallacy 10: <u>*Truancy*</u> *is related to poor attitudes, home problems, lack of motivation and other factors which have* <u>*nothing to do with*</u> *their preferred* <u>*learning style*</u>.

truancy has

nothing to do with students' learning style

Studies of secondary school truants revealed that when their learning style preferences were catered for and <u>their time preferences</u> where <u>matched</u> to their academic schedules, their <u>attendance improved</u> dramatically. Their attendance and learning

time preferences matched attendance improved

Sometimes
when you
reach for a dream,
you have to leave
something
behind.

motivation increased also when they were given a teacher different from the one with whom they had been truant. (1) Although we do not have a study on truancy and <u>learning styles</u> in New Zealand, we know that in some <u>high schools</u> where learning styles have been introduced, the <u>truancy rate</u> has markedly <u>gone down</u> and expulsions are now a thing of the past.

motivation increased

learning styles in high schools

truancy rate gone down

Results with learning styles worldwide challenge and disprove these old beliefs, and show that when teachers respond to students' individual learning needs, it takes as little as <u>six weeks</u> to see positive results such as <u>increased academic achievement</u> and <u>a decrease in discipline problems</u>. As many practitioners have experienced, even at-risk students begin to learn and feel better about themselves, and teachers no longer despair having them in their class. And even if not every teacher embraces learning styles enthusiastically, the <u>knowledge</u> about <u>diversity in the classroom</u>, a few changes in teaching methods, the insight that the one-style-fits-all approach is outright wrong – all that works wonders in <u>improving classroom management</u>. The unexpected but always <u>positive results</u> delight teachers and students alike.

six weeks to increase academic achievement and decrease discipline problems

knowledge about diversity in classrooms

improves classroom management; positive results

5. Secrets of successful teaching – flexibility and matching styles

From whatever has been said about better teaching, learning styles, student-centred approaches and individualized instructions, there are two more aspects which will not remain secrets any longer:

1. <u>Matching students' learning styles</u> with the <u>appropriate teaching styles</u> will always lead to successful interaction between teachers and their students, and result in improved learning outcomes as we have seen in this chapter.

   matching students' styles with teaching styles

2. <u>High flexibility</u> for achieving genuine style matches is maybe more important, and teachers need to be confident in choosing their methods and strategies, and must be prepared to try something else when the usual methods don't work. But this 'something else' should not be trial and error, but

   high flexibility of teachers

ARANUI HIGH SCHOOL

PO Box 15-019
Christchurch 6
New Zealand

Principal G J Plummer
Phone (64 3) 388-7083
Fax (64 3) 388-7913

27 August 1996

Barbara Prashnig
Creating Learning
PO Box 5422 Wellesley St
AUCKLAND

Dear Barbara

I have had some wonderful feedback from your course on Friday. 99% of the staff were bubbly and enthusiastic when they returned to school.

I am very impressed that you were able to work so effectively with such a diverse group. I had felt some trepidation about the cost and disruption of having a large group of teachers out for the day but the results certainly justify the effort.

I now have a substantial group of staff members who are aware of the basic concept involved in learning styles and know that that will begin to impact on our classroom programmes.

Once again, thank you for a very effective day's in-service training.

Yours sincerely

GRAEME PLUMMER
Principal

based on a sound knowledge of students' learning style needs. But isn't that what teachers are supposed to do anyway, you might ask. Supposed maybe, but very few teachers are actually flexible enough to change their methods according to their students' learning needs because most teachers have a very limited repertoire of teaching methods – remember, they have all been trained by the same analytical system – and when the few well-known strategies don't work, they are soon at their wits' end, blaming everyone and everything else for their students' failure and finally give up on them.

change methods according to students' learning needs

Another reason for this unfortunate situation is the fact (again based on research findings and our own experiences in data collection) that teachers are among the least flexible people of all professional groups. The majority have very strong preferences based on analytic, left-brain dominance, paired with very strong beliefs about what's right and wrong in learning. They find it very hard to flex and adjust, prefer to stay with what they know, even when this knowledge is outdated, and generally resist change. Often I hear from cynical teachers that there is no need for them to change because their methods have been around for the last 150 years, have worked for many students and if someone has to change it is surely the students who should get their act together! This is a very regrettable state of mind, far more often found among high school and university teachers than among primary school educators. This attitude needs to change because too many students really suffer from such inflexibility and are often lost for good for lifelong learning. For those of you who have already accepted the notion that everyone can learn, you will agree that this is a standpoint that is no longer acceptable.

teachers least flexible people, have very strong preferences, are left-brain dominant, have strong beliefs

resist change

students suffer from teachers' inflexibility

It is quite obvious that educators need to become more flexible, and teachers who are now working with learning styles realize that it is they who have to be the most flexible person in class. Highly flexible people usually get on well with others and you probably remember one or other teacher who was well liked by everyone, who always found a way to get on with others and were a great inspiration for the young ones.

teacher has to be most flexible person in class

SIX CONDITIONS OF QUALITY SCHOOLS

Courtesy of Malfroy School, Rotorua

6. Quality schools and quality teaching

Some years ago, when the corporate world was
brimming with TQM – Total Quality Management –
which appeared under various names, based on
the work of Dr W. Edwards Deming, quality was
defined as goods or services having characteristics
required by customers and having been produced
without wasted human or non-human resources. (2)
As TQM is both a management method and
a philosophy, it has been widely used in large
organizations, often overemphasizing strategies,
techniques, systems or practices, and at the same
time forgetting people and their individuality.
That might have been the reason why TQM in
education has not taken hold and has been seen
as a much too theoretical system needing to be
strictly followed. However, the desire to create
quality schools is often reflected in a school's
mission statement but its implementation can
get bogged down in too much bureaucracy.

**quality –
goods or services
produced without
wasted resources**

**quality schools
mission statement**

Through my work with learning styles I also
became involved in the long-term planning of
change processes in schools and the issue of
quality surfaced again. As I did not favour an all
too pragmatic approach, I discovered some very
useful ideas in William Glasser's books on quality
which can be easily combined with learning styles
and creative learning methods. In his first book,
*The Quality School, Managing Students Without
Coercion*, he describes very clearly that the purpose
of any organization, public or private, is to build
a quality product or perform a quality service, that
the workers in the organization must do quality
work and that the job of the managers is to make
sure that this occurs. In every school, the students
are the workers and right now almost none are
doing quality work in class.

**quality combined
with learning styles and
creative learning methods**

**in schools students are
the workers not doing
quality work in class**

Glasser describes it graphically like this: 'Picture the students in a required academic
class at a randomly selected secondary school as a gang of street repair workers. If they
were working as hard as the students are doing in class, half or more would be leaning on
their shovels, smoking or socializing, perfectly content to let the others do the work. Of
those who were working, few would be working hard, and it is likely that none would be
doing high-quality work.' (3)

CREATIVE INTELLIGENCE

1. PREPARATION:
gathering information and exploration

2. INCUBATION:
a period of processing in the mind and body

3. THE 'AHA!':
an exciting point of insight

4. VERIFICATION:
insuring the integrity of the insight

5. IMPLEMENTATION:
*putting the information and insights
into a usable framework*

From: *Rhythms of Learning* by Chris Brewer and Don Campbell

While <u>students know what quality is</u>, recognize it when they see it and generally believe they are capable of doing quality work in class, all but a few admit that they <u>have never done it</u> and have no plans to do it in future. What's the reason that so many students are <u>not really interested</u> in participating, let alone in <u>producing quality work</u> at school? The most often quoted reason is not that <u>work is too</u> hard, but that it is boring; '<u>boring</u>' meant that they could not relate to the learning task and that it was <u>not satisfying students' needs</u>.

students know what quality is

have never done it

not really interested in producing quality work

work is too boring

not satisfying their needs

And this brings me to the most important message in Glasser's second book, *The Quality School Teacher*:

<u>The six conditions of quality schoolwork</u>:

six conditions of quality

1. *There must be a warm, supportive classroom environment*.
   Without a strong, friendly feeling between students and staff there can be no quality schoolwork and, above all, there must be trust.

   warm, supportive classroom environment

2. *Students should be asked to do only useful work*.
   No student should be asked to do anything that does not make sense, like memorizing or rote learning. Whatever they do has to have some use – practical, aesthetic, artistic, intellectual or social.

   students do only useful work

3. *Students are always asked to do the best they can*.
   That means students must be given the necessary time to make an effort to produce quality work. They are used to covering ground, not learning, and have hardly ever attempted to do quality work.

   do the best they can

4. *Students are asked to evaluate their own work and improve it*.
   Self-evaluation is the most difficult to implement but is essential to achieve constant improvements in students' efforts to produce quality work.

   evaluate own work and improve it

5. *Quality work always feels good*.
   It is sad that so few students feel good in their academic classes now. Not only do students feel good as they succeed in doing what they know is quality, but also their teachers and parents feel good observing the process.

   quality work feels good

Multiple Intelligences Checklist

Mark those statements that apply to you:

Linguistic Intelligence:
_____ Books are very important to me.
_____ I can hear words in my head before I read, speak or write them down.
_____ I get more out of listening to the radio or a spoken word cassette than I do from television or films.
_____ English, social studies and history were easier for me in school than maths and science.
_____ I have written something recently that I was particularly proud of or that earned me recognition from others.

☐ Total

Logical-mathematical Intelligence:
_____ I can easily compute numbers in my head.
_____ Maths and/or science were among my favourite subjects at school.
_____ I'm interested in new developments in science.
_____ I like finding logical flaws in things people say and do at home and work.
_____ I feel more comfortable when something has been measured, categorized, analysed or quantified in some way.

☐ Total

Spatial Intelligence:
_____ I prefer looking at reading material that is heavily illustrated.
_____ Geometry was easier for me than algebra at school.
_____ I can generally find my way around unfamiliar territory.
_____ I often see clear visual images when I close my eyes.
_____ I like to draw and doodle.

☐ Total

Bodily-kinesthetic Intelligence:
_____ I find it difficult to sit still for long periods of time.
_____ I engage in at least one sport or physical activity on a regular basis.
_____ My best ideas often come to me when I'm out for a long walk or a jog, or when I'm engaged in some type of physical activity.
_____ I often like to spend my free time outdoors.
_____ I would describe myself as well co-ordinated.

☐ Total

6. *Quality work is never destructive*.
   It is not quality to achieve good feelings
   via the addictive use of drugs or to harm people,
   living creatures, property or the environment. (4)

**quality work is
never destructive**

Please consider if all these conditions of quality
are already to be found in your school and what
it means on a daily basis for all parties concerned;
or, if only some apply, what the reasons are that
not all six conditions are present yet and what
could be done to improve the situation.

**quality conditions
in your school**

improve the situation

7. Many ways of being intelligent

One of the myths surrounding education is the
notion that human beings have a general capacity,
called *intelligence*, to deal with all the different
situations a human being will encounter during
his or her lifetime. For a long time people believed,
and many still do, that this general capacity is
fixed for a particular individual and varies in its
quantity from person to person.

**general capacity
intelligence**

In recent years Harvard Professor of Education
Howard Gardner has been one of many who
made a major contribution to our understanding
of human intelligence by shattering the 'fixed IQ'
myth. He developed Multiple Intelligence theory
(MI) based on neurobiological research which
indicates that the human brain is an extremely
complex organ with a much greater capacity for
learning than currently used by human beings.
Originally, Gardner defined at least seven
different intelligences which all work together in
the brain as an integrated whole, yet each in itself
identifiable and capable of enhancement. (5)

MI theory

**seven
different intelligences
integrated whole**

More recently, there has been debate about
additional intelligences, and Gardner always
maintained there could be many more faculties
which meet his criteria for intelligence. In 1996 one
more was added, the 'naturalist's' intelligence, but
the main focus is still on the basic seven, of which
all human beings possess varying degrees – in
Gardner's terminology people's 'biopsychological
potential' which they develop over a lifetime. (6)

additional intelligences

naturalist

**biopsychological
potential**

Multiple Intelligences Checklist continued

Mark those statements that apply to you:

Musical Intelligence:
_____ I can tell when a musical note is off-key.
_____ I play a musical instrument.
_____ I have a pleasant singing voice.
_____ I know the tunes to many different songs or musical pieces.
_____ I often make tapping sounds or sing little melodies while working, studying
       or learning something new.

| | Total

Interpersonal Intelligence:
_____ I have at least three close friends.
_____ I enjoy the challenge of teaching another person, or groups of people, what I
       know how to do.
_____ I like to get involved in social activities connected with my work, church or
       community.
_____ I would rather spend my evenings at a lively social gathering than stay at
       home alone.
_____ When I have a problem, I'm more likely to seek out another person for help
       than attempt to work it out on my own.

| | Total

Intrapersonal Intelligence:
_____ I regularly spend time alone meditating, reflecting or thinking about
       important life questions.
_____ I have attended counselling sessions or personal growth seminars to learn
       more about myself.
_____ I am self-employed or have at least thought seriously about starting my own
       business.
_____ I keep a personal diary or journal to record the events in my inner life.
_____ I consider myself to be strong-willed or independent-minded.

| | Total

Adapted from *Seven Kinds of Smart* by Thomas Armstrong (7)

The original <u>seven intelligences</u> described by
Gardner are:

seven intelligences

1. *Linguistic intelligence*: as the ability to read and/
   or write well. People who are strong in this area
   also have highly developed auditory skills, their
   vocabulary is extensive and spelling is easy.

   Linguistic

2. *Logical-mathematical intelligence*: as the ability
   to reason, calculate and handle logical thinking.
   People who are strong in this area are highly
   capable of analysing and classifying information,
   to theorize and create patterns and hypotheses.

   Logical-mathematical

3. *Visual-spatial intelligence*: as the ability to think
   in pictures and images, see things in relationship
   with others, to navigate, take great photographs
   and to perceive the visual world accurately. People
   who are strong in this area often have the skill to
   paint or sculpt, even with little or no sight.

   Visual-spatial

4. *Musical intelligence*: as the ability to sing, play
   instruments, compose, appreciate and produce
   rhythms, pitch and form of musical expression.
   People who are strong in this area are able to
   carry a tune, have a good musical ear and are
   sensitive to sounds in the environment.

   Musical

5. *Bodily-kinesthetic intelligence*: as the control of
   body movements and the capacity to handle
   objects skilfully, enabling people to express
   themselves physically, to be active in sports and
   to 'know' things with their body. Movement
   and physical activities are very important.

   Bodily-kinesthetic

6. *Interpersonal intelligence*: as the ability to work
   and interact sensitively with other people, to have
   social responsibility and compassion. People
   who are strong in this area can listen effectively,
   negotiate, handle conflicts, co-operate and get
   along well with diverse groups of people.

   Interpersonal

7. *Intrapersonal intelligence*: as the ability to access
   and understand one's inner feelings, weaknesses,
   strengths and desires, reflect on experiences, think
   about thinking (metacognition) and discriminate
   between inner emotional states. People here often
   have strong opinions and prefer to be by themselves.

   Intrapersonal

MY UNIQUE BLEND OF
H. GARDNER'S MULTIPLE INTELLIGENCES
- SCORING -

Plot your bar graph on the grid below, according to your self-assessment scores, to come up with an intelligence profile that is currently relevant to you.

Effortless skill and consistent levels of high achievement and success **5**

Effortless skill and consistent levels of high achievement and success **4**

Effortless skill and consistent levels of high achievement and success **3**

Effortless skill and consistent levels of high achievement and success **2**

Effortless skill and consistent levels of high achievement and success **1**

L Linguistic **L/M** Logical-mathematical **S** Spatial **B/K** Bodily-kinesthetic **M** Musical **Inter** Interpersonal **Intra** Intrapersonal

MI theory offers a <u>useful framework</u> for curriculum design in schools, and if it is true that there are developmental changes in intelligence through the schooling years, learning experiences must contain opportunities to develop all seven, and Gardner challenges schools to provide experiences for students to develop the different 'ways of knowing'.

useful framework

If you are interested in finding out your personal blend of intelligences, the short <u>questionnaire</u> on pages 206 and 208 will give you a general <u>profile of your multiple intelligences</u> which you can create on page 210.

questionnaire
your profile of MI

Although the MI theory has been enthusiastically welcomed in the USA and tried out by many educators around the world, there has also been confusion, exaggeration and misunderstandings about how to implement this <u>theoretical framework</u>, and I often find that <u>multiple intelligences</u> are being <u>confused with learning styles</u>. I believe that MI made a valuable contribution to make the elusive concept of intelligence more tangible and, utilized carefully by well-trained teachers, it can be a very useful concept to enhance classroom teaching.

theoretical framework
MI confused with
learning styles

Since the publication of Daniel Goleman's book, *Emotional Intelligence: Why It Can Matter More Than IQ*, the debate about academic and life achievements based on intelligence has been expanded by one more dimension – emotionality. According to collated results of brain research contained and interpreted in this best-selling book, <u>EQ (Emotional Quotient) matters more than</u> a person's IQ because, as Goleman argues, our present view of human intelligence is far too narrow, and our emotions play a much greater role in thinking, decision making, even logical reasoning, than is commonly acknowledged. This concept really expands on Howard Gardner's two *personal intelligences* in his MI framework, focusing on the full range of <u>emotional and relationship abilities</u> rather than only on one's mental processes.

EQ (Emotional Quotient)
matters more than IQ

emotional and relationship
abilities

The model of <u>emotional intelligence</u> was first proposed by Salovey and Meyer in 1990 and contains the five following domains:

emotional intelligence

SUCCESSFULLY INTELLIGENT PEOPLE

- motivate themselves and learn to control their impulses

- translate thought into action and know when to persevere

- are initiators and know how to make the most of their abilities

- have a product orientation and are not afraid to risk failure

- don't procrastinate, complete tasks and follow through

- spread themselves neither too thin nor too thick and accept fair blame

- are independent and have the ability to delay gratification

- have the ability to see the forest and the trees

- seek to surmount personal difficulties and reject self-pity

- focus and concentrate to achieve their goals

- have a reasonable level of self-confidence and a belief in their ability to accomplish their goals

- balance analytical, creative and practical thinking

Robert J. Sternberg

1. _Knowing one's emotions_: self-awareness, recognizing a feeling when it occurs, crucial for self-understanding.

   knowing one's emotions

2. _Managing emotions_: handling feelings so they are appropriate, the capacity to soothe oneself and shake off anxiety, gloom and irritability.

   managing emotions

3. _Motivating oneself_: emotional self-control, delaying gratification and stifling impulsiveness, essential for paying attention, reaching mastery and achieving creativity.

   motivating oneself

4. _Recognizing emotions in others_: empathy and attunement to the subtle social signals indicating what others need or want, one of the fundamental 'people skills'.

   recognizing emotions in others

5. _Handling relationships_: social competence and abilities underlying popularity, leadership and interpersonal effectiveness. (8)

   handling relationships

No one can seriously dispute that these abilities are crucial to live a satisfying, happy life (whatever that might mean to the individual) but, considering the alarming statistics about social ills, particularly in the USA, they seem to be a barometer of dropping levels of emotional competence which does not bode well for the future of society. Goleman states that surveys over the past twenty years are proof that children today, on average, are emotional illiterate as they are doing more poorly in these specific ways: (9)

   abilities to live satisfying, happy life

   children today emotional illiterate

- **Withdrawal or social problems**: preferring to be alone; being secretive; sulking a lot; lacking energy; feeling unhappy; being overly dependent.

- **Anxious and depressed**: being lonely; having many fears and worries; needing to be perfect; feeling unloved; feeling nervous or sad and depressed.

- **Attention or thinking problems**: unable to pay attention or sit still; daydreaming; acting without thinking; being too nervous to concentrate; unable to get mind off thoughts; doing poorly on school work.

- **Delinquent or aggressive**: hanging around kids who get in trouble; lying and cheating; arguing a lot; being mean to other people; demanding attention; destroying other people's things; disobeying at home and at school; being stubborn and moody; talking too much; teasing a lot; having a hot temper.

STAFF TRAINING IN STYLE

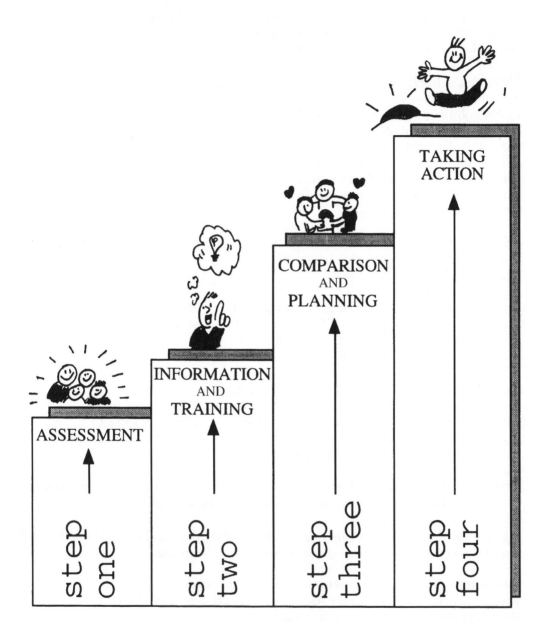

If you as a teacher or parent are struggling with any of these issues with your students or children, Goleman's book makes exciting reading, offers valuable insights into the amazing <u>emotional circuits in the brain</u> and gives practical advice on how to deal with these problems from a different angle.

emotional circuits in the brain

Considering the sad statistics about young New Zealanders in the areas of school failure, drug and alcohol abuse, violence, unwanted teen pregnancy, depression and teenage suicide, it seems that this nation, too, has a problem with <u>emotional competence</u>, and maybe even with their moral one as well. Robert Coles, in his very good book, *The <u>Moral Intelligence</u> of Children*, points out that every child is a witness of grown-up morality – or lack thereof (10) and I can highly recommend this book for adding a new and thought-provoking dimension to the intelligence debate.

emotional competence

moral intelligence

That is the reason why I have now built the notions of multiple and emotional intelligences into my training programmes because I consider them extremely important and they actually enrich the learning styles and diversity concepts.

8. Staff training in style – how to increase motivation and skills

Teachers, principals, administrators and managers in virtually all Western countries are suffering from <u>heavy workloads</u> due to changes in their present educational systems and radical new curriculum developments, causing severe <u>stress and burnout</u>.

heavy workloads

stress and burnout

However, instead of having staff in schools who out of <u>despair and frustration</u> often fit into the categories of Traditionalist ('good ol' days'), Do Nothings (retired on the job), Verbal Abusers, By-the-Book Bureaucrats, Meeting Dominators, Narrow-Minded Nit Pickers, Chronic Complainers, Blind Followers, Sceptics, Sarcastics and Cynical Inflexibles, institutions could have competent people on their staff who <u>feel at ease</u> with the demands made on them, honestly <u>love the work they do</u> and who are <u>open to change</u>.

despair and frustration

feel at ease
love their work
open to change

DISC Model

The DISC Model suggests that people generally display one of the four basic behavioural styles

DOMINANCE:
High Ds are interested in the new, the unusual and the adventurous. They love a challenge. They have one goal in mind – that is to make things happen – and happen now. When results are at stake, it brings out the best in them. They are great problem solvers and will work long hours, continually, until a tough problem is solved.

INFLUENCE:
High Is want to be liked and usually like others – sometimes indiscriminately. They have the ability to talk smoothly, readily and at length. They will not be overlooked, or uninvolved. Is are consistently trying to inspire you to their point of view. They are great motivators and work well with people.

STEADINESS:
High Ss are generally easygoing and relaxed. They like to build a close relationship with a relatively small group of associates. Ss are usually very dependable, predictable and loyal. They operate well as members of a team and co-ordinate their efforts with others with rhythm and ease.

COMPLIANCE:
High Cs are humble, precise and will do whatever is expected of them to the best of their ability. They strive for a stable and orderly life and tend to follow procedures in both their business and personal life. They are systematic thinkers and workers, precise and attentive to details they perceive as important.

The DISC Model is based on the book *The Emotions of Normal People* by William Moulton Marston (12) and was computerized in the 1980s. Presently there are 21 versions of various reports available, and DISC Reports can be ordered through Creative Learning Company (address in Appendix II).

A simple four-step plan based on matching styles can bring about enhanced collaboration, increased productivity, <u>better skills</u>, improved performance among teaching and administration staff, greater <u>job satisfaction</u>, more pride and higher motivation for everyone.

better skills

job satisfaction

Many schools in New Zealand have already gone through this programme or are in the process of retraining their staff by following this plan, which also has relevance for European schools, as my ongoing work shows in these regions.

Step I: Assessment

a. All teachers are assessed for their individual <u>learning style</u> with LSA (Adult Version) and their teaching style with the TSA-Education (<u>Teaching Style</u> Analysis)

learning style

teaching style

b. All board members are assessed for their <u>working style</u> with the WSA

working style

c. All administrators are assessed for their personal <u>administration style</u> with EFL (Administrator Version) Excellence for Learning – DISC. (11)

administration style ·

Step II: Information and Training

a. Discussions about different working, teaching and administration styles among all staff – learning to understand and <u>appreciate diversity</u>

appreciate diversity

b. Explanation of different profiles through trained facilitator, and considering practical ramifications of different styles for daily work

c. <u>Review</u> of administrators' and board members' styles with <u>management group</u>

review
management group

d. <u>Review of teachers' styles</u> and implications for their classroom teaching

teachers' styles

e. <u>Assessing students</u> in primary, intermediate and secondary years with the LSA Jun. or Sen.

assessing students

f. <u>Training teachers</u> in the use of the LSA and TSA instruments and application of their results; <u>explanation</u> of <u>students' learning style profiles</u> on an individual and group basis to students and <u>involving parents</u> in this process.

training teachers
explaining
students' LSA profiles

involving parents

Step III: Comparison and Planning

a. Comparing teachers' and administrators' <u>perceptions of each other</u>

each others' perception

TSA - Ed

Sample Group

Members: 10

Group Percentages

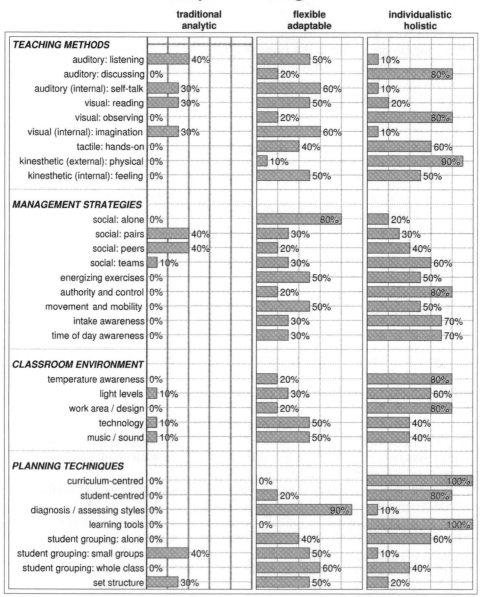

	traditional analytic	flexible adaptable	individualistic holistic
TEACHING METHODS			
auditory: listening	40%	50%	10%
auditory: discussing	0%	20%	80%
auditory (internal): self-talk	30%	60%	10%
visual: reading	30%	50%	20%
visual: observing	0%	20%	80%
visual (internal): imagination	30%	60%	10%
tactile: hands-on	0%	40%	60%
kinesthetic (external): physical	0%	10%	90%
kinesthetic (internal): feeling	0%	50%	50%
MANAGEMENT STRATEGIES			
social: alone	0%	80%	20%
social: pairs	40%	30%	30%
social: peers	40%	20%	40%
social: teams	10%	30%	60%
energizing exercises	0%	50%	50%
authority and control	0%	20%	80%
movement and mobility	0%	50%	50%
intake awareness	0%	30%	70%
time of day awareness	0%	30%	70%
CLASSROOM ENVIRONMENT			
temperature awareness	0%	20%	80%
light levels	10%	30%	60%
work area / design	0%	20%	80%
technology	10%	50%	40%
music / sound	10%	50%	40%
PLANNING TECHNIQUES			
curriculum-centred	0%	0%	100%
student-centred	0%	20%	80%
diagnosis / assessing styles	0%	90%	10%
learning tools	0%	0%	100%
student grouping: alone	0%	40%	60%
student grouping: small groups	40%	50%	10%
student grouping: whole class	0%	60%	40%
set structure	30%	50%	20%

Please note: the above graph shows the percentage of selected group members in all three categories, adding up to 100%.

b. <u>Comparing</u> main areas of their Teaching Style Profiles as well as their learning, management and administration <u>styles</u>

comparing

styles

c. Working out strategies for <u>positive interaction</u> and <u>team building</u>

positive interaction
team building

d. Comparing students' and teachers' profiles using individual and group profiles

e. Planning for <u>in-service staff training, meetings and projects</u> using strategies which are suitable for different styles, which help with personal growth, which are motivational and enhance co-operation.

in-service staff training
meetings and projects

Step IV: Taking Action

a. <u>Implementation</u> of new strategies for staff interaction, training and teaching methods; classroom performance based on learning styles and creative, accelerated learning

implementation

b. Compulsory <u>management training</u> for all administration and board members, but optional for teaching staff

management training

c. <u>Monitoring</u> increase in productivity and performance of staff; carrying out adjustments if necessary

monitoring

d. <u>Documentation</u> of positive changes among staff and effects on students, parents and the wider community (for full change programmes see pages 299 and 301).

documentation

When personality types are understood, diversity in administration and management styles is cherished rather than levelled out, <u>teaching</u> and <u>behavioural styles are matched with students' learning styles</u> in daily classroom situations, and educators will experience less stress and burnout, and <u>more pride and job satisfaction</u>. Principals and administrators will be able to do their high-pressure jobs with <u>greater effectiveness</u>, and the community at large will be more satisfied with the services provided by educational institutions.

teaching and behavioural
styles matched with
learning styles

job pride and satisfaction

greater effectiveness

Individually as well as a group, this new breed of educators and administrators will certainly be able to <u>make a difference</u>, not only to their own lives but also to the lives of their students and their families in our fast-changing world.

make a difference

If we accept that no two human beings learn the same information at the same time the same way, we also have to accept that, if schools introduce learning styles and individualized instruction, all students have a <u>much greater chance</u> to <u>fully develop their learning potential</u>, despite social, economic, gender, ethnic and/or cultural differences.

greater chance to fully develop learning potential

These are truly <u>revolutionary thoughts</u> compared to traditional views that 'learning disabilities and underachievement are facts of life which can't be changed' as one high school principal put it so succinctly. Although these new concepts might sound as if a revolution was about to happen, I know from experience that wherever learning styles, student-centred teaching and creative, accelerated learning (so called holistic teaching methods) are being introduced, it is rather an <u>evolutionary process</u> because of resistance being encountered on the way.

revolutionary thoughts

evolutionary process

The reason is that human beings seem to <u>respond to change</u> in the way Arthur Schopenhauer described it so well: (13)

response to change

'All truth goes through three stages:
at first it is ridiculed,
then it is violently opposed,
and finally it is accepted as self-evident.'

Looking at the illustration on the opposite page, reflect on changes your organization has already undergone and how you and other people responded, particularly when the change or 'truth' was unwelcome. Or think about the changes you have gone through in your private life and how you reacted before you were capable of seeing the 'truth' and welcoming the change.

For our own, our children's sake and for the sake of the many adults who are still carrying <u>negative memories of learning</u> through their lives, let's hope that this particular truth – accepting, <u>appreciating</u> and catering for <u>human diversity</u> in any <u>learning or working process</u> – will be widely accepted sooner rather than later.

negative memories of learning appreciating human diversity in learning and working

1. How you learn and work is how you live

From our investigation into <u>style differences</u> in the areas of learning, teaching, working, stress management, communication and partner choice, it is already more than obvious that the way we do things doesn't end here – style differences go far beyond that. It is appropriate to say that learning and working styles are not only that – they are really <u>life styles</u>. The main differences are once again the basic ones: <u>analytics, holistics and flexibles</u>. No matter how well you play roles in your work environment, when you go home you either slip into another role and act out another style, or most of the time you revert back to your true style. It is easy to imagine how (when not understood and appreciated) these <u>style differences cause problems</u> on a daily basis, not only in the workplace, but also between partners and among family members.

style differences

life styles
analytics, holistics, flexibles

style differences can cause problems

Just consider this:
- Are you a person who needs lots of stimulation which you get by creating dramas at home, by causing disruptions with people at work or by pursuing somewhat dangerous hobbies?

- Or are you the type who doesn't like to socialize very much, enjoys sitting quietly at home reading a good book and gets stressed out at work when no one else does?

Style differences based on <u>left/right-brain processing</u> deeply affect even seemingly unimportant aspects of our daily lives, like:

left/right-brain processing

- cooking: <u>analytics</u> usually need a <u>cookbook</u> and follow recipes very diligently; <u>holistics</u> usually <u>throw together something creative</u>, unable to repeat the same dish twice;

cooking
analytics – use cookbook
holistics
throw something together

- squeezing the <u>toothpaste tube</u>: <u>analytics</u> always squeeze it from the end, <u>roll it up</u>, close the cap; <u>holistics</u> always <u>make a mess</u>, squeeze it from the middle, never roll it up and can't be bothered to put the cap on, which drives true analytics crazy;

toothpaste tube – analytics
roll it up
holistics – make a mess

STYLE DIFFERENCES
of strongly analytical/holistic people

cooking

toothpaste tube

shopping

- or consider shopping: analytics make shopping lists, plan every purchase and spend their money – even if they have lots of it – very wisely and never on unnecessary items; holistics, however, do all of that spontaneously; they loathe shopping lists, and when they do write one, they usually leave it at home, and they hardly ever know precisely where their money has gone. And so it goes on. The examples on the opposite page illustrate these situations and show you a more humorous view of style differences.

shopping – analytics make shopping lists

holistics – spontaneous loathe shopping lists

Reflect on your own relationships and you will realize the number of examples is endless. Marriages, the most committed form of relationships, go wrong when husband and wife fail to acknowledge, or resent, each other's complementary differences even after years of living together.

relationships

**marriages
go wrong
fail to acknowledge, resent
complementary differences**

So, what's the message in all that? You may have already guessed and it can't be said often enough: Know Thyself! It might sound like a paradox, but the better you know yourself, the more chances you have to understand others and the more likely it is that you will get on with them.

2. Some things never change – the real YOU

Increased self-knowledge will give you yet another advantage: you will realize who you really are, what makes you tick, what you can change and what you can't. By understanding your personal style features, your preferences, your flexibilities, your dislikes and even your intelligences more accurately, you will also realize what your core qualities are. These insights are particularly important when you are under stress or encounter adverse situations. Based on the unique way your brain works, you will always fall back into your basic style features under such conditions because your brain will go into survival mode. It has to, because under threat it cannot and will not consider options; all it will do is help you survive, whatever 'survive' might mean to you. And that can sometimes be a nasty surprise when you don't know the basic patterns

self-knowledge

core qualities

**basic style features
brain goes
into survival mode**

Most people live ...
in a very restricted circle
of their potential being.
They make use
of a very small portion
of their possible consciousness,
and of their soul's resources
in general,
Much like a man who,
out of his whole organism,
should get into a habit of using
only his little finger.

William James

of your behaviour, your thinking, learning or
acting – in other words, your real YOU.

Let me illustrate this with the following example:
When things are going well, everything is to your liking, your needs are met and you can
do things your way, you will most certainly feel comfortable, probably enjoy yourself and
also be able to display flexibility when necessary and appropriate. You cruise along, are
satisfied with your accomplishments, probably like yourself for that, you notice that you
are in harmony with others, you are nice to them and they are nice to you. And then
something happens – something unexpected and unpleasant, upsetting the whole pleasant
scenario. Unless you are an incredibly balanced person or know yourself extremely well,
you will notice that within a very short period of time – often within moments – your
behaviour and your style changes, most often to the negative. In such situations people
often display behaviour so very different from their usual one, and do or say things they
later regret. These can be times when people hardly recognize their partners or workmates
because all of a sudden they are so different from their usual self. Often they don't even
recognize themselves, may get very upset and wonder what has got into them. These
mechanisms can repeat themselves time and again, and people have no clue how to break
their patterns.

Unless you learn what makes you tick and how
your personal style features affect you in every
situation, you have no chance of <u>controlling your
behaviour</u>, let alone preventing your <u>emotions
control you</u>. But when you know yourself, your
core features, your strengths and weaknesses, your
boundaries, your breaking points, you can develop
strategies to prevent going over the edge because
you know how you would react automatically if
you didn't know yourself. Like it or not, <u>some</u> of
your <u>style features will never change</u>, particularly
your biological ones (see pages 72 and 74) as they
are responsible for <u>who you are</u>. You'd better learn
to live with them, use them to your advantage and
<u>capitalize on your strengths</u>. Remember: you are
a special human being with a unique brain and a
unique style combination, and although you cannot
control what happens to you, it's always in your
power to control how you react.

**controlling your behaviour
or emotions
control you**

**some style features
will never change**

who you are

capitalize on strengths

3. Match and mismatch – where do you fit?

There are at least <u>three fatal consequences</u> from
not knowing your true style, being unaware of
all your preferences: it <u>affects your daily life</u>,
how you <u>feel about yourself</u> and how you

three consequences

**affects daily life,
feel about self,**

WORK SMARTER, NOT HARDER

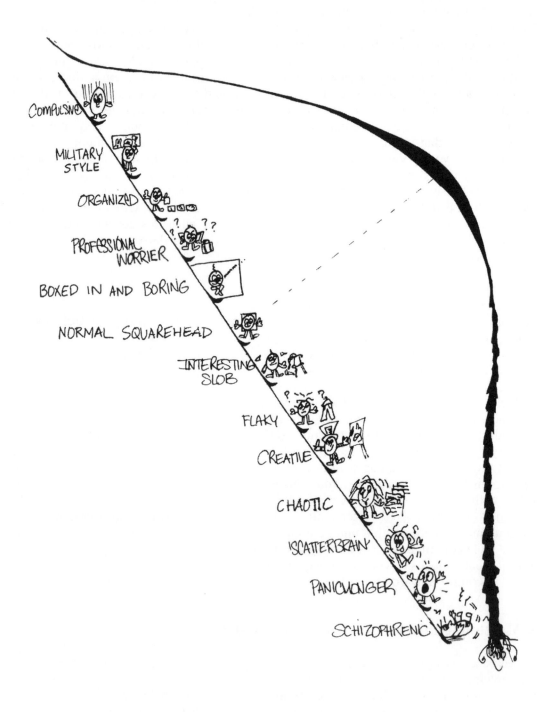

perform at work. It's a vicious circle: the more you suffer from these consequences, the more you are inclined to adopt different styles and play different roles in addition to your social roles.

work performance

By not knowing what your real strengths and preferences are, you will often unconsciously try to fit into other people's requirements and do things *their way* which might not be *your way*. That's very often the reason why so many people in their jobs lose motivation, or despair at tasks they think they can't do.

not knowing strengths and preferences

their way not your way

The following example illustrates this process:

example

You might have experienced that you quite like doing a job or a difficult assignment but the way it has to be done, because 'that's the way we do things here', does not really suit you. You find it hard, so you try harder; you try out different roles, different approaches to get the task done, but despite all your efforts, it actually drives you crazy after a while. You are frustrated and feel stressed out. Then you either throw in the towel (if you can), get more miserable until the thing is finally over, or delegate it to someone else who probably experiences half the stress and might even enjoy doing the job you couldn't come to terms with!

way to be done

does not suit you

frustrated
stressed out

Your final conclusion is: you are not suited for such tasks, you'll never be able to do these things and you should probably change your job! WRONG! You just experienced a typical example of mismatched styles. It's not true that you were not suited to the job but your style was not compatible with the way the job was supposed to be done! It had nothing to do with your capability of carrying out the task; if it had been possible to do it *your way*, it might have been a lot easier and you might have enjoyed the process more.

not suited

change job

mismatched styles
your style
not compatible

capability

easier
more enjoyable process

The majority of people who leave their jobs don't do it because of their inability but out of frustration about the way they have to do it.

frustration

My Best Practices

**To become aware of your learning strategies,
your 'Best Practices', answer the following questions.
Take your time to really think and reflect.**

1.   How I like to learn: _____

       _____

2.   Where I like to learn: _____

       _____

3.   When I like to learn: _____

       _____

4.   Why I learn: _____

       _____

5.   When I don't learn: _____

       _____

6.   What stops me from learning: _____

       _____

When you <u>know your style</u> you can, most of the time, <u>work through your preferences</u> and avoid playing roles or following trial-and-error approaches; no longer do you have to do tasks the 'hard' way, no longer do you have to believe you are just not good at difficult jobs.

know your style
work through preferences

The more often you work with <u>mismatched styles</u>, the more you will come to believe that you are not good at anything, which means you will struggle to be <u>persistent in your work performance</u>. Due to its importance it's worth repeating: it is not your <u>lack of ability</u>, it is mainly a <u>mismatch</u> between your style and the way you are made to do a job (or learn, if you are a student). This is the reason why so many people become <u>successful after they leave</u> environments which didn't suit them any longer; they had outgrown the style of the organization they were in before – family, educational institution, large corporation, government body, and so on. Finally they were allowed to do things their way and to their surprise it worked! If they had really <u>known their own style</u> and their true preferences <u>before they set out to do new things</u>, you can imagine how much easier it would have been to be <u>successful</u>.

mismatched styles

persistent in work
performance
no lack of ability
but mismatch

successful
after leaving

know own style
before doing new things

successful

Maybe you can relate to this story:

Just imagine a boy growing up with siblings in a family where strict rules and regulations are the norm. From an early age on it is obvious that this child is a 'misfit'. He struggles through school, leaves without qualifications, does not want to go to university as his parents had hoped and is also not interested in working in the family business. He doesn't get much support for his 'weird' ideas as his interests are totally different from all the other family members' interests; only his grandmother stands by him and helps him to follow his dream. With the help of his father he tries several jobs, but without success, and finally leaves home and his disappointed parents behind. His teachers have told him he'll never make it, never come to anything and his parents have finally given up on him. By travelling the world he gains life experience, saves some money and is finally able to realize his dream. Away from his family he experiences success based on his true talents and he becomes rich and famous. Everyone who knew him as a child can hardly believe his transformation – only his grandmother, who always believed in his special gifts, who always said 'I know it, one day you'll make it,' would not have been surprised if she could have lived to see his success; she always knew.

Do you know of people who have had similar experiences?

In a room full of

Weird Johns,

Weird John is just John – normal.

Just as Straight Sally,

Careful Henry and Emotional Mary

are normal in their own tribes –

simply Sally, Henry and Mary.

Ned Herrmann

4. Redefining the 'normal' – dare to be different

Since interest in <u>brain functions</u> is increasing,
brain research is no longer the exclusive domain
of medical science. People want to know more
about left- and right-brain dominance, and it is now
possible to observe our daily lives from the aspect
of brain functions; what's even more exciting,
we can influence that functioning.

brain functions

In his book, *The Creative Brain*, Ned Herrmann
finds a new way of <u>describing what 'normal'</u>
means: 'Brain dominance technology gives us ...
new ways to look at normalcy and define it more
appropriately.'

describing 'normal'

Two of these <u>new definitions</u> are:
1. 'normal means belonging to a tribe of
    <u>similar people</u>' and
2. 'being <u>normal</u> includes <u>being unique</u>'. (1)

new definitions

similar people
normal – being unique

The traditional view is, as Herrmann explains,
we are normal if we are like everybody else
in our school or in our community. We are
even <u>more normal if we are like everybody else</u>
in our social group, our gang or our tribe.
People who aren't like the rest of the tribe
'are not normal', a phrase that carries a
very negative connotation because it says,
'that person does not belong to our group,
he or she is different and does not share our
beliefs, language and expectations'. But human
beings obviously need to belong and that's a
dilemma for so many people these days – they
feel they don't belong anywhere any longer.
For teenagers that mindset can have disastrous
consequences, often leading from isolation to
depression and, via despair and hopelessness,
to suicide.

more normal if
like everybody else

In the context of the Working Style Analysis,
being normal means having one of the <u>many</u>
<u>possible style combinations</u> and stretches across
the full brain processing scale (the entire 'brain
dominance spectrum', as Herrmann calls it). If
this assumption is true and the scale has universal
applicability, each <u>uniquely different</u> person in this

many possible
style combinations

uniquely different

'The qualities that make for a happy and genial life

are these: a small estate with fruitful vineyards,

a fire to curtail the rigours of winter, a contented

mind, a strong and healthy body, frankness tempered

by tact, congenial associates, happy guests, a table

spread with simple viands, wine not in excess but

enough to drive away care, yet virtuous with all,

sound sleep to make dark hours fly, no longing

for change, just contentment with what you are,

no fear of death, nor yet a desire for it.'

Free quotation of an ancient Roman poet

world with a completed style analysis is indeed
<u>normal</u>. By understanding their own profiles, their
left/right-brain dominance and the true meaning
of human diversity, people can now come to terms
with <u>why they are the way they are</u>. As a result of
having their own working style assessed, we see
many people finally coming to terms with who
they are and feeling OK about themselves, often
<u>appreciating</u> their own <u>uniqueness</u> for the first
time in their life.

normal

**why they are
the way they are**

appreciating uniqueness

The message of hope behind all these insights is
that <u>differences are not only normal</u>, they are <u>also
positive</u> and enable people to live more creatively,
appreciating and using diversity to make change
easier to handle. When we learn to appreciate
style differences more – in ourselves and others –
we are capable of making better choices in
education, our professions and personal lives.

**differences not only
normal – also positive**

Above all, <u>accepting and acknowledging diversity</u>
in our families, relationships, schools, companies
and organizations can lead to top performances
and tremendous productivity gains as well as to
<u>new values and attitudes</u> in human beings,
something we need more than anything else
right now in our far from peaceful and often
uncaring world.

accepting diversity

new values and attitudes

To remind the reader how diversity can become
normal (the new 'norm'), go back to Chapter 3,
page 53, and read why some people in education
<u>dare to be different</u>, dare to take risks, dare to
go against traditional beliefs about teaching and
learning, and dare to <u>accept</u> and <u>welcome</u>
<u>diversity in their classrooms</u>.

dare to be different

**accept/welcome diversity
in classrooms**

5. Do you have a quality life?

When we are born we do not know what the basic
components of a quality life are – survival, love, fun,
personal power, freedom – but we all are capable
of knowing what feels good, what feels bad and the
difference between the two. Immediately after birth,
we become aware that it is <u>better to feel good</u> than
bad and quickly learn that it feels good to eat

better to feel good

Five Basic Needs of a Quality Life

Survival

Personal Power

Freedom

Fun

W Glasser

because all <u>survival behaviours feel good</u>. Almost immediately we also learn that it feels good to be <u>loved</u> and, later, to love. Based on our ability to feel good, we also learn how important it is to <u>have fun, to be free</u>, and to have some control over what happens to us and around us, which is <u>power</u>. Glasser maintains that these basic needs are built into our genetic structure, and from birth we must devote all our behaviour to attempt to satisfy them. (2)

survival behaviours feel good
to be loved
have fun, to be free

power

Quality, therefore, is anything we experience that is consistently satisfying one or more of these basic needs. It is important to understand that <u>maintaining</u> the <u>quality of our lives</u> is so vital that for many of us it can become a matter of life and death. For example, we are probably the only living creatures who, given all the means of physical survival, still may choose to <u>commit suicide</u> when we desperately feel lonely or powerless. People still choose to die because they believe the <u>quality of their life is so low</u>, and there is so <u>little chance it will improve</u>, that their existence is no longer tolerable and <u>death is a more favourable option</u>. This is particularly tragic when young people have reached that conclusion, and given the world's highest rate in teenage suicide in New Zealand, there is obviously a dramatic lack of what they perceive as quality in their lives. To help prevent more of these sad incidents we need to look at our own lives first and how we as parents and educators can <u>create quality for ourselves</u> and at the same time for our <u>children</u> and students.

maintaining
quality of life

commit suicide

quality of life very low
little chance to improve
death a more
favourable option

create quality for
ourselves and our children

I invite you to honestly consider your own life and check it out for the five <u>basic needs</u> constituting a <u>quality life</u>:

basic needs of quality life

1. Is your <u>survival</u> guaranteed? Do you live in physical, emotional, financial comfort?

survival

2. Is there <u>love</u> in your life? Do you love and are you being loved? If not, how does it feel?

love

3. Do you have <u>personal power</u>? Can you control what happens to you and around you? And if not, how do you react?

personal power

4. Do you have <u>freedom</u> of choice, thought, action? Are you free to move, to speak, to be yourself?

freedom

5. Do you have <u>fun</u> on a daily basis? Are you able to experience joy and delight regularly?

fun

1. Partner choice and personal styles

The old saying 'opposites attract' could not be
more true when it comes to choosing a partner
for a personal relationship. It seems that we are
generally attracted to someone who has all
the style elements we either don't have ourselves
or would like to have. For business or working
relationships, however, a different pattern seems
to be true – we tend to choose people who are
rather similar in their working style. We can relate
to our colleagues and superiors much better
when they think and work like us. Significant
style differences in this area usually lead to
serious conflicts unless the two parties
respect and appreciate each other's diversity.

choosing a partner

**style elements we
would like to have**

**similar working style
with colleagues
think and work like us**

**serious conflict unless
respect diversity**

But for couples, different rules apply. Time and
again I have seen that both partners, though
compatible in many ways, display needs at the
opposite end of the scale in their individual
Working Style Analysis.

couples – different rules

display opposite needs

Although the following descriptions are very
general and there are many exceptions to these
rules, they are nevertheless widely applicable
to couples and often lead to misunderstandings:
she is an impulsive, holistic thinker, most of
the time following her intuitions and feelings,
he is a reflective analytic, usually going by
his logical mind and rationalizing everything;
he hardly ever feels the cold, she does; one is
a 'night owl', the other an 'early bird'; he needs
mobility and is kinesthetic/tactile, she prefers to
sit quietly and is more auditory/visual; one always
prefers noise and/or music when concentrating,
the other needs absolute quiet; and on it goes.
The combination of opposites is endless.

**impulsive, holistic
intuition and feelings
reflective, analytic
logical and rationalizing**

**night owl – early bird
kinesthetic/tactile
auditory/visual
noise, music
absolute quiet**

Let's leave it to psychologists to explain why we
feel attracted to our opposites. I can only advise
you what to do when these style features begin to
cause problems, which in the long run might, and
often do, cause the breakdown of the relationship.
With climbing divorce rates, increasing numbers
of single-parent families, and too many children

attracted to opposites

**can cause problems and
relationship breakdowns**

♀ ♂

DIFFERENCES

Often detached	Often emotional
Often obsessed with sports	Sports less important
Talk mostly about 'things'	Talk mostly about 'people'
Less talkative in private	Less talkative in public
Take things literally	Look for hidden meanings
Less responsive listener	More responsive listener
Focus more on solutions	Like to discuss problems
Less willing to seek help	Seek help readily
Often seek conflict	Tend to avoid conflict
Fearful of commitment	Eager for commitment
More sadistic	More masochistic
More sex-oriented	More love-oriented
Have fewer close friends	Have many close friends
Less trusting	Often too trusting
Shop out of necessity	Often shop for enjoyment

Based on an original idea from *He & She – 60 Significant Differences*

Between Men & Women by Cris Evatt

coming from broken or reconstituted families,
it is <u>more important than ever to understand our</u>
<u>different styles</u>. It is not enough to accept them
grudgingly. We need to <u>appreciate our diversity</u>
and make it work to our advantage so that
attractions don't become repellents. But what
can we do?

important to understand
different styles
appreciate diversity

2. When attractions become repellents

In the <u>beginning of a relationship</u> we are usually
fascinated by the way our chosen one behaves and
goes about things because it's all <u>new and exciting</u>.
We tend to appreciate, often glorify, style features
we like and readily overlook the ones we are not
too comfortable with. When the relationship
continues and the initial firestorm has cooled off
a little, you can bet that <u>real style differences</u> are
now <u>surfacing slowly</u> but steadily. As you learn
more about each other, you discover quite
a few aspects which are so different that you get
a little <u>concerned about your compatibility</u>.
But you are still very much in love and you tell
yourself that all these little '<u>bad habits</u>' will
eventually <u>disappear</u> over time, that he or she
will <u>change for the better</u>.

beginning of relationship

new and exciting

real style differences
surface slowly

compatibility questioned

hope bad habits
disappear or
change for the better

Then something occurs which will remain
a <u>mystery</u> for you if you don't know anything
about styles: despite your attempts to <u>change</u>
or 'fix' <u>your partner</u>, he or she stubbornly
<u>remains more or less the same</u> and your
<u>disillusionment</u> as well as disappointment <u>grows</u>.

mystery
change or
fix partner
but remains the same
disillusionment grows

The <u>diversity which had attracted you</u> to your
partner in the first place begins to <u>cause further</u>
<u>uneasiness</u>. You are amazed that many of these
originally <u>fascinating features</u> have long <u>lost</u>
<u>their attraction</u> and begin to bother you because
they just <u>don't fit your style</u>. But you still love
your mate very much, so you tell yourself again
'if I try harder <u>maybe he or she will change</u>
and then we will be <u>totally compatible</u> and
<u>really happy</u>'.

diversity attracted you
causes uneasiness

fascinating features
lost their attraction
don't fit your style

will maybe change
be totally compatible,
really happy

As this unfortunately only happens in love stories,

DIFFERENCES – SIMILARITIES
in general

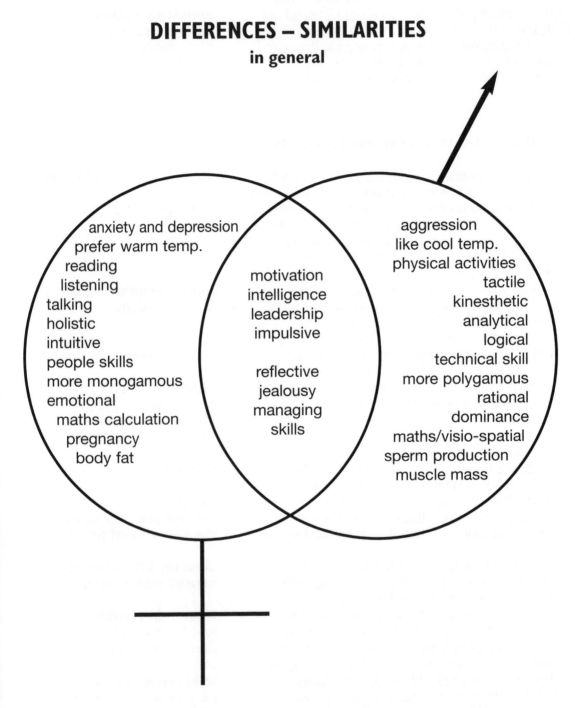

anxiety and depression
prefer warm temp.
reading
listening
talking
holistic
intuitive
people skills
more monogamous
emotional
maths calculation
pregnancy
body fat

motivation
intelligence
leadership
impulsive

reflective
jealousy
managing
skills

aggression
like cool temp.
physical activities
tactile
kinesthetic
analytical
logical
technical skill
more polygamous
rational
dominance
maths/visio-spatial
sperm production
muscle mass

Relationships between men and women can be much more successful when
there is a recognition of inherent biological differences, a respect for one
another's diversity and a valuing of shared qualities. (1)

you are now entering the either sad or dramatic
stage of your relationship where these early
attractions have finally turned into repellents.
And like a disease they are slowly destroying
your love and compassion.

**early attractions
turned into repellents**

Here you have only two choices: either to leave
the relationship (something an ever-increasing
number of people do these days) or to stay, trying
to figure out what's going on, getting counselling
or just hanging in, hoping for the best. People
who leave usually follow the same patterns and
are bound to make the same mistakes in their new
partner choice until they begin to really understand
how diversity works. Those who stay often learn
to put up with less than acceptable situations,
believing it's their destiny to suffer.

two choices:

leave or stay

hoping for the best

make same mistakes

It could have been much easier had you just
known both your own and your partner's style,
respected each other's diversity, cherished your
compatibility, and worked to overcome your
differences so that you could truly complement
each other and grow together.

**much easier
partner's style
respected diversity**

**complement
grow together**

The great danger in not understanding
true style differences between partners is that
one is quick to judge different preferences as
something that should be changed for good, and
to misinterpret different behaviour as something
the other partner does to us on purpose to make
life harder. When we consider that, in particular,
biological style features of a human being
change very little over a lifetime, cannot be
altered easily by sheer will and seem to manifest
themselves as habits, it is not hard to comprehend
why we always fight a losing battle with
our partners by trying hard to change them,
improve them and fix them.

**not understanding
true style differences
misjudge preferences**

misinterpret behaviour

**biological features
change very little**

**become habits
fight losing battles
trying to change,
improve, fix them**

If you want a clearer picture about yourself in
this particular area, please look at the biological
style elements displayed on page 72, and mark
the ones which are true for you. Do it without
compromising, without considering present
circumstances, or taking into account how you
have to do things right now.

**biological
style elements**

We love each other's physical differences,
but we can only love each other's
differences of character, mind, values
and sensitivity once we actually
understand them.

There are thousands of marriages
beached on the bleak sands of
mutual incomprehension.

'Why on earth does he or she
react so differently from me?'

From *Brainsex*, A. Moir and D. Jessel

Ask your <u>partner</u> to do the same if you wish, then <u>compare the results</u>. You might be surprised by how many <u>differences</u> you have discovered and pleased to see in which <u>areas</u> you both are <u>truly compatible</u>.

partner
compare results
differences

truly compatible areas

We can conclude the <u>mystery about attractions becoming repellents</u> in following the thoughts so accurately expressed by Anne Moir and David Jessel in their book *BrainSex*: 'It is hard to understand nature's plan in arranging this <u>inherent incompatibility</u> between the two sexes of the species. Maybe if we all felt and thought alike we would soon get bored with each other. But sex would surely be less of a disaster area if these <u>differences were recognized and understood</u>. Science is doing what it can, by producing the evidence that the minds of men and women are different. The rest is up to us.' (2)

mystery about attractions
becoming repellents

inherent
incompatibility

differences
recognized and understood

3. That's not what I meant!

Many books have been published over the past few years describing <u>communication differences</u> between males and females, containing valuable exercises and giving lots of advice on how to <u>overcome these difficulties</u>.

communication differences

overcome difficulties

These differences are already obvious in young children, where <u>girls</u> are more '<u>person-centred</u>' and <u>boys</u> are more '<u>thing-centred</u>'; these features carry on in adult communications, where <u>women talk mostly about people</u>, their problems, reactions and responses. Even when women talk about careers these days, a great deal of these work-related conversations are about people. <u>Men talk</u> mostly <u>about business, sports and politics</u>, often about cars, gadgets and tools. They can discuss at length how things are made, how they work, how to fix them and how they affect the world. Many <u>men get irritated</u> by women's highly personal subject matters, and many <u>women are bored</u> by male topics and cannot understand how someone can get excited about a car engine or results in sports competitions. (3)

girls – person-centred
boys – thing-centred

women talk about people

men talk about
business, sports and
politics

men get irritated
women are bored

Conflict Resolution 'NewStyle'

Remember at least three conflicts you had in the past and try to find answers to the following questions:

1.   *How did these conflicts start?*

_____

_____

_____

_____

_____

2.   *Who or what fuelled them?*

_____

_____

_____

_____

_____

(Continued on page 248)

The answers to these questions and your knowledge about diversity should give you a clear insight into your patterns and how to avoid them in future.

The book with the same title as the heading of
this sub-chapter by Deborah Tannen explains so
brilliantly that growing up in different parts of a
country, having different ethnic and class back-
grounds, even age and individual personality,
all contribute to different conversational styles
which can cause disappointment, hurt and blame.
Very appropriately for the differences between
male and female talking patterns, she describes
that male–female conversations are always cross-
cultural communication. By culture she means
the combination of habits and patterns acquired
from past experiences because boys and girls
grow up in different worlds, even if they grow
up in the same house, and as adults they 'live'
in different worlds, reinforcing patterns
established in childhood. (4) We also have to
do away with the conventional wisdom and
'common-sense' making us believe that the
more time people spend together, the better they
will understand each other. If you don't know
yourself and your partner's style – not only in
conversation but also in learning, working and
living – you will not be able to overcome the
differences which attracted you in the first place.

**different
conversational styles**

**male–female conversations
always cross-cultural
communication**

**more time together –
better understanding
of each other**

differences

4. I just can't understand you!

The failure to communicate is one of the basic
facts of life. Given our new understanding about
style differences women need no longer complain
about men's lack of communication, because
men's brains are structured that way. And yet,
she truly wants him to express himself, *he* wishes
she wouldn't press him. In the book *BrainSex*
a familiar male complaint is described and a
contrasting female viewpoint given: '"She always
says I don't talk to her. I don't understand.
I am sure she knows what I'm thinking but that
isn't good enough for her." ... "Sometimes
he listens, but he hardly ever talks to me. It's hard
to talk to a drunk, and yet it's the only time he
shows me any real feelings." Alcohol breaks down
the barriers between the discrete compartments
of the male brain.' (5) Physiologically speaking,
in the female brain, the centres of reason and
emotion are more closely connected. Therefore

failure to communicate

style differences

**familiar male complaint
female viewpoint**

Conflict Resolution 'NewStyle'

3.   *How did you feel during the conflict?*

_____

_____

_____

_____

_____

4.   *What did you think about your counterpart(s)?*

_____

_____

_____

_____

_____

5.   *Who or what terminated the conflict?*

_____

_____

_____

_____

_____

The answers to these questions and your knowledge about diversity should give you a clear insight into your patterns and how to avoid them in future.

she is better equipped to analyse, rationalize and verbalize her emotions. Something many of us have long known intuitively is now finally being acknowledged by scientists: the fact that male and female brains work differently.

verbalize emotions

male and female brains work differently

Taking all the obvious and not so obvious male and female differences into account, I believe knowing one's personal style, true preferences and brain processing functions should be the starting-point for any attempt to try to understand diversity and deal with differences. It just makes any human interaction so much more successful and takes the guessing out of the process.

knowing one's personal style

makes human interaction more successful

Eric Jensen, in his book *The Learning Brain*, has a whole section called 'Sex and Gender' in which he sums it up very nicely: 'Males and females truly live in a different world created by the processing of very different sensory information.' (6)

different world processing of different sensory information

5. Conflict resolution 'NewStyle'

Most of the stress in major relationships stems from the misconception that men and women are essentially the same. That's the reason why *he* cannot understand why *she* spends so much time agonizing over their relationship, and *she* cannot comprehend why *he* spends so much time tinkering with the car or working and/or playing on his computer. Life would be much easier if we only acknowledged how different we are from each other.

misconception men and women the same

agonizing over relationship

tinkering with the car

different from each other

Next time you encounter conflict of opinion, dissatisfaction, impatience or miscommunication with people at work or with your loved ones, you can be sure it's due to style differences. Practise some new approaches and surprise the people around you with more flexibility and greater understanding of different needs and styles. You could respond to different styles either by matching their style – which means you learn to do things 'their way' even if it is not 'your way' (this method will make you more flexible and is usually a success recipe for creating great rapport

conflict of opinion dissatisfaction, impatience

style differences

more flexibility greater understanding

matching styles

make you more flexible

How MARTIANS (males) cope with stress

- become focused and withdrawn
- feel better by solving problems
- lose temporary awareness of everything else
- do not burden others with their own problems
- retreat, go quiet and find solutions
- do something else to forget problems
- become distant, forgetful, unresponsive
- on solving the problem become attentive again

How VENUSIANS (females) cope with stress

- become overwhelmed and emotionally involved
- feel better by talking about problems
- continue talking about logically unrelated problems, worries, frustrations
- openly talk about their problems and feelings
- share feelings of being overwhelmed
- need loving friends
- become emotionally involved in other people's problems
- by talking and being heard, the stress disappears

MARTIANS NEED TO:

- Listen without offering solutions
- Help solve problems without quick-fix attitude
- Feel trusted and appreciated

VENUSIANS NEED TO:

- Talk about their problems and feelings
- Accept without giving advice or criticism
- Have their feelings validated

Based on an idea from: *Men Are From Mars, Women Are From Venus* by John Gray

with the people around you) or you could do it
by showing <u>more love or compassion</u> for
the other person whose behaviour is different
from yours and up to now has often upset, even
outraged you, because you didn't understand
their style.

more love, compassion

You'll be pleased to discover how much <u>easier
interaction</u> on any level of a relationship will be
when you practise <u>conflict resolution 'NewStyle'</u>.
The exercises on pages 246 and 248 should help
you to make this change process more effective.
There is now a vast variety of books available
on this topic; the ones which are practical and
have helped me most are listed in the section
Bibliography and Further Reading.

easier interaction

**conflict resolution
'NewStyle'**

6. A true love story in style

The 21 years of my second marriage (now totally resurrected from its ruins) are a glowing
example of what happens if neither partner truly understands style differences and
diversity. Had I known then what I know now about different styles and non-preferences,
biological needs and diversity, I would have saved myself and my family a lot of money,
disappointment, heartache and despair. I would have realized that our daily frustration
and uneasiness came from misunderstanding and misinterpreting different brain
processing styles which created adverse behaviour. But, as we are discovering right now,
it is never too late to learn more about ourselves and different styles. With love, tolerance
and understanding we now actually enjoy each other's diversity and are totally committed
to create a successful, long-lasting relationship.

This didn't happen until we both had our WSA and LSA profiles and sat down to compare
them, element by element. Although we thought we had known each other, we got a real
shock by discovering that I am naturally much more analytic than my husband! For all
these years, particularly during highly emotional times, he had obviously found it very
hard to be always logical, reflective ('cool, calm and collected') in our discussions
because that was the way we generally interacted. I had no clue that he actually wanted
to be much more spontaneous and carefree, which I often saw as just silly or
irresponsible. As we both did not know ourselves as we could have, and were not used to
communicating in matching styles, we got into misunderstandings, arguments,
disappointment, bitterness, the lot. The result was that we split up and were determined
never to get back together again. But then, after a year and a half of separation, we started
talking again – business only at first – and in this process we rediscovered our
compatibilities, and with more insight into style differences we were also able to
overcome mismatched areas of our styles with humour. It's still not all milk and honey,
but we have learned to appreciate each other on a very different level, and the deep love
which was always there can now blossom again in a very different climate, based on
friendship and true understanding of human diversity.

1. Like father – like son?

In previous chapters we have discussed at great length matches and mismatches between teachers and their students, between partners in private relationships, and now it is time to look at style differences between parents and their offspring. As you already know, opposites attract when it comes to partner choice and therefore it is no surprise that married couples usually have style preferences at the other end of the scale; they are usually diametrically opposed to each other, particularly in their biological style features. But how about children?

style differences between parents and their offspring

When we talk about style differences and similarities, please note that we only talk about natural, biological children of a couple; we are not talking about adopted children or children from reconstituted families. Research carried out in the USA only dealt with biological offspring because the question of interest was, how do genetics influence learning styles? For many the answer will be surprising, but when we consider the difficulties we often have with our children, it's not hard to accept that the first child has very different learning styles from its father or mother. Only the second or third child resembles one of the parents or a sibling in their style features.

biological children

how genetics influence LS

first child
different learning styles

So, if you have only one child, don't expect it to be like you although it might have many similarities and compatible areas, particularly in the learned or conditioned areas (like motivation, conformity, responsibility, structure and variety) of your style profiles. However, in the biological elements you will find a style combination usually not matching yours and that can lead to ongoing, often seemingly unresolvable conflicts, particularly during teenage years. But even earlier on, conflicts based on style differences become visible, often between fathers and their sons, based on the differences in analytic and holistic styles. The majority of children are still strongly holistic when they begin school, but most fathers, being strongly analytic, expect their sons to be rational, logical, highly responsible and

biological elements
not matching parents

conflicts

between fathers and sons

most children
strongly holistic
most fathers
strongly analytic

The easy part is learning how
to do new things.

The hard part is giving up
what we normally do.

more formal when it comes to school work. The boy whose brain works very differently despairs because nothing is ever good enough; he knows he can't meet his father's high expectations, and finally either gives up or becomes rebellious. <u>Mothers</u>, who are generally <u>more right-brain dominant</u>, <u>understand the needs</u> of their sons <u>intuitively</u> better but can often do very little to help resolve the conflict between fathers and their sons, and so everyone suffers in their own way.

mothers
more R/B dominant
understand needs
intuitively

Later on we will see how styles can be matched and conflicts resolved with the help of understanding learning styles, and family life can be much more harmonious – something we all need these days.

To accommodate the style needs of one child can be difficult enough but to get on in peace with your spouse and with several children can sometimes seem impossible; yet again, a <u>knowledge of</u> one's own and <u>everyone else's styles in the family</u> can be a <u>great help</u>. As we now know there is hardly ever the same style between parents and their first child, but the situation is very different when we consider the second and third child in a family.

knowledge of everyone's
styles in the family
great help

2. This is such an easy child!

How often have you heard this exclamation, usually uttered by a parent who already has experienced some disharmony with another (or some other) of their children? Research and our own work with learning and working styles has shown that the <u>second</u> and more often the <u>third child</u> of a couple can <u>resemble one parent</u> very strongly <u>in its style</u> and that's why it gets labelled 'easy'. It is 'easy' because a <u>style match</u> always <u>feels good</u>; you are on the same wavelength and understand each other even without words. Wherever there is a true style match between parent and child there is a <u>mutual understanding</u> which cannot be reached when there is a mismatch present.

second or third child
can resemble one parent
in its style
style match feels good

mutual understanding

In practical terms this might mean that both of you want it quiet when you concentrate, or that you love to do physical things together, or that you

I believe that imagination is stronger than knowledge –

That myth is more potent than history.

I believe that dreams are more powerful than facts –

That hope always triumphs over experience –

That laughter is the only cure for grief.

And I believe that love is stronger than death.

Robert Fulghum

share the same interests in reading, talking and
listening, or that you both are early birds or night
owls. In any case, you will have many areas of
compatibility leading to shared interests, which   **shared interests**
leads to more closeness. You want to be together   **more closeness**
because you enjoy each other's company very much.
In some families this can lead to favouritism and
exclusion of the other children, even the spouse,
creating disappointment and a lot of unhappiness.

Whenever you have such a situation in your own
family, make sure you and your partner fully under-
stand styles and diversity, have the whole family   **styles and diversity**
assessed, and begin immediately to discuss style
differences and similarities, because it is crucial
that all family members understand the reasons   **reasons for**
for conflict as well as harmony.   **conflict and harmony**

How to utilize the results of learning and working
style profiles will be discussed at the end of this
chapter, and you will find some useful hints for
clearing the air and improving the family climate.

3. Homework – the never-ending battle in some families

One area in which style mismatches between parents   **style mismatches**
and their children can lead to constant frustration,   **parents and children**
irritation, even fights, is that of homework. All
parents know homework is important and most
children resent it. How come that in the same family
there is no problem with homework for some kids,
they sit down, do what needs to be done, seem to
cope well with even loads of homework and the end
product is always neat and tidy? And then there are
these other children for whom homework is nothing   **homework:**
but a constant struggle: they don't want to do it,   **constant struggle**
always have something more important to do, and
when they finally sit down to get on with their
homework, don't stay with it, find every possible
interruption and usually end up with half-finished,   **interruptions,**
shoddy work. And their work area – you can't even   **half-finished**
look at the mess! There is no wonder, you think,   **work area – a mess**
that they can't produce good work under such
conditions: their school books strewn all over the
place, the radio blaring (if you allowed it), food
everywhere, and in the midst of it your daughter,

Dialogue between Parent and Tactile Child at Homework Time

Child: 'Mum? I need some help – I don't <u>get</u> this!'

Mother: 'That's because you aren't even <u>looking</u> at it! How do you <u>expect</u> to learn anything that way? It's not written on the ceiling, you know! As usual – you're just not <u>trying</u>.'

Child: 'I <u>am</u> trying, but it's too <u>hard</u>! I just don't <u>get</u> it, that's all!'

Mother: 'Look, Sharon, I don't have time for this nonsense. You pay attention to your work, and don't let me see you staring out the window or up at the ceiling. Keep your eyes on your page and try again – and please don't bother me with any more of your ridiculous excuses!'

Adapted from *Try To Feel It My Way* by Suzette Haden Elgin

or more often, your son – <u>slouching</u>, not sitting on the chair, or most of the time <u>lying</u> stretched out <u>on the floor</u> or on the bed. You go out of your way to help them, support them, sometimes even do parts of the homework for them, just to get these daily unpleasantries out of the way. You try your best, <u>you get frustrated</u>, your nerves are at break point, you plead, cajole, <u>even threaten</u>, and when you have succeeded for a few days, the moment comes and you are back to square one – the <u>child doesn't want to do homework</u>. Despite all your efforts, deep down you know there is not much you can do about this hopeless situation and finally <u>you give up</u> educating them HOW to do homework properly and leave them to themselves.

**slouching,
lying
on the floor or bed**

**you get frustrated,
even threaten**

**child doesn't want
to do homework**

you give up

Sounds familiar? I can feel for you because that was the scenario we had in our house all through our daughter's high school years – it was a <u>constant battle</u> and usually <u>all of us were the losers</u>. I could not understand why my daughter sometimes would do her homework in no time, although the quality was not the best, but at least she did it, and at other times she would just forget, leave it half finished or find excuses for not doing it at all – and then she would go to school without it.

**constant battle
all of us were the losers**

I had no clue why she was so <u>resistant to doing homework</u>. I knew she was bright and could produce very good work – if she was interested and wanted to, but I didn't know how to make her WANT to learn. For years I had given her what I thought was <u>good advice</u> on how to do homework, and I know for many of you the following sounds very familiar because we have all heard it from our parents and said it to our children. Whenever it was time for homework (usually right after school or after a short snack after coming home from school) I would say to my daughter: 'Go to your room, switch off the radio, turn on the lights, take out your books, sit at your desk – upright please – and do your homework.' For me this was <u>the only thinkable way of doing homework</u>; that's how we had to do it and that's how everyone does it, because it's <u>the right way</u> to do it, right?

**resistant to doing
homework**

good advice

**the only way
to do homework**

the right way

Wrong! Once I found out about learning styles

A mind once stretched

by a new idea

can never go back

to its original dimension.

Oliver W. Holmes

I realized how wrong I was and that <u>the way a child</u> is <u>forced</u> to do homework can totally <u>switch off</u> its <u>willingness to learn</u>. I still regret that I found out about different learning styles when my daughter was in her last year at high school and I would never have guessed how she could learn best because <u>her style</u> is so <u>very different from mine</u>. Can you guess what she would have needed to do her homework with more enthusiasm?

forced way
switches off
willingness to learn

her style
very different from mine

She would have worked best in the middle of the living room on the floor, with the cat and the dog close by, with healthy drinks and nibbles, with dim light and the radio going (with the appropriate learning music of course – see Chapter 6) and with me around, in case she needed my help. On top of that she would have needed learning tools she could manipulate to keep her hands busy instead of doodling or chewing pencils.

If the described scenario seems crazy to you, as it did for me when I first heard it, it is true that <u>learning with</u> what we call <u>'distractions'</u> is the style which works best for many children, particularly when they are more <u>holistic, right-brain dominant</u>. You just have to accept that fact. Research has proven it and we have seen it hundreds of times that children with these style needs (often under-achievers at school) could perform much better, WANT to learn this way and actually do it very successfully. Have your <u>children's learning styles assessed</u>, let them try to study in their own way, <u>set</u> <u>some basic rules</u> (like you can do it your way when you clean up your 'mess' afterwards and when your school performance improves), and <u>watch them succeed</u>.

learning with
'distractions'

holistic, R/B dominant

have children's learning
styles assessed,
set basic rules

watch them succeed

I can guarantee you that not only their attitude towards learning will improve but also the daily battlefield around homework will disappear, and you will have a much <u>more relaxed atmosphere</u> in your own home. Even if it makes you shudder when you watch your child do homework that way, <u>ACCEPT</u> that <u>your child has a different style</u> and learning needs. The best you can do to really help and support is to understand and let your child be the wonderful person he/she is meant to be.

more relaxed atmosphere

accept your child's
different style

Do not confine
your children
to your own learning.
For they have been born
in another time.

Hebrew Proverb

4. Messy rooms – minefields in our family homes

Now we have tackled one area which can cause
big problems in a family for years, let's look at
another one, equally <u>unpleasant</u> but not with such
serious consequences as refusing to do homework.
It's <u>messy rooms</u>, for which teenagers are famous.
Again we have to ask ourselves, how come that
one child is tidy and keeps their room in order, just
as the parents want it, and that another child can
never be tidy, lives in a 'pigsty', as many desperate
parents call their children's living quarters; <u>even if
they do tidy up</u>, the <u>mess creeps in immediately</u>, or
the mess is shoved under beds or into wardrobes
and cupboards, an activity these children have
developed mastery in. As if such <u>'bad habits'</u>
were not bad enough, they are usually to be found
<u>in children</u> who also have <u>problems with doing
their homework</u>, whereas their high-achieving
siblings often display the welcome skills of being
tidy and organized in their rooms. Just as you like it.

unpleasant

messy rooms

**even if they tidy up,
mess creeps back in**

bad habits

**in children with
homework problems**

So, why is it compounded in some children and no
matter what we do, nothing seriously works? I
remember a time when the mess in our daughter's
room started spilling out into the rest of the house.
We set a rule which said, whatever you do in your
room is none of our business, as long as you keep
the mess confined to it. However, that didn't work
in the long run, because there came a day when we
couldn't open the door and the room was virtually
no longer accessible. We were at our wits' end and
when I started to tidy up, there arose another fierce
conflict because now she couldn't find anything!

Does this sound familiar too? Have you, like me,
argued about untidy rooms, complained about the
<u>mess in the kitchen or bathroom</u>, despaired over
shoes, clothes and school bags flung into a corner
or dropped in the middle of the hall? Again, I wish
I had known about different learning styles long ago;
it would have given me the insight into the profound
<u>difference between analytic and holistic</u> human
beings (see Chapter 5); it would have explained to
me that more left-brain dominant people (like many
parents) are tidy, well organized, look after their

messy kitchen/bathroom

**difference between
analytic and holistic style**

AGE (approximate)   DEVELOPMENT

Conception – 15 months   Reptilian Brain
Basic survival needs – food, shelter, security and safety
Sensory development starting with vestibular system, then hearing, tactile, smell, taste and finally
seeing – rich sensory activation
Motor development moving from reflexes to core muscle activation, neck muscles, arms and legs
leading to rolling over, sitting, crawling and walking – motor exploration

15 months – 4 ½ years   Limbic System/Relationship
Understanding of self/others, self/emotions, self/language
Emotional exploration; Language exploration/communication;
Imagination; Gross motor proficiency; Memory development; Social development

4 ½ years – 7 years   Gestalt Hemisphere Elaboration
Whole picture processing/cognition   Image/movement/rhythm/emotion/intuition
Outer speech/integrative thought

7 – 9 years   Logic Hemisphere Elaboration
Detail and linear processing/cognition
Refinement of elements of language
Linear maths processing
Reading and writing skills development
Technique development – music, art, sports, dance, manual training

8 years   Frontal Lobe Elaboration
Fine motor development – skills refinement
Inner speech – control of social behaviour
Fine motor eye teaming for tracking and foveal focus (2-dimensional focus)

9 – 12 years   Increase Corpus Callosum Elaboration and Myelination
Whole brain processing

12 – 16 years   Hormonal Emphasis
Learning about body, self, others, community, and meaningful living through social consciousness

16 – 21 years   Refining Cognitive Skills
Whole mind/body processing, social interaction, future planning and play with new ideas and
possibilities

21+   Elaboration and Refinement of the Frontal Lobes
Global/systems thinking
High-level formal reasoning
Insight
Refinement of fine motor skills
Refinement of emotions – altruism, love, compassion

From *Smart Moves* by Carla Hannaford (1)

things and keep them in order, whereas the more right-brain dominant people (like teenage children) are sloppy, disorganized, don't look after their things and don't keep them in order. They are 'scatterbrains' and find it very hard to 'get their act together', they are the risk takers, are impulsive and most of the time don't see the consequences of their actions. Whether you like it or not, that's the way they are and usually they don't change their basic style very much, although many will learn – often the hard way – that being organized and tidy has its advantages. They learn to function in this manner, but if they don't have to be that way, they can easily fall back into disorganization bordering on sloppiness.

R/B dominant teenagers

'scatterbrains'
impulsive risk takers

don't change
basic style very much

disorganization
sloppiness

Once you understand these style features, you can help your child to become a bit more organized, but be warned, logical reasoning will not do the trick. There are some very good books available which give good advice on how to deal with disobedient youngsters and you will find these books listed in the section Bibliography and Further Reading.

help child
become more organized
but no logical reasoning

5. I wish I could bring up my children all over again!

After this host of new insights many of you might now say this wish with a sigh, as I did. Yet, one cannot rewrite the past but it's never too late to apply knowledge of different learning styles, even to your grown-up children. I realized that, although I couldn't undo many of the things I had said to my daughter when it came to learning (some of which I regret), I can utilize my new-found insights in all my interactions with her. Despite our distinctly different styles (remember, she is an only child and so profoundly different from me in many ways), we have lots in common and can always capitalize on these common features, complementing each other.

never too late

lots in common

As we both know our strengths and weaknesses it has become much easier to communicate, to discuss things and to get on with each other. Our relationship has improved dramatically (which is probably also due to our getting older and wiser) because we now understand and respect each other for who we are

know our
strengths and weaknesses

understand and respect

'All it takes to make a difference is
the courage to stop proving I was
right in being unable to make a
difference ... to stop assigning the
cause for my inability to the
circumstances outside myself and
to be willing to have been that way,
and to see that the fear of being a
failure is a lot less important than
the unique opportunity I have to
make a difference.'

Werner Erhard

as human beings and not because we are mother and daughter. I am eternally grateful for having found out about learning styles and that it was not too late, although our rift during her late teens was profound and I thought we would never be able to bridge the gap again. But like with my husband, never say never again.

Finally I have also <u>overcome my guilt feelings</u> about the mistakes I made by not understanding her style because at any time I tried my best. Had I known better, I would have acted differently, and I can only advise you to <u>apologize</u> for forcing your style onto your children and get on with your life. <u>Enjoy your children</u> the way they are, stop nagging, help and support them in becoming who they are meant to be, and appreciate every day you can spend with them.

overcome guilt feelings

apologize

enjoy your children

6. Learning styles as new family therapy

These days many people are in <u>rocky marriages</u>, filled with strife and conflict. Less dramatic, but more common, is the situation that after several years of marriage, many people don't like their spouses anymore (see Chapter 9), and this is fertile ground for <u>fighting</u>. But at the same time, both parents are often deeply concerned with the well-being of their children. It seems to be a plain fact – at least statistically – that either <u>separation</u> or fighting in response to an unhappy marriage is likely to <u>harm your children</u> in <u>lasting ways</u>, as Martin Seligman, author of the excellent book, *Learned Optimism*, points out. (2) He has done years of research on <u>pessimism and depression</u>, and recommends that, if you care about your children, you step back and think twice or three times before you fight. <u>Being angry and fighting</u> are NOT <u>human rights</u>. Fighting is a human choice, and it's your child's well-being, more than yours, that may be at stake. Research shows that the following chain of events is common: parental fighting or separation leads to a <u>marked increase in the child's depression</u>. The depression itself then <u>causes school problems</u> and the child becoming even <u>more pessimistic</u>. School problems combined with this newly minted

rocky marriages

fighting

separation

harms children in lasting ways

pessimism and depression

being angry and fighting are not human rights

increase in child's depression causes school problems, increases pessimism

Until one is committed,
there is hesitancy, the chance to draw back,
always ineffectiveness.
Concerning all acts of initiative (and creation),
there is one elementary truth
the ignorance of which kills countless ideas
and splendid plans:
that the moment one definitely commits oneself,
then Providence moves too.
All sorts of things occur to help one
that would never otherwise have occurred.
A whole stream of events
issues from the decision,
raising in one's favour
all manner of unforeseen incidents
and meetings and material assistance
which no man could have dreamed
would have come his way.

W. H. Murray:
The Himalayan Expedition

pessimism maintain depression, and a <u>vicious cycle</u> has begun. <u>Depression</u> now becomes a <u>permanent</u> way of life for your child. (3)

vicious cycle
depression becomes
permanent

Long-lasting depression is always one of the vital ingredients <u>leading to suicide</u> and, as recent statistical figures from New Zealand teenagers are on the rise, it is time to consider what else can be done to help families in trouble. Unless the whole situation is already out of hand, and drug abuse, violence and even crime are taking place, we have found that a <u>knowledge</u> of the <u>children's learning</u> and their <u>parents' working styles</u> are an extremely useful tool for <u>family counselling</u>. We have many reports from families where the knowledge about style differences has improved the family climate dramatically, changed the way family members interact, and has brought back the <u>appreciation</u> and <u>love</u> between parents and their children.

leading to suicide

knowledge of
children's learning and
parents' working styles
for family counselling

appreciation and love

In a <u>family coaching session</u> where parents and children bring along their WSA and LSA profiles, style differences are discussed, similarities pointed out and mismatches explained. For many families it is the very first time at such a session that they actually <u>listen and talk to each other</u>, and that their style features are taken seriously because they are printed black on white. It can be very emotional for all family members to clarify misunderstandings and confusions, long-held grudges and false beliefs about each other, and maybe learn to see their nearest and dearest through very different eyes. Such an interpretation of one's own profile can also lead to <u>renewed self-esteem</u> through better self-understanding and <u>more tolerance</u> towards others, as we know there are no good or bad styles.

family coaching session

listen/talk to each other

renewed self-esteem
more tolerance

With <u>soothing music</u> in the background and the skilful <u>help of a family coach</u>, people who before had a communication breakdown begin to talk to each other and find a way to get on in the future. For families with teenagers, career choice is often a point of friction, and a good understanding of the adolescent's style features can often resolve conflicts in this area. Many people told us that such a family coaching session was <u>more constructive</u> and more useful than <u>counselling sessions</u>.

soothing music
help from family coach

more constructive than
counselling sessions

1. Breaking an old myth – no pain, no gain

Thinking back to our school days and to any other
formal learning or studying we ever had to do,
it was usually hard, frustrating, stressful and often
boring. This has left many of us with a negative
attitude towards learning, with the uneasy feeling
that learning is painful; we came to believe that
there is no gain without pain. Haven't we heard
this from our parents, teachers and instructors?
After all, they are the experts – they should know!

formal learning
hard, frustrating, stressful
often boring

learning is painful
no gain without pain

Not quite. Because they had a strong belief
in this old myth – it had become their personal
mindset, their own paradigm which kept them
repeating it, making their children's, students'
and their own lives unnecessarily hard. It was
unimaginable to them – and still is for many –
that learning can actually be enjoyable and easy
and have long-lasting, positive results.
The same goes for work – if it's too easy,
let alone enjoyable, it can't be worth much.

strong belief
old myth
paradigm

unnecessarily hard

learning enjoyable and easy
positive results

How then can we do away with these old myths?
As Ronald Gross, in his book *Peak Learning*,
explains, it is possible for anyone who wants
to try, because the principles of 'peak learning'
are based on some fundamental truths about
learning and growing that can liberate us from
over-reliance on schooling.

do away with old myths

principles: 'peak learning'

The main principles are:
a) Adults who take care of their own learning
   often master more things and master them better
   than those who rely on being taught. They tend
   to be more motivated, retain more of what
   they have learned, and make better use of it
   in their private and professional lives.

take care of own learning

more motivated

b) Adults learn in different ways from children.
   They have a different sense of themselves, of their
   time, and of what's worth learning and why. As
   adults we finally realize no one can learn for *me*,
   anymore than someone can eat for me. Education
   is something I must tailor to myself, not something
   I can get ready-made in institutions of learning.

adults learn differently

education
tailored to self,
not ready-made

SAID
is not yet heard,

HEARD
is not yet understood,

UNDERSTOOD
is not yet agreed,

AGREED
is not yet applied,

APPLIED
is not yet implemented.

c) <u>No particular learning style is in itself superior</u> to another. How you learn, as Gross puts it, depends on your temperament, circumstances, needs, tastes or ambition. (1) However, he also says that <u>success in learning</u> depends not on the subject itself or the conditions (how, where and when) of learning, but basically on the <u>learner's engagement</u> – his or her fascination with the subject.

no style is superior

success in learning

learner's engagement

Although I fully agree with the above statements in general, I have to disagree with this last one. Research into learning styles, backed up by our own experience with working styles, shows that for many people, except for the highly flexible, <u>learning to a great extent *does* depend</u> on the <u>how</u>, <u>where</u> and <u>when</u>. It is very important that the <u>conditions of learning</u> are <u>matched with the learner's individual style</u>. Only then will motivation and persistence increase, performance improve and <u>information become knowledge</u> for the learner.

learning depends on how, where, when learning conditions matched with learner's style information ~ knowledge

As we have seen, anyone can become a successful or so-called 'peak learner' with ease and no pain. The first and most important step, however, is to <u>know yourself</u>, your true working or learning style and do it <u>*your wa*</u>y when it comes to information intake.

know yourself do it your way

2. Acceptance – the first step to change

These arguments for becoming more successful, not only in learning or work situations but also possibly in running your life, sound quite plausible you might think, but then ... you have all your <u>past learning experiences</u> – and most of them were <u>not pleasant</u>. You think you know yourself, and you have strong evidence that learning or information intake is really <u>not that easy</u> (you even have written proof for that on your school reports and certificates). As you are a curious person, open to learning new things, you have also assessed your own working style, and studied your profile and report. You are really <u>keen to improve your learning</u> and concentration skills

past learning experiences not pleasant

not easy

keen to improve learning

My Flow State

Think about work or study situations where everything seemed to go smoothly. You were on a real performance high and the result was better than you expected. To be able to repeat such 'flow states' more often you must become aware of **HOW** you did things to be able to duplicate these successful strategies in future.

Become aware of the following conditions under which you did the job so well:

1. Physical environment – where were you – inside/outdoors? Was it warm/cool? How about music, other sounds?
2. Time of day – when did you do the work?
3. Your physical needs – did you sit still, move around, eat, drink? Could you take breaks?
4. People – did you work with someone else, a group, or were you alone? How about instructions/guidelines?
5. State of mind – how did you feel – before, during, after the task? Were you eager, excited – even before you started? What kept you going?

Make a list of these important ingredients of your mental 'flow state' and reflect on how you can ensure these are the conditions when you need to do tasks. Your Learning Style Analysis (LSA) Report will give you further suggestions for peak performance.

but you are not quite sure how. The old beliefs about your learning abilities are still very strong and you are not yet quite comfortable with your newly discovered strengths which are your preferences in the profile.

but old beliefs about learning abilities strong

As with anything new, you have to take the first step – to accept your true abilities. Even if you have never realized that you possess such-and-such strengths, accept that you *do* have them. You can trust yourself and your style. Observe how you do things when you are in a 'flow state', when everything seems to come easily. Continue practising your abilities and strengths and you might be surprised about the outcome!

accept true abilities

trust yourself, observe flow state, when everything comes easily

To help you in achieving mental peaks more often in your work, your studies or other activities, you'll find some useful considerations opposite. They can be even more useful if you watch how other people reach, and operate in, a 'flow state'; also think about more examples from your own life.

3. The more you know, the more you can know

Whether you experience some drastic changes, some minor changes or no changes at all in your self-perception after you discover your own learning or working style, one thing is for sure: the more you know about yourself and how your brain works, the more you know about your strengths and weaknesses and how you tick, the more you can capitalize on that knowledge. You will be able to live your life your way instead of following other people's advice, even if it's well meant.

know yourself

strengths and weaknesses

live your life your way

The more knowledge you have about the way you take information in, the more you will be able to do it and the easier it will be. It's similar to exercising muscles you have hardly ever used before: in the beginning you might be a little sore, but the more you exercise these muscles, the better you will become, and the better you will feel and perform. With learning ability it goes even further: the more you activate your brain *your way*,

more knowledge about information intake makes it easier

activate brain your way

CHAOS EXERCISE

Sit back and relax.
Think about something that was once a big issue for you,
something which confused you greatly.
Remember how you were desperate for a while
because you didn't know what to do?
Write down what you did to gain clarity and how you felt
when you finally found a solution or saw a way out.

_____

_____

_____

_____

_____

_____

_____

_____

_____

_____

_____

_____

_____

_____

_____

the more it will want to learn, take information in, store and retrieve it. This is the fuel that <u>keeps</u> your <u>motivation going</u>. Diana Beaver, in her book *Lazy Learning*, describes how to 'make the best of the brains you were born with', as the subtitle states, and suggests some very simple but effective structures and strategies to find out how you learn best. (2) Similar exercises can be found on pages 4, 276 and 280.

keep motivation going

With <u>greater self-knowledge</u> and a range of easy, suitable strategies described throughout this book, you will not only be <u>more effective</u> in learning, studying or working, you will also <u>enjoy</u> it more and experience <u>more satisfaction</u> with your results. You might even become addicted to your own learning ability!

greater self-knowledge

more effective

enjoyment, satisfaction

4. Out of chaos comes new order

From what you have read so far about learning and working styles, human diversity, brain functions and information intake, and what you learned from the tests and exercises I invited you to do, you have perhaps gained a very <u>complex picture</u> about yourself and the people you know.

complex picture

You might think, 'I wish I had known all that twenty years ago' or 'Why doesn't everyone know about this?' You might be delighted about what you discovered or not be very pleased at all. Whatever reaction you might have to this wealth of knowledge, you will probably experience <u>mental confusion</u> too.

mental confusion

If I can go by the reactions I have seen in thousands of people exposed to the concept of learning or working styles, you are not alone. Most of them went through a phase of total confusion after accepting human diversity and style as the basis of successful learning, working and interacting. <u>Old beliefs</u>, paradigms and past experiences <u>fight an inner battle with</u> the <u>new knowledge,</u> the unthinkable and the truly unbelievable. However, deep down we might have known intuitively that diversity is the truth.

old beliefs
fight inner battle
with new knowledge

Educational change is like
being on a rotten boat,
with a mutinous crew,
sailing into uncharted waters.

Only the person not rowing has
time to rock the boat.

It's hard to know what to do at this stage:
throw out everything you have believed about
yourself, other people and how true learning
works and adopt these somewhat strange new
principles, or try to <u>combine old and useful beliefs</u>   **combine old, useful beliefs**
<u>with new insights</u> and leading-edge knowledge.   **with new insights**

During this phase many people go back and forth
in their thinking from 'Oh, it can't be true, it's
all a bit over the top, too idealistic,' to 'What if
it's true, what if styles really hold the key to so
many unsolved mysteries?' back to 'I can't be
bothered, I've got so much else to do ... but what
if it could help solve some problems we have
at work, at school, with so-and-so right now?'

This ties in with the <u>chaos theory</u> pioneered by   **chaos theory**
mathematicians and physical scientists since the
early 1970s and explained by James Gleick in
the best-seller *Chaos: Making a New Science*.
It says that chaos, or the tendency to <u>unpredictable</u>   **unpredictable behaviour**
<u>behaviour</u>, lurks in practically every real-world
system, yet <u>order arises spontaneously</u> in those   **order arises spontaneously**
systems (3) – so chaos and order occur together.
Furthermore, more often than not, <u>chaos is the</u>   **chaos is the**
<u>normal operating state</u> of a system! (4)   **normal operating state**

Given that our brain is an open system, always
in flux, constantly rearranging thought patterns
through sensory input, it is possible that <u>the brain</u>   **brain**
<u>is designed for chaos</u>, and that this instability   **designed for chaos**
creates purposeful activity and direction. (5)
Once we are <u>through this state of inner chaos</u> –   **through inner chaos**
no one knows how long this will last, one never
knows how and when the breakthrough is going
to happen – we are definitely <u>bound to reach</u> a   **reach**
<u>higher level of clarity</u>, a new way of thinking,   **higher level of clarity**
a <u>new perspective</u>.   **new perspective**

Whether it creeps up on you slowly and unnoticed
or whether you have one big, mighty '<u>Aha</u>'   **'Aha'**
or many small ones, I can assure you, it's a
<u>very pleasant feeling</u> and you might like to   **pleasant feeling**
experience it time and again. That's the point
at which you finally get '<u>hooked</u>' <u>on learning</u>.   **'hooked' on learning**

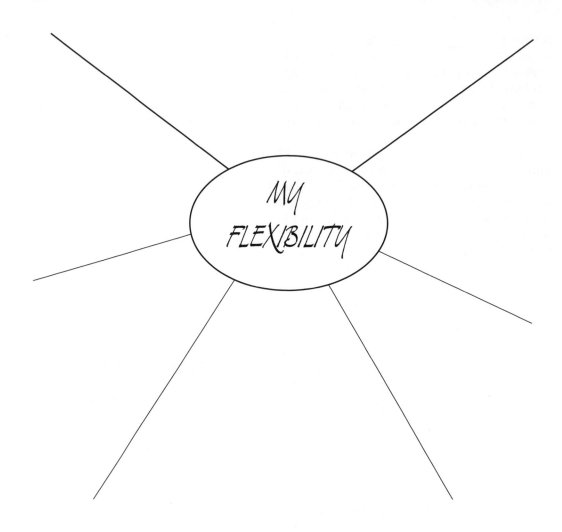

See results from your LSA or WSA profile and write down/draw
the elements in which you are flexible.

How to get questionnaires and computer-generated WSA/LSA profiles – see Appendix II

Learning climates of surprise, suspense, even
provocation, slight uncertainty and disorder can,
if properly orchestrated, lead to better, joyful
learning and more satisfying understanding.

**joyful learning and
satisfying understanding**

When people reach this new stage of awareness,
something else might occur in their brains,
impacting on their information processing ability
and learning skills: they discover they are capable
of things they thought they could never do,
their learning abilities broaden and their
self-esteem increases.

new awareness

**learning abilities broaden
self-esteem increases**

With these new mental skills another phenomenon
occurs: their flexibility strengthens and they
experience perhaps that ...

flexibility strengthens

5. Flexible is beautiful

In the process of understanding diversity we have
learned that human beings are uniquely different
from each other in their preferences and needs,
unearthed the profound differences between
holistics and analytics, and also discovered
the importance of the biological aspects of a
person's learning or working style profile.

**humans are
uniquely different**

**holistics and analytics
biological aspects**

Now we must add on one last but probably the
most important aspect to make the picture complete:
human flexibility. When looking at any Working
Style Profile, you can see one's preferences
(people usually have between three and fifteen
strong preferences); non-preferences that can
become weaknesses when continually used
instead of one's preferences; and question marks
indicating inconsistencies or contradictions about
certain aspects. The bulk of the information,
however, usually shows your overall flexibility.

**most important is
flexibility
style preferences**

non-preferences

**question marks indicate
inconsistency/contradiction**

overall flexibility

Although it is very important to be aware of
all your strengths and non-preferences, it is
probably even more important to know
your flexible areas because combined they can
become a personal strength in itself, and are
often the only feature which will help you
survive difficult situations.

**important to know
flexible areas,
become a strength**

Sample of Flexible Profile

 LSA - Jun   Ken

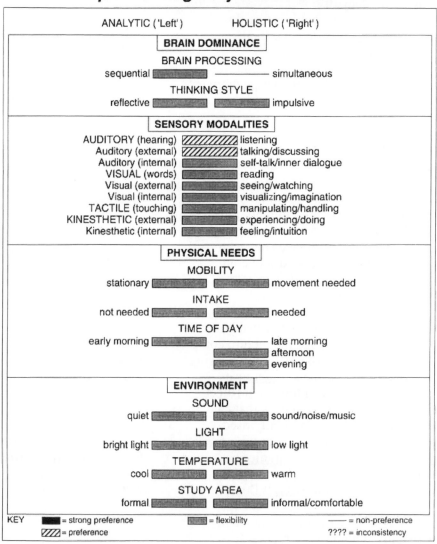

Graph 1. Biologically Based Elements

ANALYTIC ('Left')   HOLISTIC ('Right')

BRAIN DOMINANCE

BRAIN PROCESSING
sequential ▨▨▨ ——— simultaneous

THINKING STYLE
reflective ▨▨▨ ▨▨▨ impulsive

SENSORY MODALITIES

AUDITORY (hearing) ▨▨▨ listening
Auditory (external) ▨▨▨ talking/discussing
Auditory (internal) ▨▨▨ self-talk/inner dialogue
VISUAL (words) ▨▨▨ reading
Visual (external) ▨▨▨ seeing/watching
Visual (internal) ▨▨▨ visualizing/imagination
TACTILE (touching) ▨▨▨ manipulating/handling
KINESTHETIC (external) ▨▨▨ experiencing/doing
Kinesthetic (internal) ▨▨▨ feeling/intuition

PHYSICAL NEEDS

MOBILITY
stationary ▨▨▨ ▨▨▨ movement needed

INTAKE
not needed ▨▨▨ ▨▨▨ needed

TIME OF DAY
early morning ▨▨▨ ——— late morning
▨▨▨ afternoon
▨▨▨ evening

ENVIRONMENT

SOUND
quiet ▨▨▨ ▨▨▨ sound/noise/music

LIGHT
bright light ▨▨▨ ▨▨▨ low light

TEMPERATURE
cool ▨▨▨ ▨▨▨ warm

STUDY AREA
formal ▨▨▨ ▨▨▨ informal/comfortable

KEY   ▪▪ = strong preference   ▨▨ = flexibility   ——— = non-preference
▨▨ = preference   ???? = inconsistency

Considering our fast-changing world, the
changing shape of work, as Gordon Dryden
and Jeannette Vos describe it so succinctly in
their excellent book *The Learning Revolution*,
and the estimation that people in the workforce
of the future will be changing their profession,
not only their jobs, up to five times during their
working life, it will be more necessary than ever
to be flexible and adaptable.

changing shape of work

**changing professions
up to five times**

flexible and adaptable

Self-knowledge and flexibility will be the two
most important qualities – for employees and
managers as well as for people who want to be
successful in training, teaching and learning.
The same goes for anyone who wants more
than just to survive, who wants to thrive
in the times ahead and live a rich, fulfilled life.

self-knowledge, flexibility

Highly flexible people (like those in the sample
profile shown on pages 282 and 284) have the ability
to use both left- and/or right-brain processing skills
equally well and can, according to the requirements
of the situation, respond easily, either the analytic
or the holistic way. They can effortlessly adjust to
different conditions in their environment and have
hardly any strong needs or preferences. They are
appreciated for being all-rounders and are usually
very easygoing, accommodating, and most of the
time not overly ambitious.

highly flexible people

left/right-brain skills

**analytical or holistic
adjust effortlessly**

At work these people are generally the appreciated
all-rounders, colleagues who are most of the time
willing to do anything and are always prepared
to help anyone.

**at work
all-rounders**

People with no preferences at all, just flexibilities,
usually display average performance and will
hardly ever become leaders. Unless something
triggers their interest or motivation deeply,
they are usually content with their roles for
quite a long time.

**no preferences
average performance**

content with their roles

Strong flexibility in the sensory areas (visual,
auditory, tactile, kinesthetic) means that such
people need information intake and learning
through all their senses. Doing it through one or
two modalities only is not quite enough for

sensory flexibility

through all senses

Sample of Flexible Profile continued

 LSA - Jun _____   Ken

Graph 2. Conditioned/Learned Elements

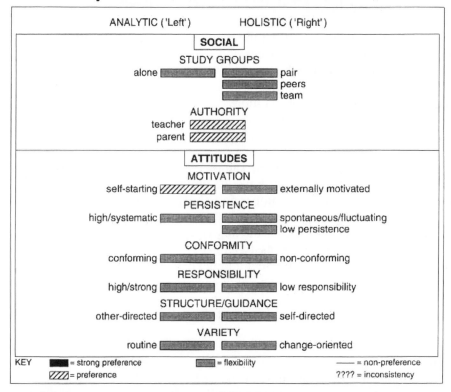

DIFFERENCES BETWEEN BIOLOGICAL AND LEARNED ELEMENTS:
The results on page 2 represent your biological needs when concentrating, reading for information or learning something new and difficult. Preferences and non-preferences in these areas are usually hard to change and remain mostly stable over a lifetime. When they are mismatched over a longer period of time they will influence learning motivation, persistence and responsibility in a negative way. For lasting learning success, make sure that your strong preferences are being matched most of the time.
The results on page 3 reveal your conditioning, and show with whom you learn best and what your attitudes are when it comes to learning something new and difficult. These elements are not stable in your profile and can change quite rapidly. This usually happens when there are changes going on inside you or in the world around you. To be successful at school it is very important that you develop positive attitudes and always attempt the best you can do because your preferences become your strengths when you use them wisely.

their brain. They need a <u>multisensory approach</u>. That's why <u>creative</u>, <u>accelerated learning methods</u>, taking into account all the senses, seem to be particularly useful for anyone with high flexibility in their perceptual areas.

**multisensory approach
creative, accelerated
learning methods**

Being <u>flexible</u> in one's <u>thinking style</u> means that these people can be either <u>quick</u> and <u>impulsive</u> in their thinking or they can <u>slow down</u> and <u>reflect</u> on things before they make decisions. The true advantage is they can adjust their thinking style easily to match the diversity of situations or problems. This gives them a <u>greater capacity</u> to <u>understand</u> what's going on and enables them to <u>respond more appropriately</u>. Given the great complexity of human life these days in our Western societies – privately and professionally – it is almost a <u>necessity to be highly flexible</u>, at least in our thinking style, because <u>mental rigidity</u> (either strongly analytical or holistic, left- or right-brain style) will <u>not be sufficient</u> to cope with our <u>fast-changing world</u>. The future belongs to flexible thinkers!

**flexible thinking style
quick and impulsive
slow down and reflect**

**greater capacity of
understanding
respond appropriately**

**necessity to be flexible
mental rigidity**

**not sufficient for
fast-changing world**

So, how can you become more flexible if you have been using more or less only one kind of thinking style for many years? The good news is that <u>mental flexibility</u> can be <u>learned</u> like any other skill. <u>Through practice</u> every human being can become more flexible in their thinking style.

**mental flexibility – learned
through practice**

In his book *The Right Brain Manager*, Harry Alder takes a clear stand against the way in which <u>Western culture</u> generally values most highly those skills which reflect <u>left-brain dominance</u>. Such skills as <u>logical or mathematical ability</u> and <u>sequential or analytical reasoning</u> are focused on throughout higher education and professional training and are vital to all scientific methods. The <u>abilities located in the right brain</u>, however, tend to be <u>neglected, even suppressed</u>, because the imaginative powers of the right brain are not valued highly. Such an <u>imbalance</u> is bound to affect a person's <u>overall abilities</u> and may be the cause of <u>losing the intuitive powers</u> of the creative part of the brain. (6)

**Western culture
left-brain dominance
logical/mathematical ability
sequential/analytical skills**

**right-brain abilities
neglected, suppressed**

**imbalance
overall abilities
losing intuitive powers**

How to
Increase my Flexibility

Considering your preferences and your non-preferences,
think how you could become more flexible.
(Write down what you could do)

- Instead of _____

  I could _____

- Instead of _____

  I could _____

- Instead of _____

  I could _____

People have been trained through formal education into being more analytic, using predominantly logical thinking; it would <u>help analytics</u> to <u>use their intuition more often</u> and enhance their right-brain thinking skills. <u>Holistics</u>, on the other hand, who often have a hard time in our left-brain dominated society, could <u>practise logical thinking</u> and use their left-brain, analytical skills more often. This way, not only their <u>flexibility would increase</u>, but also their <u>brain power would be enhanced</u>.

help analytics
use intuition more often
holistics

practise logical thinking

flexibility increased
brain power enhanced

If you want to begin your own '<u>flexibility training</u>' I invite you to try out the suggested exercises on the opposite page. Not only are they fun, they will also give you an insight into your existing <u>thought patterns</u>, some of which you have been building up over a lifetime. The more often you <u>repeat certain mental patterns</u>, the more they are likely to <u>become</u> 'habits'; many of them may even have manifested themselves as <u>bad habits</u>! The only way <u>to get rid of these</u> is to <u>become aware</u> of them in the first place, observe how they no longer serve you, and then consciously get rid of them until you have <u>developed new patterns</u> which are more appropriate or which make you more flexible, or even more 'likeable'.

flexibility training

thought patterns

repeat mental patterns
become 'habits'
bad habits
to get rid of by
becoming aware

developing new patterns

6. Get familiar with your new self

If, by any chance, through reading the book or doing your WSA Profile, you have found out that the style you have been displaying and using up to now is <u>not really your true style</u> (you may have discovered that you are much more holistic, right-brain dominant than you had thought or allowed yourself to be, or that you have more analytic style features than you believed you had), rest assured. You are in the company of numerous people – intelligent, successful human beings who have lived all their lives <u>without really knowing</u> what <u>their true preferences</u> are, like myself.

not your true style

without knowing
their true preferences

Since I discovered my true self and became <u>clearer about</u> my <u>strengths and weaknesses</u>, I have been utilizing my style features differently and have gained a <u>new awareness</u> about myself and other

clearer about
strengths and weaknesses

new awareness

RISK

- To laugh is to risk appearing a fool.

- To weep is to risk appearing sentimental.

- To reach out for another is to risk involvement.

- To expose feelings is to risk exposing your true self.

- To place your ideas, your dreams,
  before the crowd is to risk their loss.

- To love is to risk not being loved in return.

- To live is to risk dying.

- To hope is to risk despair.

- To try is to risk failure.

But risks must be taken because the greatest
hazard in life is to risk nothing.
The person who risks nothing, does nothing,
has nothing, is nothing.
He may avoid suffering and sorrow, but
he simply cannot learn, feel, change, grow, love, ... live.
Chained by his certitudes, he is a slave:
he has forfeited freedom.
Only a person who risks is free.

                                                            Anonymous

people. Even if your reaction to some of the results in your profile might be: 'But that's not me' or 'That's not how I do it', think again, because such a reaction could be a sign of <u>not having used your true style</u>, and the cost is probably stress, exhaustion, frustration and dissatisfaction. Therefore trust your profile if the results are valid, <u>experiment with your flexibilities</u> and <u>practise your new-found strengths</u>. In the beginning it might be a bit awkward, you might even experience a slight slump in your performance or efficiency because you are now <u>changing old routines and habits,</u> but trust your own abilities, they will give you greater ease and more success in whatever you do in future. Believe me, your <u>true self</u> is <u>the best you can have</u> – everything else is pretence and costs a lot more energy.

not using your true style

**experiment with flexibility
practise your strengths**

**changing
old routines and habits**

**your true self –
the best you can have**

7. See how far you have come – a checklist for change

Now that you have hopefully found a whole new world of possibilities opening up for you, answer the questions on the <u>learning attitudes</u> checklist again in the 'How I Feel About Learning' post-test on page 302. <u>Compare</u> how you scored before you began reading this book with how you have scored now. Has <u>anything changed</u>?

learning attitudes

compare

anything changed?

Have you scored higher? If not, ask yourself if you actually wanted to change your attitudes towards learning and working and why not. <u>Reflect</u> on what might be the reason for your unchanged mindset and consider if it is useful for you to continue in the same way. If your answer is 'Yes', that's good, but if your answer is 'No', maybe you could go over certain chapters of the book again, complete some exercises, talk to people or read some more books. It could be the beginning of a great discovery.

reflect

If something HAS changed, you are on your way to becoming a <u>skilled brain user</u>, a more effective and <u>satisfied learner</u>. That will definitely help you in whatever you do – it might even help you to finally live the life you have always wanted.

**skilled brain user
satisfied learner**

Congratulations!

1. The new drug of education

'If students receive an <u>ecstatic high from successful learning</u> in a pleasant, fun, socially comfortable and caring environment, then drugs have no allure,' wrote Lyelle Palmer, Professor of Education and Director of the Office of Accelerative Learning at Winona State University, back in 1990. (1) Over ten years later, as creative, accelerated, student-centred learning and teaching methods are spreading around the world, new paradigms in education and <u>new standards of classroom practice</u> are producing results in achievement far beyond the old norms of any subject matter, age group or social setting.

**ecstatic high from
successful learning**

**new standards
of classroom practice**

These new methods, <u>based on learning styles</u> and a better understanding of <u>how the brain works</u>, have re-inspired teachers, re-energized students and given parents new hope.

**based on learning styles
how the brain works**

Many components of this new approach are not new at all – they have been researched and used for many years. What is <u>new is the system</u>, the total package in which they are now being used, taking into account the <u>sequence of preparation and presentation</u> of curriculum content, and the <u>holistic view</u> of matching students' needs and teaching styles in a positive, <u>emotionally supportive</u> learning environment.

new system

**sequence of preparation
and presentation
holistic view**

emotionally supportive

This new way of teaching is in <u>stark contrast</u> to <u>traditional educational settings</u> where much of the time is spent on complaining, finding negative aspects and pointing out mistakes; where students' individual needs are not considered really important or even valid; and <u>negative expectations</u> prevail on either side.

**stark contrast
traditional education**

negative expectations

Under such conditions the energies of teachers and students alike are depleted very quickly, and then the climate is one of <u>resignation, boredom</u>, complaint, <u>frustration</u> and <u>hopelessness</u>. The resulting attitude of all concerned is one of '<u>getting by</u>', not only at school but often in life.

**resignation, boredom,
frustration, hopelessness**

getting by

The Three Learning Zones

> *Think about your own schooling or training —*
> *when and how frequently have you been in each zone?*

LEVEL OF DIFFICULTY IN LEARNING

GROAN ZONE:
Learning seems painful,
difficult and uncontrollable.

FLOW ZONE:
Learning seems challenging
but manageable.

DRONE ZONE:
Learning seems boring,
slow and dull.

SCOPE OF YOUR ABILITY– Skills, Attitudes, Strategies

Based on an idea from *Peak Learning* by Ronald Gross

As explained throughout the book, when <u>styles</u>
<u>are matched</u>, methods are truly <u>student-centred</u>
and brain processing is understood, teachers
become energized and inspired, and students
experience a <u>positive learning environment</u>,
remarkable <u>creativity</u> and <u>retention rate</u> as well as
self-discipline, joy, <u>high</u> responsibility and
<u>motivation for learning</u>.

matched styles
student-centred methods

positive environment
creativity and retention

high learning motivation

Learning under such favourable conditions
is brain-friendly, fast and easy. Students quickly
develop a <u>positive self-image</u>, show relaxed
attentiveness during classes and display
an <u>eagerness for learning</u> – they want more,
more, more.

positive self-image

eagerness for learning

Even if teachers (particularly in high schools)
may find it hard to believe, <u>learners</u> under
such favourable conditions can really <u>get</u> '<u>high</u>'
<u>on their own abilities</u>, experience learning as
an exciting adventure, and can actually get
<u>addicted to learning</u>. This 'natural high'
produced by these new educational strategies has
<u>far-reaching implications</u>: drug use and alcohol
abuse, which have reached frightening proportions
among the younger age groups in New Zealand
and in many other countries, can be stopped when
students begin to feel good about themselves and
experience learning success and higher self-esteem.

learners
get 'high'
on own abilities

addicted to learning

far-reaching implications

When this is achieved, their need for <u>killing</u>
<u>emotional pain through drugs disappears</u>.

killing emotional pain
through drugs disappears

Although I accept that this particular social problem
is much more complex, it is also true that we
as educators can do a lot to help students who have
experienced nothing but rejection, negative
expectations, underachievement, frustration
and desperation combined with low self-esteem
during their years of schooling, and make them
<u>feel better about themselves</u>.

feel better about selves

When we accept these students are not 'thick,
lazy, slow or stupid', as often labelled by their
teachers, and also <u>not learning disabled</u>, as often
described by psychologists, when we appreciate
they are just '<u>learning different</u>' and provide them

not learning disabled

learning different

New Zealand Schools
having Partially or Fully Implemented
Learning Styles

PRIMARY/INTERMEDIATE SCHOOLS (5–12 yrs of age)

Forbury School
Glendowie Primary
Katikati Primary
Alexandra Primary
Bucklands Beach Primary
St Anne's School
Kenakena Primary
Te Puna School
Te Moana School
Raroa Normal School
Ponsonby Intermediate
Hillpark School
Lincoln Heights Primary
Rotorua Primary
Sumner Primary
Pinehill School
Papamoa School
Somerville Intermediate

Frankton Primary
Hillsborough Primary
St George's Preparatory
Wakaaranga School
Tokoroa North School
St Martin's Primary
Northland Primary
Outram School
St Dominic's School
Raumanga Middle School
Tamatea Intermediate
Inglewood Primary
Woodlands School
Malfroy School
Waikari School
Stratford Primary
Pukekohe North Primary
Van Ash Deaf Education Eentre

SECONDARY (12–18 yrs of age)

Hamilton's Fraser High School
Nayland College
Christchurch Girls' High School
Pakuranga College
Katikati College
Craighead Diocesan School
Henderson High School
Hamilton Girls' High School
Sacred Heart College
Hornby High School
Temuka High School
Waitaki Boys' High School
Porirua College
Howick College

Kamo High School
Hamilton West High School
Pukekohe High School
Hamilton Boys' High School
Waimea College
Sacred Heart College
Rotorua Lakes High School
Waitakere College
Kawerau College
Linwood High School
Papanui High School
Taradale High School
St Paul's Collegiate School
Queen Elizabeth College

Source: Creative Learning Company, Auckland (February 2004)

with opportunities for successful learning, we will have done more for them and their future life than just trying to ensure they – and their school – achieve better grades.

There is plenty of evidence that these holistic methods produce a high level of productivity and caring, independence and deep respect for human diversity. Considering our fast-changing world, these are certainly the attitudes we need to develop in our children to enable them to take personal responsibility for their own learning and for making positive choices in life. Instead of becoming helpless victims, they have abundant opportunities to choose success for themselves.

high level of productivity, caring, independence respect for human diversity

personal responsibility positive choices in life

2. The 'School of the Future' based on learning styles

When I began conducting in-service training programmes for schools I became acutely aware that single seminars and workshops sometimes achieved personal changes for individual teachers but could definitely not bring about a change for the whole learning culture of their institution. Out of that consideration grew a programme which has been extremely successful here in New Zealand and overseas and which is still growing. The programme is called 'School of the Future based on Learning Styles and Quality' and is based on the notion that for any change in education, if it is to be successful, there have to be three vital ingredients:

in-service training programmes

New Zealand and overseas

changes in education to be successful three ingredients

1. *A Basic Philosophy* which says that students possess unique learning style preferences and that educators must adopt a new view of education, recognizing and valuing the uniqueness of each human being, and accepting that both teachers and students have distinctly different abilities to absorb and retain new information.

basic philosophy

educators must adopt new view of education

2. *A Model* which helps educators to identify and administer assessment instruments, providing a suitable framework for capitalizing on individual differences in students' learning abilities.

a model

suitable framework

PRINCIPLES FOR RESTRUCTURING

based on **VISION, PIONEERING SPIRIT** and **PEOPLE NEEDS**

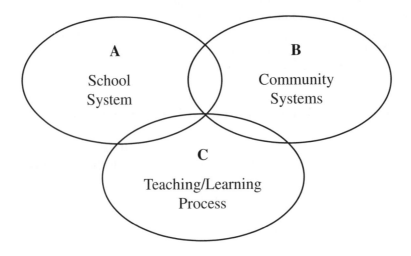

They need to:

A. include the organizational restructuring of the school system itself

B. be related to changes and needs in the community and society

C. focus on the restructuring of the teaching/learning process

3. _The Transformation_ – after having adopted and identified a suitable model, the challenge then is to establish <u>practical guidelines</u> for transforming a rigid teacher-centred traditional school and classroom situation into an exciting, <u>child-centred learning environment</u> suitable for any age group. To accomplish this, the school needs to invest time and resources to <u>train their existing staff</u> in learning styles and leading-edge teaching methods. Educational leaders, principals, teachers and parents need to agree on and implement policies which support such change programmes. (2)

the transformation

practical guidelines

**child-centred
learning environment**

train existing staff

Dryden and Vos, in the second edition of their book _The Learning Revolution_, give a detailed description for planning tomorrow's schools and how to transform a nation's education system by recommending the following <u>12-step programme</u>:

12-step programme

1. *Schools as lifelong, year-round community resource centres*
   It can fulfil the role of an information resource centre, regarding education as a whole-of-life process involving families.
2. *Ask your customers first*
   Entire communities can be involved in planning a new school and where it has been done, results are inspiring.
3. *Guarantee customer satisfaction*
   Like with successful businesses, schools should be based on building and keeping satisfied customers – their students and parents.
4. *Cater to all intelligence traits and learning styles*
   With the most important single innovation – multiple intelligences and learning styles – school dropout rates could be greatly reduced.
5. *Use the world's best teaching techniques*
   Changes in education will only be successful with a major emphasis on teacher training and continual retraining, and one of the keys are accelerated, integrative learning techniques.
6. *Invest in your key resources – teachers*
   The world's most thoroughly researched educational breakthroughs are not being modelled at universities and teacher training colleges, and tomorrow's teachers are not being trained in these methods.
7. *Make everyone a teacher as well as a student*
   Many problems of staff 'burnout' could be solved by involving parents, grand-parents and the community in the teaching process – and students too.
8. *Plan a four-part curriculum*
   It consists of personal growth, life skills, learning-to-learn programmes and content, and is as important in continuing education as in childhood and during teenage years.

The **AIDA** Principle

Awareness – see, hear (about learning styles)

Information – read (about practising schools)

Decision – OK to go ahead – plan implementation

Action – start programme (on a school-wide basis)

9. *Change the assessment system*
There are numerous efforts worldwide to change this key principle of school reform; the most important ones are doing away with traditional teaching and testing, involvement of the whole person, self-assessment and critical thinking.

10. *Use tomorrow's technology*
Interactive computer–satellite–video–television and electronic games technology provide the catalyst that will finally force a much-needed change in the teacher's role – from information to transformation.

11. *Use the entire community as a resource*
Many successful change models underscore the common-sense of moving schooling away from the traditional classroom.

12. *For everyone: the right to choose*
As the world has not only become one giant electronic, automobile, fast-food and financial services market but also a major one-world educational market, the days of school monopoly on education are rapidly coming to an end. (3)

If you as a reader are a <u>principal</u>, <u>administrator</u> or <u>politician</u> dealing with educational matters, the above mentioned facts and philosophies should give you enough food for thought so that you hopefully in all earnest begin to contemplate how you can <u>instigate change</u> in the educational institution you are responsible for or involved with. The following process will help you in carrying out this task with the best possible preparation for hitches and glitches on the way.

principal, administrator, politician

instigate change

3. Nine steps to being a change agent in your school

Years ago, when I visited Linda MacRae-Campbell at Antioch University in Seattle, she gave me an article which describes 'how to do what must be done' when you want to start a revolution at your school. I have recommended this process to many schools over the years, and it has never failed to produce results. <u>Individuals</u> willing to serve as <u>instigators of change</u> will encounter formidable resistance as they work at the forefront, but with <u>strategies</u> and <u>co-ordination</u> these 'change agents' can successfully topple the entrenched traditions.

individuals
instigators of change

strategies and co-ordination

Step One: Identify a need for reform within the school
A starting-point for many schools will be writing a new mission statement that specifies the school's philosophy, goals and values, and addresses serious concerns such as underachievement, discipline problems, dropout rates, high stress among teaching staff, lack of parental involvement and other problem areas.

True change and higher human adaptation

are not made by resistance to the old habits.

Change is not a matter of NOT doing something;

it is a matter of doing SOMETHING ELSE.

Da Avabhasa

Step Two: Seek supporters for change
The number of people who must be convinced of a new concept or approach is approximately 15 to 20 per cent of a school's population; strong advocates for the change project need to be identified from both within and outside the school, and their support actively sought.

Step Three: Create and communicate an action plan for the change
It's wise to begin with small projects that will succeed within the first few months. The projects should be well organized and co-ordinated to reduce the open scepticism abundant among traditional school staffs. For major restructuring efforts, plan a minimum of three to five years.

Step Four: Secure the needed resources
Identify and secure human resources as well as material needs. These might include consultants, training programmes, financial resources and definitely additional time for the staff involved.

Step Five: Acknowledge the emotional reactions
As a change agent you must anticipate personal reactions to change; a typical emotional cycle has been identified through research, and includes five stages:
1. uninformed optimism
2. informed pessimism
3. hopeful realism
4. informed optimism
5. rewarding completion. The 'Implementation Dip' is another phenomenon encountered in restructuring and means a frustrating decline in performance or work quality is experienced for a while.

Step Six: Anticipate problems, identify problem-solving skills
Predictable problems during any restructuring process are attitude and emotional issues, lack of co-ordination or communication, lack of resources, and unanticipated crises. Active problem-solving methods are extremely important for the project(s) to be successful.

Step Seven: Share the leadership
For widespread change to become firmly implanted, it is necessary to share the control of the project and work collaboratively with others.

Step Eight: Anchor innovation very quickly to classroom practice
For new classroom practices to be implemented, a combination of support and pressure is required, and change efforts that are quickly linked to the classroom are perceived as relevant and important; ongoing staff development is necessary.

Step Nine: Embed the innovation into organizational practice
Once implemented, measured and refined, innovations become part of school life and restructuring efforts become embedded in the school's philosophy, budget, policies and administration. Never forget to celebrate the progress! (4)

HOW I FEEL ABOUT LEARNING

Post-test

Please respond to these statements by ticking the appropriate box –
do it fast, without analysing.

		True	False
1.	If I really want to learn something, I have to do a lot of studying and repetition	☐	☐
2.	Learning is something very interesting and pleasant for me	☐	☐
3.	I think I have a good memory	☐	☐
4.	Learning is hard work most of the time	☐	☐
5.	I think I've always been a good learner	☐	☐
6.	I wish I could concentrate better	☐	☐
7.	I don't think I'm very intelligent	☐	☐
8.	Often I think 'If only I didn't forget everything so quickly'	☐	☐
9.	If I can learn something new, I get the feeling of deep satisfaction and contentment	☐	☐
10.	If I think back to my time at school, I think 'Oh no! I'm glad that's over!'	☐	☐
11.	I think learning is very hard for me	☐	☐
12.	I know I learn quickly	☐	☐
13.	Learning has hardly ever been fun for me	☐	☐
14.	Learning gives me satisfaction, happiness and contentment	☐	☐
15.	I can't imagine that I'll ever be able to master a difficult subject (e.g. a foreign language, mathematics) easily	☐	☐
16.	Foreign languages have always been my favourite subject	☐	☐

For scoring see page 324

4. Unity through diversity – is it possible?

During my years of studying every possible
aspect of this new discipline, by learning from
the masters in their field as well as from my own
teaching experience in formal education settings
and in business training, I have experienced:
- so many diverse and yet parallel movements,
- so many different schools of thoughts,
- so many unique and yet similar avenues to the
  one common goal – to help people learn better.

help people learn better

Many fine scholars in this field have researched
phenomena, gained most useful insights into
the mystery of human learning and have created
methods, techniques and tools to enhance learning.
Alas, many scholars are only capable or willing
to see their own approach. Unless they collaborate
with other specialists, they only theoretically accept
the other specialists in their field and hardly ever
look outside their own discipline. Most academic
researchers find it very 'unscientific' to blend
different techniques or tools, often refusing even
to discuss possibilities of combining their own
with other experts' methods.

many scholars researched

methods, techniques, tools

only see own approach

refuse
combining own with other
experts' methods

Thus the developmental process is slowed down
and they deprive themselves and others of greater
possible successes.

The conclusion has to be: it is not really important
who invented what, when and where, and whose
ideas, programmes or approaches are the best.
The most important is what serves the learner.
What can help them best in coming to terms with
difficulties during the learning process? Which
programmes or techniques will match someone's
unique style? How successful and satisfied have
learners been during the learning process? How
much have they gained and grown personally?
Was there fun and enjoyment, or boredom, stress
and frustration? And finally, is the learned
information retained and useful to the learner?

most important
what serves the learner

match unique style
successful, satisfied

fun and enjoyment

information retained,
useful to learner

As learning has become such a frustrating activity
for so many people, it is no longer enough only to

My Strengths and Weaknesses

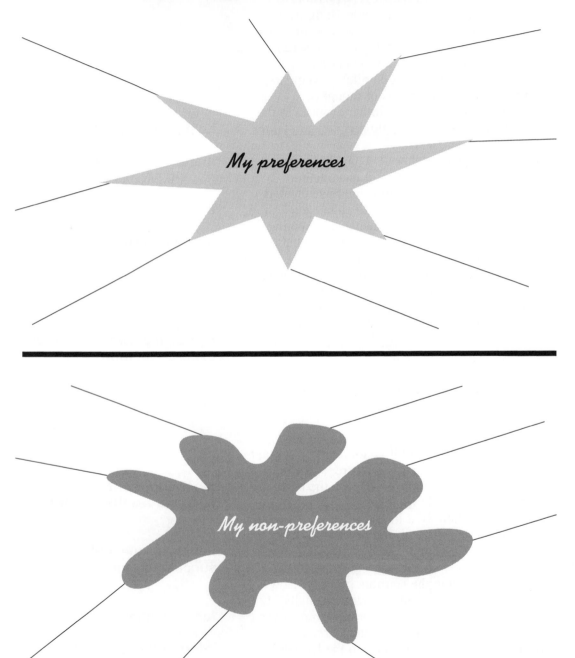

<u>acknowledge</u> (sometimes grudgingly) one another's contributions in the fields of education, brain research, sociology, psychology, cognitive science, management and business training.

acknowledge

It is high time that <u>specialists join forces</u> to create the synergy necessary for helping individuals, educational institutions, small businesses and large corporations as well as communities around the world in <u>coping with change</u>, capitalizing heavily on diversity, and finding more satisfactory ways of learning, working, training, studying, communicating, interacting and effective information intake.

specialists join forces

cope with change

Unless these leading forces in their different fields manage to create <u>unity through diversity</u> by recognizing and accepting that they all somehow work for the same cause – to further the development of the human race by <u>enhancing our knowledge</u> about the most powerful force in human beings – the <u>brain's unlimited ability to learn</u> – valuable insights will remain undiscovered, people will continue to struggle and many good ideas will be lost for ever.

unity through diversity

enhance knowledge

brain's unlimited ability to learn

5. Focus on strengths and manage weaknesses

One of the <u>most damaging</u>, <u>unwritten rules</u> many families, schools, companies and organizations follow is: 'Let's <u>fix what's wrong</u> and let the OK things take care of themselves.' As so accurately described in the book *Play to Your Strengths*, such systems are set up to catch people's weaknesses rather than build on their strengths:

damaging, unwritten rules

fix what's wrong

- <u>business managers</u> spend most of their time <u>working with their weakest performers</u>, trying to eliminate their mistakes;
- almost all <u>social work is focused on problems</u> instead of helping people to become really self-sufficient;
- parents usually point out their own children's shortcomings, and <u>teachers always concentrate on their students' lowest marks</u> rather than on their highest. (5)

**managers
work with
weakest performers
social work focuses
on problems**

**teachers concentrate
on students' lowest marks**

To deal with any situation successfully

you need to know

YOURSELF

and how to handle your weaknesses;

you also need to know

YOUR STYLE

and how to utilize your strengths.

B. Prashnig

We tend to focus our energies on <u>fixing weaknesses</u> while <u>ignoring strengths</u> because we have been conditioned to believe that fixing weaknesses will make everything all right, strengths can take care of themselves, success is the opposite of failure and practice makes perfect.

fixing weaknesses
ignoring strengths

What happens when we <u>follow these myths</u> is that fixing weaknesses will only ever achieve <u>average results</u>; <u>excellence is developed</u> solely by <u>focusing on strengths</u>.

by following myths –
only average results;
excellence develops by
focusing on strengths

Apart from arts and sports, personal strengths are not considered as important areas of professional development. So many people never discover their real talents and only achieve <u>mediocre performance</u> because they focus on their weaknesses and <u>neglect their strengths</u>.

mediocre performance

neglect strengths

The <u>study of failure</u> can give very misleading information about what needs to be improved. It is also a widespread <u>false belief</u> that if we can <u>identify weaknesses</u> we are then able to <u>turn them into strengths</u>.

study of failure

false belief
identify weaknesses
turn them into strengths

One of the most damaging beliefs, for adults and particularly for young people while they are still impressionable, is the saying: 'If so-and-so can do it, you can do it.' The assumption that 'anyone can do anything' assumes that <u>all people are clones</u>, possessing <u>identical abilities</u>, totally <u>disregarding human diversity</u>. As common-sense and research into style differences tell us, we are all different, equipped with a <u>unique combination of strengths</u>. The saying should be rephrased into: 'If someone can do it, those with the same strengths can do it.'

all people are clones
identical abilities
disregard human diversity

unique combination
of strengths

So far it has become quite clear that for achieving any success at all it is essential to focus on one's strengths. But how can we <u>manage our weaknesses</u>?

how to manage weaknesses

Again, Clifton and Nelson give great advice which fits perfectly into my notion of diversity and can be applied by interpreting the Working Style Analysis for adults and the Learning Style Analysis for students of primary and secondary schools:

HOW THEY HANDLE

TIME

Left-Brain Processors	Right-Brain Processors
Strong Analytic Thinkers	**Strong Holistic Thinkers**

Left-Brain Processors
Strong Analytic Thinkers

- highly organized
- overly punctual
- plan their time
- like to use time planners
- keep diaries/journals
- love to-do lists
- want daily routine
- plan activities in advance
- get upset when time
  schedules are disrupted
- live within 'real' timeframes
- prefer morning hours

Right-Brain Processors
Strong Holistic Thinkers

- disorganized
- difficulty being on time
- tend to lose track of time
- find time planners very stressful
- only keep diaries if they have to
- hate to-do lists
- find routine limiting
- do things spontaneously
- have problems following
  time schedules
- live with 'diffused' time concept
- prefer late afternoon/evening

Based on observations, experience and reports from people

- learn how to find out how good people can be by <u>identifying their strengths</u> rather than their weaknesses;

identify strengths

- learn how to stop wasting time <u>working on your weaknesses</u>;

stop working on weaknesses

- learn how to double and triple your productivity or effectiveness by <u>exercising your strengths</u>. (6)

exercise strengths

As we'll see later, there is <u>no magic formula</u> for dealing with weaknesses. They can be removed but they cannot be transformed into strengths. The goal, therefore, is to manage our weaknesses so our <u>true strengths</u> can be <u>freed up</u> to develop and become so powerful that they ultimately <u>make our weaknesses irrelevant</u>.

no magic formula

true strengths freed up make weaknesses irrelevant

This is an attitude good, loving parents as well as brilliant, caring teachers seem to understand intuitively; but the majority of teachers, particularly in our high schools, seem only to be focused on weaknesses, therefore making their own and many students' learning life miserable. It's time to heed the message and act on it.

6. Know who you want to become and go for it!

The more you know yourself, the more you know who you are, the more you will be able to become who you are truly meant to be. Some years ago, when I heard statements like these, I could not see any meaning in them and found them rather weird. They sounded odd and my well-trained analytical mind rejected them. I had been an academic for such a long time that I had <u>somehow forgotten</u> that there is <u>more to life than logic</u>, well-founded arguments, <u>reasoning</u> and belief systems which categorically stated that what doesn't make sense can't possibly exist.

forgotten more to life than logic reasoning

However, I had always felt there was <u>something missing</u> from my very successful academic life as well as my private life. I really did not know what it was until my <u>awareness grew</u> and I learned about things I had never learned at school, during my training as a teacher or at university, even studying psychology. I learned fascinating facts

something missing

awareness grew

THE BEST PREDICTOR

OF FUTURE SUCCESS

IS PRIOR SUCCESS.

about the human brain and how it works, how learning processes influence us in whatever we do, and that <u>brain patterns</u> are <u>powerful mechanisms</u> which either limit us or further us in our <u>personal development</u>.

brain patterns
powerful mechanisms
in personal development

Deeper insight into diversity and <u>personal growth</u> came when I began to attend seminars and started reading books about personal growth. Slowly I began to understand that we can truly determine who we want to be and how we can actually <u>shape our own future</u> by developing our <u>untapped brain power</u> and applying strategies to <u>use our mental strengths</u> much more effectively.

personal growth

shape own future
untapped brain power
use mental strengths

Among the hundreds of books on <u>self-development</u> (and there are many excellent ones on the market), I found the books and tapes by Anthony Robbins, *Unlimited Power* and *Awaken the Giant Within*, some of the most useful. All his recommendations, theories and practical exercises are based on <u>how the brain works</u> and how our brain patterns influence our development in life. 'Properly run,' he states in his remarkable book *Unlimited Power*, 'your brain can make your life greater than any dream you've ever had before.' (7)

self-development

how the brain works

The ultimate <u>success formula</u> he advocates is very simple: <u>know your outcome</u>, <u>take action</u>, know what results you are getting, and have the <u>flexibility to change</u> until you are successful. Robbins' books are full of success stories and I know many people who are constantly following this formula with great results. I, myself, have been using this formula for the past eight years with great success, especially in my business. But only by combining it with thorough <u>self-knowledge</u>, by understanding, experiencing and accepting my own and other people's uniqueness could I fully appreciate why this approach works so well. It all depends on how you <u>use your brain power</u> and what you do with what you have got.

success formula
know outcome, take action

flexibility to change

self-knowledge

use your brain power

People who never ask themselves in what direction they are presently going (or if they follow their current direction, where they will be in five or

ten years' time, and is this where they want to go)
tend to miss out on a lot in life and will not be able
to shape their own future. If, however, they begin
to ask questions, learn more about themselves,
their style, their needs, their preferences, and
accept and appreciate diversity, they will find
that life gets easier, efforts are more worthwhile
and they will become masters of their own destiny.

shape their own future

appreciate diversity
life gets easier
masters of own destiny

7. Walk your talk – dance your story – celebrate your glory! (8)

Years ago I had a cooking apron with the following
words printed on it: 'What you see is what you get.'
I found it an amusing saying, nothing more.
Later, when I had learned more about diversity,
style differences and how people learn to play roles
until they don't know any longer who they really
are, suddenly, in the light of human diversity
and brain functioning, this sentence took on
a deeper meaning. I imagined how it would be
if we could all be ourselves at all times, if we
could only stop pretending that we are something
or someone we are not, if we could most of the
time 'walk our talk'.

style differences how
people learn to play roles

could be ourselves
stop pretending

walk our talk

The more I thought about role playing and
observed masked behaviour, the more I began to
ask why? Why are we doing this? Why can't we
be who we are? And then it dawned on me:
most people don't know who they are, because
they never really bothered to find out, they never
dared to discover their real self, their own unique
style. They were living their lives mostly by other
people's standards and expectations, using up
all their mental and physical energy to play these
roles, never knowing why they were so exhausted,
stressed, frustrated, confused and burnt out.

masked behaviour

people don't know
who they are
real self – unique style

With the use of style analysis instruments, people
suddenly gain deep insights into themselves,
their own needs and preferences, and their own
uniqueness. They learn what makes them tick
and realize why they and others do things.

style instruments
deep insights

In many conversations with people who had
their styles assessed with our instruments, I have

Sit back and relax and think about yourself. Think about all the things that you don't like about yourself, things you would like to change or improve. Draw or write them down in the left-hand column. After two minutes switch your mind over to things you like about yourself, things you are proud of or you have been successful in. Write or draw these in the right-hand column. Compare the two lists and now you have an indication where you need to start your change process.

What I don't like about myself	What I like about myself

discovered the <u>power of self-knowledge</u>. Those
with low self-esteem and very uncertain beliefs
about themselves gained the most from their
new insights. Getting their profiles, interpreting
them and learning that there is nothing 'good'
or 'bad' about styles, they finally began to
<u>believe in themselves</u>, and to see their past
failures and their whole self in a different light.

power of self-knowledge

believe in themselves

Equipped with these new insights they could now
be true to themselves and <u>help themselves</u> in their
own way. They saw who they were, what <u>qualities</u>
they had, that it is OK to be who they really are,
and that they are <u>good enough</u>. By learning more
about themselves and appreciating their unique
qualities, people also learned that they <u>don't have
to take themselves and life so seriously</u>, that they
can experience what one movie title describes as
'the (un)bearable <u>lightness of being</u>' and not only
'walk their talk' but also '<u>dance</u>' <u>their unique story</u>.

help themselves
qualities

good enough

don't have to
take themselves and life
seriously
lightness of being
dance their story

We know that life is never plain sailing, that there
will always be ups and downs, but with greater
self-knowledge and better understanding of
human diversity it is much easier to cope with
whatever happens, keep one's integrity, remain
true to oneself and <u>celebrate one's own greatness</u>.

celebrate own greatness

Even if people have a lot of negative beliefs about
themselves, they can consciously <u>change their
brain pattern</u> (with know-how and patience) to
produce a more <u>positive self-image</u>, which in turn
leads to <u>greater understanding</u> and tolerance
as well as to <u>more brain power</u>.

change brain patterns

positive self-image
greater understanding
more brain power

For those of you who are keen to begin the change
process now, the exercise on the opposite page
is a good starting-point; with repeated use you
will notice how your negative beliefs will slowly
but surely be replaced by positive ones. Once
you have acknowledged your negative beliefs,
your brain will help you to get rid of them,
especially when you keep practising and stay
focused on the positive ones.

If people can <u>appreciate and cherish</u> their and
others' <u>uniqueness</u>, they are also more capable of

appreciate and cherish
uniqueness

If a child lives
with approval,
he learns to live
with himself.

Dorothy Law Nolte

It is a great sign
of mediocrity
to praise always
moderately.

Vauvenargues

recognizing strengths, sharing successes and appreciating achievements. When people are ready for that, they will be strong enough to take praise and be able to <u>celebrate their glory</u>. Everyone wants <u>recognition</u> and it is virtually impossible ever to give too much <u>praise</u> for achievement, especially to children. Knowing how powerful <u>positive reinforcement</u> is, it is really sad to see how overlooked praise is in most areas of life, in our families, in business and in education.

celebrate their glory
recognition
praise

positive reinforcement

Clifton and Nelson have devoted a whole chapter to <u>celebration</u> in their interesting book *Play to Your Strengths*. There they describe many examples of significant <u>improvement of productivity</u> when recognition for someone's work is received and they state: 'In the largest sense, people are attracted to that which is celebrated, and people do what they are celebrated for.' (9)

celebration

productivity improvement

As every educational institution has its own <u>styles of celebrating</u>, you need to understand your own <u>need for recognition</u> and must find ways to fulfil it. Consider the following questions, answer them honestly and see how you can <u>celebrate your personal strengths</u>:

styles of celebrating
need for recognition

celebrate strengths

1. Are you getting enough recognition in your current work/school (home) environment?
2. What kinds of recognition can you expect over the next two or three years at work, at your studies (or at home)?
3. How could you get more?
4. If you are not getting the recognition you know you deserve, what can you do?

If you think you don't need any rewards, or that's not your sort of thing, rethink your attitude. As many studies have shown, <u>personal rewards</u> are an important part of <u>building personal strengths</u>; they stimulate your brain to better performance and can come in many forms. One should never forget that young people and old need to <u>celebrate their uniqueness</u>, their achievements.

personal rewards
building strengths

celebrate uniqueness

What is Success?

To laugh often and love much;
To win the respect of intelligent persons
and the affection of children;
To earn the approval of honest critics
and endure the betrayal of false friends;
To appreciate beauty; to find the best in others;
To give of one's self without the slightest
thought of return;
To have accomplished a task, whether
by a healthy child, a rescued soul, a garden patch,
or a redeemed social condition;
To have played and laughed with
enthusiasm, and sung with exaltation;
To know that even one life has breathed
easier because you have lived;
This is to have succeeded.

8. And there is still so much more to learn

'The more you know the more you can know' is
another statement that is best understood in light
of our unlimited brain capacity and lifelong learning
ability. In the past I believed that my memory was
not that great, but once I began to apply these
<u>new brain-based methods</u> to my own learning,   **new learning methods**
I was amazed how much more information I could
absorb, retain and access whenever necessary.
I also found, together with my new-found self-
knowledge, it was much easier to understand
difficult concepts (although I knew I had a 'high IQ'
and during my schooling was considered
'very intelligent', I still had my doubts).

The amount of information I have taken in over
the past few years in the field of creative learning
and human diversity is much much greater than
everything I had ever learned during my 21 years
of formal education – from primary school to
university. It might sound boastful, but
<u>my memory has improved dramatically</u>, I feel   **greatly improved memory**
younger and <u>more energetic</u>, <u>enjoy life more</u>,   **more energetic**
I do more and accomplish more. (I even   **enjoy life more**
learned to play golf, something I never thought
I could master!) I also know more and am capable
of passing on information better, faster and more
effectively.

All these changes are still quite new to me and it
took a while to get used to this new 'Me'. For
a long time, while I was observing these often
dramatic <u>changes in my abilities</u>, I kept asking   **changes in my abilities**
myself 'Why?', 'How come?', 'What's happening
in my head?', and so on. In hindsight the answers
seem very simple: I began <u>using my preferences</u>   **using my preferences**
more consciously, surrounded myself with people
who complemented me in my style, created
learning environments which matched my style
and learned to <u>manage my weaknesses</u>. In short,   **manage my weaknesses**
I dared to <u>do things</u> '<u>My Way</u>' without limiting   **do things 'My Way'**
others in my environment to do things 'their way'.

But most importantly, by using my brain according
to my strengths and unique style, I also <u>increased</u>   **increased my flexibility**

He
who knows much about others
may be learned,
but he
who understands himself
is more intelligent.

He
who controls others
may be powerful,
but he
who masters himself
is mightier still.

Lao-tsu

my flexibility, my <u>tolerance for diversity</u>, and my love for human beings in general. Over the years, I have seen similar developments in virtually everyone who has embraced diversity and adopted <u>new attitudes</u> towards themselves, their own learning abilities, their work and other human beings in general.

tolerance for diversity

new attitudes

However, the <u>greatest changes</u> I have experienced so far have been in my <u>personal life</u>: in my <u>transformed relationships</u> with my husband, as described in Chapter 9, and the vastly improved relationship with my daughter, as described in Chapter 5. I am now even working with her – she has re-joined our company and we both love it. Again, I never thought this would be possible, but as experienced before, never say never.

greatest changes
personal life
transformed relationships

Because I am a very private person, it was not easy for me to reveal these deeply <u>personal experiences</u>. However, I had to do it for everyone who is going through hard times with their loved ones themselves, and still struggles to find better ways of getting on. I also had to do it for the simple reason that we need to fully <u>understand human diversity</u>.

personal experiences

understand diversity

It is obvious that, by utilizing new scientific insights and brain-friendly teaching techniques, by acquiring self-knowledge and becoming more flexible, and by dealing with our nearest and dearest in different ways, we are not only capable of learning, doing and knowing more, but we can also seemingly <u>become better people</u> on our lifelong journey, able to help ourselves and others to live, learn and grow – particularly our children.

becoming better people

Since the second edition of this book I have visited many schools in many countries and worked with many wonderful educators. I feel privileged and grateful for being part of this quiet but profound <u>shift in thinking</u> about learning and teaching <u>on a global scale</u>. I have seen incredible changes in previously 'hopeless' learning situations, countless projects being instigated and witnessed even more long-term, <u>sustainable changes</u> in schoools.

shift in thinking
on a global scale

sustainable changes

And that gives me great <u>hope for the future</u>.

hope for the future

In possession of
more developed minds,
people will be able to find
within themselves
the elements needed
to build a new society.

Luis Machado

Before I conclude my attempts to open your minds to the joys of human diversity and its effects on our daily lives, privately and professionally, I would like to thank you sincerely for reading the book and taking an interest in a topic which has grown ever closer to my heart over the past few years.

Depending where you are on your path to discovering, accepting and appreciating diversity, particularly in learning, teaching and life situations, this book will either have provoked your thoughts, stimulated your interest, given you some answers or new perspectives or generated more questions than answers. When any of the above happens, we know that your brain is learning, and usually learning fast, and that is good for you, because only by stimulation and new input is it possible to develop your mental capacities.

No matter who you are or where you are in your development right now, I hope this book has inspired you to take action, to *do* something to help yourself and others to learn, teach, study, work, concentrate and communicate better. Hopefully it will also help you to achieve your goals, to develop your full potential and to be the best you can. You deserve it! I am sure you will agree with me: to master any situation successfully you need to know yourself, your style, your strengths and weaknesses.

This book is a more specific 'How to' guide to deeper self-knowledge, to better learning and teaching methods, and to managing yourself, your children and your life more satisfactorily with the help of learning, teaching and working styles.

If the revelations or the exercises in this book have helped you to come to terms with some nagging questions or doubts you might have had about your own style or your learning abilities, I do hope that each chapter has given you some insights, some 'Ahas!', some comfort even, so that you can say: 'Now I understand!'

I also want you to know that you are not alone in your struggle to make sense of other people, your children or even yourself. Thousands of people around the world have the same difficulty in understanding themselves, are often puzzled by their own and other people's reactions to learning, teaching or life situations, and wonder (like I did for years) what's going on inside their heads and how they could come to terms with what makes them tick.

If you are a teacher, I hope I have not offended you. If you are a parent, I hope I have shown you some ways to support your children in learning. And if you are a person who wants to learn, I hope I have given you plenty of food for thoughts.

As I am always looking for better and more exciting ways to help people help themselves, I would be delighted to hear from readers who have already used our TSA, LSA or WSA instruments and the diversity approach in their school, family or workplace. Your feedback, your ideas for improvement, your creative applications and/or your general experiences with this new tool would be greatly appreciated. Please write to me; you can find our address in Appendix II.

How I Feel About Learning

<u>SCORING</u>: Circle your results for each statement.

Quest.	True	False	Quest.	True	False
1	-2	+2	9	+2	-1
2	+1	-1	10	-1	0
3	+1	-2	11	-2	+2
4	-1	+1	12	+2	0
5	+1	0	13	-1	+1
6	-1	0	14	+1	-1
7	-1	+1	15	-2	+1
8	-1	+1	16	+2	0

Please add up all the + and – figures. Subtract the minus result from the plus result.
You will either have a zero, a plus or minus end result.

<u>RESULTS</u>

+9 to +19 points: You have a high learning motivation and a very positive attitude towards learning. Learning in general is fun for you and you always gain a lot from learning situations.

+8 to -8 points: Your learning attitude is average, neither very positive nor really negative. By working through this book you have (had) the opportunity to gain a totally new learning experience. This will definitely change your attitude towards learning into a more positive direction.

-9 to -17 points: You have a rather negative attitude towards learning. Maybe you should ask yourself the following questions and try to answer them honestly:

1. Can I really prove that I am a poor learner? Maybe I have just adopted one teacher's negative remarks from the past?
2. Can I really prove that I have a poor memory – in general or only when I am learning difficult content?
3. Is there really any proof that I cannot concentrate?
4. Is learning always a drag for me? Maybe the reason for that lies in the methods used.
5. What was the reason for why learning has been little fun for me in the past? Perhaps my learning style has never been taken into account?

Chapter 1
1. Dunn, Rita and Dunn, Kenneth. *Teaching Secondary Students Through Their Individual Learning Styles: Practical Approaches for Grades 7–12.* Boston: Allyn and Bacon, 1993. p. 2.

Chapter 2
1. Dellinger, Susan. *Psycho-Geometrics: How to Use Geometric Psychology to Influence People.* Englewood Cliffs, NJ: Prentice Hall, 1989. pp. 1–12.
2. Dunn, Rita and Dunn, Kenneth. *Teaching Secondary Students Through Their Individual Learning Styles: Practical Approaches for Grades 7–12.* Boston: Allyn and Bacon, 1993. p. 25.
3. Grinder, Michael. *Righting the Educational Conveyor Belt.* Portland, OR: Metamorphous Press, 1991. pp. 16–17, 19–21.
4. McCarthy, Bernice. *The 4MAT System: Teaching to Learning Styles with Left/Right Mode Techniques.* Barrington, IL: Excel Inc, 1987. pp. 35, 48–50.
5. Dunn, Rita and Dunn, Kenneth. *Teaching Elementary Students Through Their Individual Learning Styles: Practical Approaches for Grades 3–6.* Boston: Allyn and Bacon, 1992. pp. 3–5, 488.
6. Herrmann, Ned. *The Creative Brain.* Lake Lure: Brain Books, The Ned Herrmann Group, 1989. pp. 162, 218.
7. Butler, Kathleen. *Learning and Teaching in Style: In Theory and Practice.* Australia: Hawker Brownlow Education, 1986. pp. 14–16.

Chapter 3
1. Barker, Joel A. *Future Edge: Discovering the New Paradigms of Success.* New York: William Morrow & Co., 1992. p. 32.
2. _____. pp. 205–206.
3. Caine, Renate M. and Rosengren, Tennes M. 'What's happening in students' brains may redefine teaching'. *Educational Leadership,* May 1990, p. 49.
4. Campbell, Don. *The Mozart Effect™: Tapping the Power of Music to Heal the Body, Strengthen the Mind, and Unlock the Creative Spirit.* Rydalmere, NSW: Hodder & Stoughton, 1997. p. 147.

Chapter 4
1. Prashnig, Barbara. *Diversity is our Strength: The Learning Revolution in Action, a Guide to Better Living, Learning and Working.* Auckland: Profile Books, 1996. pp. 22, 109–131.

Chapter 5
1. Dunn, Rita. 'Teaching underachievers through their learning style strengths'. *A Review of Articles and Books,* Part I, Winter 1990, p. 51.
2. Elgin, Suzette Haden. *Try to Feel It My Way: New Help for Touch Dominant People and Those Who Care About Them.* New York: John Wiley & Sons, 1996. page x, preface.

3. *A Review of Articles and Books*. Part I. Learning Styles Network, School of Education and Human Services, Jamaica, NY: St John's University, 1992. various articles, pp. 64, 68, 164.
4. Treffinger, Donald J. 'Programming for giftedness and talent development', in the workbook for the 16th Annual Leadership Institute, St John's University, Jamaica, NY, 1993, p. 164.
5. _____. p. 166.
6. Zenhausern, Robert. *Hemispheric Dominance Test*. Used with permission and based on an extract given to the author in New York (1993).
7. Dunn, R., Beaudry, J. and Klavas, A. 'Survey of research on learning styles'. *Educational Leadership*, March 1989, pp. 50–51.

Chapter 6

1. *Annotated Bibliography*. Learning Styles Network, Centre for the Study of Learning and Teaching Styles, Jamaica, NY: St John's University, 1991.
2. Milgram, R., Dunn, R. and Price, G. (eds) *Teaching and Counseling Gifted and Talented Adolescents: An International Learning Style Perspective*. Westport, CT: Praeger, 1993. p. 10.
3. _____. p. 18.
4. Klivington, Kenneth A. *The Science of Mind*. Cambridge, MA: The MIT Press, 1989. p. 176.
5. Gold, Lonny. *Suggestopedia: Activating the Student's Reserve Capacities*. Paris: Trajectoires Associées, 1985. pp. 2–3.
6. Schuster, Donald. *How to Learn Quickly – An Introduction to Fast and Easy Learning*. Ames, IA: Iowa State University, 1987. p. 1.
7. Lozanov, Georgi and Gateva, Evelina: *The Foreign Language Teacher's Suggestopedic Manual*. New York: Gordon and Breach, 1988. pp. 64–66, 133, 214–226.
8. Webb, Terry W. and Webb, Douglas: *Accelerated Learning with Music – A Trainer's Manual*. Denton, TX: Accelerated Learning Systems, 1991. p. 51.
9. Rauscher, F., Shaw, G. and Ky, K. 'Listening to Mozart enhances spatial-temporal reasoning: towards a neurophysiological basis'. *Neuroscience Letters* 185, 1995, pp. 44–47.
10. Weinberger, Norman. 'Announcing a free information source in music', University of California, Irvine, CA. email: mbi@mila.ps.uci.edu

Chapter 7

1. Dunn, Rita and Dunn, Kenneth. 'Dispelling outmoded beliefs about student learning'. *Educational Leadership*, March 1987, pp. 55–60.
2. Paine, John, Turner, Phillip and Pryke, Robert. *Total Quality in Education*. Sydney: Ashton Scholastic, 1992. p. 8.
3. Glasser, William. *The Quality School, Managing Students without Coercion*. New York: Harper Perennial, 1992. pp. 1–2.

4. _____. *The Quality School Teacher.* New York: Harper Perennial, 1993. pp. 22–25.
5. Chamberlain, V., Hopper, B. and Jack, B. *Starting Out MI Way: A Guide to Multiple Intelligences in the Primary School.* Bolton: D2, 1996. p. 7.
6. Gardner, Howard. *Multiple Intelligences: The Theory in Practice.* New York: Basic Books, 1993. p. 36.
7. Armstrong, Thomas. *Seven Kinds of Smart – Identifying and Developing Your Many Intelligences.* New York: A Plume Book, 1993. pp. 18–23.
8. Salovey, Peter and Meyer, John D. 'Emotional intelligence'. *Imagination, Cognition and Personality,* Vol. 9, 1990, pp. 185–211.
9. Goleman, Daniel. *Emotional Intelligence: Why It Can Matter More Than IQ.* London: Bloomsbury Publishing, 1996. p. 233.
10. Coles, Robert. *The Moral Intelligence of Children.* London: Bloomsbury Publishing, 1997. p. 5.
11. EFL – *Excellence for Learning* (Administrator Version – computer-generated report) Software. Scottsdale, AZ: Target Training International, 1991.
12. Marston, William Moulton. *The Emotions of Normal People.* Minneapolis, MN: Persona Press, 1979. pp. 12–14.
13. As quoted in: Robbins, Anthony. *Awaken the Giant Within.* New York: Summit Books, 1991. p. 97.

Chapter 8

1. Herrmann, Ned. *The Creative Brain.* Lake Lure: Brain Books, The Ned Herrmann Group, 1989. p. 311.
2. Glasser, William. *The Quality School Teacher.* New York: Harper Perennial, 1993. p. 19.

Chapter 9

1. Ornstein, Robert. *The Roots of the Self: Unraveling the Mystery of Who We Are.* New York: Harper San Francisco, 1993. pp. 131–132.
2. Moir, Anne and Jessel, David. *BrainSex – The Real Difference Between Men and Women.* London: Mandarin, 1989. p. 111.
3. Evatt, Cris. *He & She: 60 Significant Differences Between Men and Women.* Berkeley, CA: Conari Press, 1992. p. 48.
4. Tannen, Deborah. *That's Not What I Meant: How Conversational Style Makes or Breaks your Relations with Others.* London: Virago Press, 1992. pp. 109, 110.
5. Moir, Anne and Jessel, David. *BrainSex – The Real Difference Between Men and Women.* London: Mandarin, 1989. p. 111.
6. Jensen, Eric. *The Learning Brain.* Del Mar, CA: Turning Point for Teachers, 1994. pp. 296–297.

Chapter 10
1. Hannaford, Carla. *Smart Moves: Why Learning is Not All in Your Head.* Arlington, VA: Great Ocean Publishers, 1995. pp. 82–83.
2. Seligman, Martin. *Learned Optimism.* Sydney: Random House, 1994. p. 147.
3. _____. p. 148.

Chapter 11
1. Gross, Ronald. *Peak Learning: A Master Course in Learning How to Learn.* Los Angeles: Tarcher, 1991. pp. 9–10.
2. Beaver, Diana. *Lazy Learning: Making the Most of the Brains You Were Born With.* Shaftesbury: Element, 1994. p. 135.
3. Gleick, James. *Chaos: Making a New Science.* New York: Penguin, 1988. p. 8.
4. Legge, John. *Chaos Theory and Business Planning: How Great Effects Come from Small Causes.* Melbourne: Schwartz and Wilkinson, 1990. p. 122.
5. Jensen, Eric. *The Learning Brain.* Del Mar, CA: Turning Point for Teachers 1994. p. 90.
6. Alder, Harry. *The Right Brain Manager: How to Harness the Power of your Mind to Achieve Personal and Business Success.* London: Piatkus, 1993. pp. 15–16.

Chapter 12
1. Palmer, Lyelle, L. 'Education's ecstasy explosion: the joyful experience of super-accelerative learning and teaching'. *Holistic Education Review*, Fall 1990, pp. 47–51.
2. Ingham, Joanne. 'Learning styles: challenging and transforming education'. *Innotech Journal,* Vol. XVI No. 1, January–June 1992, pp. 37–44.
3. Dryden, Gordon and Vos, Jeannette. *The Learning Revolution: Your 21st Century, Passport for Families, Students, Teachers, Managers, Trainers.* Fully revised 2nd edition. Auckland: The Learning Web Co., 1997. pp. 431–55.
4. MacRae-Campbell, Linda. 'How to start a revolution at your school'. *In Context,* Vol. 27, 1990, pp. 56–59.
5. Clifton, Donald, O. and Nelson, Paula. *Play to Your Strengths.* London: Piatkus, 1994. p. 7.
6. ____. p. 28.
7. Robbins, Anthony. *Unlimited Power.* London: Simon and Schuster, 1988. p. 348.
8. Wohlman, Gary. A quote frequently used during his workshop *Mastering Presentation Skills.* Mill Valley, CA since 1993.
9. Clifton, Donald, O. and Nelson, Paula. *Play to Your Strengths.* London: Piatkus, 1994. p. 133.

Armstrong, Thomas. *Multiple Intelligences in the Classroom.* Alexandria, VA: Association for Supervision and Curriculum Development, 1994.

_____. *The Myth of the A.D.D. Child: 50 Ways to Improve Your Child's Behaviour and Attention Span Without Drugs, Labels or Coercion.* New American Library, 1997.

Barrett, Susan L. *It's All in Your Head: A Guide to Understanding Your Brain and Boosting Your Brain Power.* Minneapolis: Free Spirit Publishing Inc., 1992.

Bonnstetter, Bill J., Suiter, Judy and Widrick, Randy Jay. *The Universal Language – DISC: A Reference Manual.* Scottsdale, AZ: Target Training International, 1993.

Bramson, Robert M. *Coping with Difficult People: Learn the Six Basic Steps that Allow you to Cope with just About Anyone.* Melbourne: The Business Library, 1981.

Brewer, Chris and Campbell, Don. *Rhythms of Learning.* Sydney: Hawker Brownlow Education, 1992.

Burns, Stephanie. *Great Lies We Live By.* Ultimo, Australia: Bramley Press, 1993.

Buzan, Tony with Buzan, Barry. *The Mind Map Book: Radiant Thinking. The Major Evolution in Human Thought.* London: BBC Enterprises, 1993.

Caine, Geoffrey, Nummela-Caine, Renate and Crowel, Sam. *Mindshifts.* Tucson, AZ: Zephyr Press, 1994.

Campbell, Don G. *Introduction to the Musical Brain.* 2nd ed. St Louis, MO: MMB Music Inc., 1992.

_____. The Mozart Effect. New York: Avon Books, 1997

_____. *The Roar of Silence: Healing Powers of Breath, Tone and Music.* Wheaton, IL: The Theosophical Publishing House, 1989.

Capelli, Glen. *Born to Learn. Advanced Learning Strategies.* Englewood: Jones Education Network, 1995 (Study Guide and video tapes)

Cherry, Clare, Godwin, Douglas and Staples, Jessie. *Is the Left Brain Always Right?* Belmont, CA: Fearon Teacher Aids, 1989.

Creating the Future: Perspectives on Educational Change. Compiled and edited by Dee Dickinson. Aston Clinton, Bucks: Accelerated Learning Systems, 1991.

Cummings, Rhoda W. *The School Survival Guide for Kids with LD** [*Learning Differences]. Minneapolis, MN: Free Spirit Publishing, 1991.

Cutter, Rebecca. *When Opposites Attract: Right Brain/Left Brain Relationships and How to Make Them Work.* New York: Dutton, 1994.

Dare to be Yourself: Knowing Who You Are – You and Others – Learning to Like Yourself – Conquering Your Fears – Going for Change. Edited by Jane Lang. Amsterdam: Time-Life Books, 1995.

Dennison, Paul E. *Brain Gym: Simple Activities for Whole Brain Learning.* Ventura, CA: Edu-Kinesthetics, Inc., 1986.

De Porter, Bobbi. *Quantum Learning.* London: Piatkus, 1993.

Diamond, Marian. *Enriching Heredity.* New York: Macmillan, 1988.

Dickinson, Dee. *New Horizons for Learning: Creating an Educational Network.* Seattle: New Horizons for Learning, 1990.

Dudink, Ad and Clifford, Pamela. *The Brain Pack.* Datchet, Berkshire: Van der Meer Publishing, 1997.

Dunn, Rita and Dunn, Kenneth. *Teaching Students Through Their Individual Learning Styles: A Practical Approach.* Reston, VA: Reston Publishing Co., 1978.

Dunn, Rita and Griggs, Shirley A. *Learning Styles: A Quiet Revolution in American Secondary Schools.* Reston, VA: National Association of Secondary School Principals, 1988.

Faber, Adele and Mazlish, Elaine. *How To Talk So Kids Will Listen & Listen So Kids Will Talk.* New York: Avon Books, 1982.

Feuerstein, Reuven. *Instrumental Enrichment.* Baltimore, MD: University Park Press, 1980.

FUNdamentals. Edited and published by Accelerated Learning Systems, Aylesbury, 1996.

Gardner, Howard. *Frames of Mind.* New York: Basic Books, 1983.

_____. *The Unschooled Mind.* New York: Basic Books, 1991.

Gilchrist, Robert. *Effective Schools: Three Studies of Excellence.* Bloomington, IN: National Educational Service, 1989.

Glass, Lillian. *He Says, She Says: Closing the Communication Gap Between the Sexes.* Sydney: Bantam Books, 1993.

Gordon, Noah. *Magical Classroom: Creating Effective, Brain-Friendly Environments for Learning.* Tucson, AZ: Zephyr Press, 1997.

Gray, John. *Men are from Mars, Women are from Venus: A Practical Guide for Improving Communication and Getting What You Want in Your Relationships.* London: Thorsons, 1993.

Green Gilbert, Anne. *Teaching the Three Rs Through Movement Experiences.* New York: Macmillan Publishing Co., 1977.

Greenfield, Susan. *The Human Brain: A Guided Tour.* London: Weidenfeld and Nicolson, 1997.

Griggs, Shirley A. *Learning Styles Counseling.* ERIC Counseling and Personnel Services Clearinghouse, Ann Arbor: The University of Michigan, 1991.

Grinder, Michael. *ENVoY: Your Personal Guide to Classroom Management.* Washington: Michael Grinder, 1993.

Hannaford, Carla. *The Dominance Factor: How Knowing Your Dominant Eye, Ear, Brain, Hand and Foot Can Improve Your Learning.* Arlington, VA: Great Ocean Publishers, 1997.

_____. *Smart Moves: Why Learning Is Not All In Your Head.* Arlington, VA: Great Ocean Publishers, 1995.

Healy, Jane M. *Endangered Minds.* New York: Simon & Schuster, 1990.

Heitkämper, Peter. *Mehr Lust auf Schule: Ein Handbuch für innovativen und gehirngerechten Unterricht.* Paderborn: Jungfermann, 1995.

Houston, Jean. *The Possible Human.* Los Angeles: J. P. Tarcher, 1982.

Howard, Pierce. *The Owner's Manual for the Brain: Everyday Applications from Mind-Brain Research.* National Library, 1994. out of print.

Hutchinson, Michael. *Mega Brain: New Tools and Techniques for Brain Growth and Mind Expansion.* New York: Ballantine Books, 1986.

_____. *Mega Brain Power – Transform Your Life with Mind Machines and Brain Nutrients.* New York: Hyperion, 1994.

_____. *Brain-Based Learning and Teaching.* Del Mar, CA: Turning Point for Teachers, 1995.

Jensen, Eric P. *Brain Compatible Strategies.* Del Mar, CA: Turning Point Publishing, 1997.

_____. *Completing the Puzzle: A Brain-Based Approach to Learning.* Del Mar, CA: Turning Point for Teachers, 1996.

_____. *Super-Teaching.* Del Mar, CA: Turning Point for Teachers, 1988.

Kline, Peter and Martel, Laurence D. *School Success.* Arlington, VA: Learning Matters Inc., 1992.

Lang, Binny and Lang, Chris. *Your Future Success: A Student's Guide to Effective Study.* Melbourne: Ashwood House, 1990.

Lazear, David. *Seven Ways of Knowing: Teaching for Multiple Intelligences.* Sydney: Hawker Brownlow Education, 1990.

MacGregor, Sandy. *Piece of Mind.* Lindfield, Australia: Creative Accelerated Learning Methods, 1993.

McPhee, Doug. *Limitless Learning: Making Powerful Learning an Everyday Event.* Tucson, AZ: Zephyr Press, 1996.

Maples, Tim. *Accelerated Learning: Effective Knowledge Acquisition.* Nelson, New Zealand: Inova Publications, 1994.

Margulies, Nancy. *The Magic Seven: Tools for Building your Multiple Intelligences.* Tucson, AZ: Zephyr Press, 1995.

_____. *Mapping Inner Space: Learning and Teaching Mind Mapping.* Tucson, AZ: Zephyr Press, 1991.

Merritt, Stephanie. *Mind, Music and Imagery: Unlocking the Treasures of Your Mind. 38 Activities With Music To Stimulate Creativity And Transform Your Life.* Santa Rosa, CA: Aslan Publishing, 1996.

Miller, Alice. *The Drama of the Gifted Child.* Originally published as *Prisoners of Childhood.* New York: Basic Books, 1990.

Mukerjea, Dilip. *Brainfinity.* Singapore: Oxford University Press, 1997.

_____. *Superbrain: Train Your Brain and Unleash the Genius Within.* Singapore: Heinemann Southeast Asia, 1996.

New Directions in Education: Selections from the Holistic Education Review. Edited by Ron Miller. Brandon, VT: Holistic Education Press, 1991.

Nicholson, John. *Men and Women: How Different are They?* Oxford: Oxford University Press, 1993.

Nummela-Caine, Renate and Caine, Geoffrey. *Making Connections: Teaching and the Human Brain.* Menlo Park, CA: Addison-Wesley Publishing Co., 1994.

O'Hara, Brendan. *The Children's Song Book.* Rye, Victoria: The F# Music Company Pty., 1991.

Ornstein, Robert. E. *The Roots of the Self: Unraveling the Mystery of Who We Are.* New York: Harper San Francisco, 1993.

Patterson, Marilyn, N. *Every Body Can Learn: Engaging the Bodily-Kinesthetic Intelligence in the Everyday Classroom.* Tucson, AZ: Zephyr Press, 1997.

Pike, Robert W. *Creative Training Techniques: Tips, Tactics, and How-To's for Delivering Effective Training.* Minneapolis, MN: Lakewood Books, 1992.

Ritt, Thomas C., Jr. *Understanding Yourself and then Others*. Tequesta, FL: People
  Concepts, 1980.
Robbins, Anthony. *Awaken the Giant Within*, New York: Summit Books, 1991.
_____. *Giant Steps. Small Changes to Make a Big Difference: 365 Daily Lessons
  in Self-Mastery*. Simon & Schuster, New York, 1994.
Rodriguez, E. and Bellanca, J. *What Is It About Me You Can't Teach? An
  Instructional Guide for Today's Educator.* Sydney: Skylight, 1997.
Rose, Colin. *Accelerated Learning*. Accelerated Learning Systems, Aylesbury, 1985.
Rose, Colin and Goll, Louise. *Accelerate Your Learning. A World of Opportunity in
  Your Hands. Introduction. Action Handbook. Six Super Skills*. Aylesbury:
  Accelerated Learning Systems, 1992.
Segal, Jeanne. *Raising Your Emotional Intelligence: A Practical Guide*. New York:
  Henry Holt and Company, 1997.
Smith, Shirley with Neller, S. *Set Yourself Free*. Sydney: Bantam Books, 1990.
Stemme, Fritz. *Die Entdeckung der Emotionalen Intelligenz: Über die Macht unserer
  Gefühle*. München: Goldmann Verlag, 1997.
Stockwell, Tony. *Accelerated Learning in Theory and Practice*. Triesen, Liechtenstein:
  EFFECT: European Foundation for Education, 1992.
Sylwester, Robert. *A Celebration of Neurons: An Educator's Guide to the Human
  Brain*. Alexandria, VA: Association for Supervision and Curriculum Development,
  1995.
Tannen, Deborah. *You Just Don't Understand: Women and Men in Conversation*. New
  York: William Morrow Company, 1990.
Van der Kley, Martin. *Disruptive Children – How to Manage their Behaviour*. New
  Zealand: Macprint Printing, Christchurch, 1992.
Wade, John. *Super Study. Mount Waverly*, Australia: Dellasta Pty, 1994.
Ward, Christine, and Daley, Jan. *Learning to Learn: Strategies for Accelerating
  Learning and Boosting Performance*. Christchurch, New Zealand: published by the
  authors, 1993.
Weiss, Daniel E. *The Great Divide: How Males and Females Really Differ*. New York:
  Poseidon Press, 1991.
Whitmore, Diana. *The Joy of Learning: A Guide to Psychosynthesis in Education*.
  Crucible, Wellingborough: The Aquarian Press, 1990.
Winebrenner, Susan. *Teaching Kids With Learning Difficulties in the Regular
  Classroom: Strategies and Techniques Every Teacher Can Use to Challenge and
  Motivate Struggling Students*. Minneapolis, MN: Free Spirit Publishing, 1996.

Articles

'Gene wars: meet man's new boss'. *Focus Magazine*. March 1998, pp. 46–52.
'How a child's mind develops: fertile minds'. *Special Report, Time Magazine*. February
  3, 1997, pp. 34–42.
'Integrative learning: discovering "genius" in every child'. *Innotech Journal*. Vol. XVI,
  No. 1 (January–June 1992): all articles.
'The Mozart Effect'. *Quality Life Magazine*. February/March 1998, pp. 20–22.

Offers the Following Training Programmes:

✍ 'Introduction to Learning Styles' for classroom teachers and educators

✍ 'Diploma in Holistic Education' – a seven-module professional development programme

✍ The 'School of the Future based on Quality and Learning/Teaching Styles' – a Management Seminar for Principals

✍ The 'School of the Future' – an INSET programme for schools

✍ 'International WSA Certification' for managers and trainers

✍ 'DISC' – Managing for Success intensive training

✍ 'Your Way – My Way' – a Partner Programme based on Styles

For updates of our programmes please check
our website:

www.creativelearningcentre.com

Regardless
of who you are
or what you have been,
you can be
what you want to be.

W. Clement Stone

How to Order CLC Products

For orders in the UK:

www.networkpress.co.uk/lsa

contact: Network Educational Press Ltd, PO Box 635, Stafford ST16 1BF
Tel: 01785 225515   Fax: 01785 228566
Email: enquiries@networkpress.co.uk

For all other orders:

www.creativelearningcentre.com

Creative Learning Company's Personal Assessment Software is easy to use and available for individual or group use, online from our website above. The website offers full reporting functionality, group profiles, print or screen-based results and storage.

Online Profiles
Upon registering you will access your own secure web pages using your username and password. From this page you are able to purchase credits, complete questionnaires and receive your profiles to view on screen, print, download as a PDF file or return and view later.

You can add more profiles at any time, and once you have five profiles or more, of any product, you can process group profiles of any combination of individuals.

Style Analysis software is currently available in the following versions:

 Working Style Analysis™

For more productive, efficient, motivated people at work, choose Working Style Analysis

 Training Style Analysis™

For more dynamic, integrated and effective training, choose Training Style Analysis

 Learning Style Analysis™

For more receptive, absorbed, successful learning, choose Learning Style Analysis

 Teaching Style Analysis™

For more effective, less stressful teaching, choose Teaching Style Analysis

Creative Learning Company
PO Box 106 239, Downtown, Auckland, New Zealand
Phone: +64 9 309 3701, Fax: +64 9 309 3708, Email: info@clc.co.nz